MONASTIC WISDOM

Trisha Day

Inside the School of Charity

Lessons from the Monastery

MONASTIC WISDOM SERIES

Patrick Hart, ocso, General Editor

Advisory Board

MONASTIC WISDOM SERIES: NUMBER TWENTY

Inside the School of Charity

Lessons from the Monastery

by
Trisha Day

Foreword by
Kathleen O'Neill, OCSO

α

Cistercian Publications
www.cistercianpublications.org

LITURGICAL PRESS
Collegeville, Minnesota
www.litpress.org

A Cistercian Publications title published by Liturgical Press

Cistercian Publications
Editorial Offices
Abbey of Gethsemani
3642 Monks Road
Trappist, Kentucky 40051
www.cistercianpublications.org

1	2	3	4	5	6	7	8	9

Library of Congress Cataloging-in-Publication Data

Day, Trisha.
    Inside the school of charity : lessons from the monastery / by Trisha Day.
        p.   cm.
    "A Cistercian Publications title."
    Includes bibliographical references (p.   ).
    ISBN 978-0-87907-020-5
    1. Monastic and religious life.   I. Title.

BX2435.D35 2009
248.4'82—dc22

                                              2009019274

For Denny
and our two sons,
Casey and Brendan

CONTENTS

FOREWORD

Among the many changes in Trappist life since Vatican II, one of the most notable has been the search for ways monasteries can assist other people in their quest for God. To some extent this new openness to "the world" is a departure from past practice; "flight from the world" is a monastic theme with a long pedigree. Although the phrase is distasteful to most of us now, the reality it enshrines—constructing an alternative environment in which Gospel values predominate—finds a modern analogue in the more popular term "countercultural." Fidelity to their counter-cultural vocation to hiddenness, silence, and prayer has always meant that monasteries erect boundaries between themselves and their culture. The monastic's primary contribution to human society is, and must remain, the presence in the world (however hidden) of lives given to adoration and intercession.

On the other hand, hospitality too has a long monastic pedi-gree. First of all, the eschatological witness of monasticism, even without any outreach to the world, is a social service the mon-astery performs in the here and now. Beyond this, monasteries of the Benedictine family (which includes the Trappist/Cistercian branch) have nearly always welcomed guests into a special sec-tion of the monastery church, where they could participate in the liturgy, at least by hearing and interior prayer. There is usually a guesthouse too, where guests may stay for some days, sharing in the prayer and silence.

But now it seems that God is asking something more of us. The primary characteristic of one called to monastic life, accord-ing to St. Benedict, is that the person be truly seeking God. Yet desire for God is the most basic human drive, not limited to those called to be monks. In our time it seems particularly hard to find understanding, assistance, and companionship on this difficult yet rewarding journey. Sometimes parish life is not sufficient to lead people to the depth of prayer and union with Christ they deeply long for. Many monasteries have sensed the depth of this longing, sensed a kinship with these fellow-seekers, and felt called by God to respond.

Here at Mississippi Abbey, in addition to the forms of hospitality already in our tradition, we have added two new forms: lay associates, and long-term guests. Formal association with lay groups, while long a component of Benedictine life, is a new phenomenon in the Trappist world. In the mid 1980s the monastery of the Holy Spirit in Conyers, Georgia, under Dom Armand Veilleux, began the first such group in the United States. In 1994 our brothers at Conyers invited the other American Trappist houses to send a sister or brother and lay friends to a meeting, if they were interested in starting such a group and wished to benefit from the experience of the Conyers group. While we could not spare a sister at the time, our brothers at New Melleray Abbey, just twenty-five minutes away from us, sent two monks, and with them went Trisha and Dennis Day.

From the time our monastery was founded in 1964, we have had an excellent relationship with our New Melleray brothers. Since both our monasteries were interested in pursuing this new apostolate, and both had lay friends also interested, we pooled our resources and formed one group associated with both communities. The first meeting of the Associates of the Iowa Cistercians was held in January 1995. Perhaps it was because there were two monasteries involved, and therefore not one clear monastic leader, or perhaps it was something in our Midwest character, but right from the beginning the leadership in our group rested with the lay folks involved—with, of course, monastic oversight and assistance. Dennis and Trisha, although eschewing any titles, in effect led the group through the first four to five years of its existence, and have continued to serve in leadership roles ever since.

I had the privilege of being the Mississippi liaison sister for the first five of those years. Our group began as an assembly of strangers, some of them with a history of alienation from the

Church, many with limited experience in prayer. Yet something drew these people to the monasteries, touching the depths of their hearts. Now they come faithfully one Saturday every month, eager to receive what the nuns and monks can teach them about the spiritual life. From the start the group has been docile to the leading of the Holy Spirit, and it has been a joy to watch them form a genuine community and grow in habits of prayer and service, a joy to acknowledge them as our spiritual sisters and brothers.

The second new form of hospitality we have developed is a Long-Term Guest program. Our guest facilities are still rather meager, and to accommodate our numerous guests we have had to limit the amount of time they may stay to about one week. In the early 1980s we began to allow women who desire a much longer time with us to spend that time in the only place where we have room, namely, within our enclosure. Space limitation was not really the only, or even the main, reason for allowing the occasional guest to come inside. Living in community with us is a quite different experience from staying in a guesthouse, allowing a far deeper penetration of the monastic way of life. Experience has shown that this has been as helpful to most long-term guests as we had hoped.

Of course, allowing guests inside does change things a bit in the monastery. We are more likely to bend the rules where a guest is concerned; for example, if a guest needs help, we will speak to her at a time or in a place we would normally keep silence. It would be untrue to say this does not have some repercussions on our life. But it is a small price to pay for the joy of sharing our riches with others who can profit from them. We do have some policies that help us maintain our monastic equilibrium: we have only one long-term guest at a time; there is always a period of at least a few months each year when we have no interior guests; only a few designated sisters are to have talks of any length with the guest (this is as much to protect the guest as the sisters!); and the guest is expected to live as we do, including limiting her contact with the outside world. Because it takes at least a week or two for guests to catch on to our basic customs, and to begin to feel at home, the minimum length of stay is a month, and over the years the average stay has been about six weeks.

Trisha Day is one of only a very few women who have participated in both these new forms of hospitality at Mississippi Abbey. Her thirst for God led her, first to the Associates of the Iowa Cistercians, and then to a three-month stay inside our monastery in 2003. As a member of the monastic community Trisha is describing, I cannot help but feel that despite her efforts to be objective, we come out sounding a good deal wiser and better than we are. But perhaps it would be fairer to say that she sees us, in some measure, as God does: with great appreciation for what is good and beautiful in our lives, and great compassion for our weaknesses. We can easily lose sight of the tremendous blessings we enjoy by virtue of our way of life. Much of what may seem praiseworthy at first sight loses its shine after years of familiarity, and like most people we begin to take for granted what we should really never stop thanking God for.

To the uninitiated, monastics may seem like highly disciplined people. But when Trisha deplores her own lack of self-control, she touches a chord that resonates in us too. In fact, one of the reasons for the high degree of structure in the monastery is precisely because many of us can't do the self-control bit on our own. We need external structures to help us do what we really want to do. Maybe, fairly extensive structures!

But more important than any structure is the working of grace. It is true that monastic practices exist for good reasons, but no group of women or men living together in Christian community can fail to be aware that it is only the grace of God that keeps the whole thing from falling apart. This grace is not merely something we deduce from the fact that we are still hanging together. No, we are often quite aware of the presence and action of the Holy Spirit in specific circumstances. It is the grace poured out from the cross of Christ that keeps the Christian monastic enterprise going. Humanly speaking, community, even Christian community, is extremely fragile at the best of times.

As a person searching for practical help in her own spiritual journey, and one moreover unwilling to inflict pious platitudes on her readers, Trisha focuses perhaps more on the sisters' efforts, wisdom, and tradition than we would do ourselves. What strikes us about our own lives is how often it is God who takes the initiative. We do what we can to grow and change, to repent and ask forgiveness, to remain faithful during long years. But we would all have given up in discouragement years ago were it not that God acts in our lives over and over, accomplishing those little miracles no efforts of ours can bring about.

Nevertheless, Trisha is undoubtedly onto something. After all, there is a reason why we enter the monastery, and a reason why we stay. Yes, the call and the initiative and the energy behind our lives originate with God. As St. Bernard said, we love God because he first loved us; and we continue to love God, because he continues to tell us that he loves us. But we come to the monastery because we need all the help we can get to hear that delicate voice of love and not to lose it amid the clamor of all the other voices in our world. For all who share this hunger for God, our prayer is that Trisha's experiences, struggles, insights, and enthusiasm may assist you on your own journey, and increase your hope in the God who is waiting for you—as he waits for us all.

Kathleen O'Neill, ocso, Mississippi Abbey
Feast of the Founders of Cîteaux, January 26, 2009

INTRODUCTION

What the Church needs is for contemplatives to share with
others their privilege of silence, worship and meditation,
their ability to listen more deeply and more penetratingly
to the Word of God, their understanding of sacrifice, their
inner vision.[1]

Thomas Merton, *Contemplation in a World of Action*

Our Lady of the Mississippi Abbey is located south of
Dubuque, Iowa, on the grounds of an estate formerly owned by
a prominent local businessman. The original home was converted
into a church, scriptorium, refectory, infirmary, and sleeping
quarters for the small group of Cistercian sisters who arrived
from Wrentham, Massachusetts, over forty years ago to found
the monastery. Situated high above the Mississippi River, with
spectacular views of Wisconsin, Iowa, and Illinois, the monastery
grounds and surrounding farmlands extend across rolling hills
and through the lush valleys of northeastern Iowa. It is a beautiful place for a monastery and I had been there many times in the
past on personal retreats, often staying in the old stone farmhouse
below the abbey that serves as one of several retreat and guest
facilities. But in the winter of 2003 I had the opportunity to move
inside the monastic enclosure and live the way the sisters themselves live.

Before I left for the monastery I had tried telling friends and
relatives where I was going and why I was looking forward to
it. But I had the feeling that most everyone thought it was a

---

1. Thomas Merton, *Contemplation in a World of Action* (Garden City, New York:
Doubleday & Company, 1973) 154.

ridiculous thing to do—although no one was unkind enough to say so. Perhaps it was unrealistic to have expected them to understand. From their perspective it made no sense whatsoever.

Fortunately I had the support of the three persons who mattered the most—my husband Denny and our two sons. Not only did Denny understand, he could also relate to the kinds of experiences I would be having because he had been through something similar the year before as a long-term guest of the brothers at New Melleray Abbey. The idea of each of us spending a prolonged period of time inside a monastic enclosure was something we started looking into as we approached retirement. We'd read a lot of books, attended seminars, and listened to what the financial counselors had to say, but there were some crucial questions that hadn't been addressed: How can we move into this stage of life reverently and with grateful hearts? How can we be more mindful of the spiritual significance of what is happening to us? What can we do to honor what is sacred about the transitions and changes we are encountering? The closer we came to retirement, the more we began to realize how important these questions were to us and to look for a way of addressing them. Our involvement with the two Cistercian abbeys with which we are associated as lay Cistercians made it possible for us to ask the superiors of both monasteries if we could come into the monastic enclosures as long-term guests. We are grateful that both of them said yes to our request. Denny retired a year before I did and went to New Melleray in January of 2002. For the next three months he prayed, worked, and lived with the monks while I remained at home and discovered for the first time what it meant to live alone. The following year it was his turn to be on his own while I went off to live with the sisters.

After he dropped me off at the abbey on that bright January morning, I stood at the window watching his car disappear around the bend in the road. We had driven to Dubuque the day before and spent the night in one of the old Victorian bed-and-breakfast inns perched high atop a bluff overlooking the Mississippi River. We enjoyed a candlelit dinner (my last chance to have meat for a while) and talked about how much we were going to miss each other in the months ahead. We polished off a bottle of good wine and joked about the incongruity of spending such a romantic evening together the night before I moved into a monastery.

I went to Mississippi Abbey because I wanted to pay more attention to what it means to believe in God. I have struggled for much of my life with issues of faith, and what better place to continue grappling with those questions than in a monastery? Saint Benedict, the founder of Western monasticism, called the monastery the school of the Lord's Service, and throughout the centuries Cistercian monasteries have been known as "schools of charity." Saint Bernard of Clairvaux, one of the great Cistercian saints, was especially fond of the expression and frequently used it as an image to describe what it means to live together in harmony and mutual respect, focused on the example and teachings of Christ. Cistercian spirituality stresses the importance of coming to the truth about oneself by looking into the depths of one's heart. It is here that one goes to find God and it is from here that one's deepest prayer emerges.

> When he came to me, he never made known his coming by any signs, not by sight, not by sound, not by touch. It was not by any movement of his that I recognized his coming; it was not by any of my senses that I perceived he had penetrated to the depths of my being. Only by the movement of my heart did I perceive his presence.[2]

The lessons to be learned inside the school of charity all have to do with the heart—that interior place where we move deep within ourselves to discover the truth of who we are and to discover what we can of God. I went to Our Lady of the Mississippi Abbey to learn how to live more intentionally and I found out that it's all a matter of being educated in the ways of the heart in order to recognize, protect, and nurture what is sacred about life.

---

2. Bernard of Clairvaux, "On the Song of Songs" in Edith Scholl, ocso, ed., *In the School of Love: An Anthology of Early Cistercian Texts* (Kalamazoo, Michigan: Cistercian Publications, 2000) 114–15.

This book is a synthesis of what I learned from a variety of sources during the time I lived inside the school of charity: from the sisters themselves, from scriptural readings and liturgical celebrations, from moments of prayer, from homilies, from monastic and other writers to whom I had access, as well as from my personal reflections and journal entries about the experiences I was having. Books like this are nothing new. Those of us who have had the opportunity to spend much time in a monastery often come away wanting to tell others about what we experienced there. But I'm convinced that what is most important about visiting a monastery for any length of time is what happens when we leave. That's why my main objective in writing this book hasn't been merely to describe what I observed during the three months I lived with the sisters. Instead, I've wanted to focus on what I'm trying to do with the things I learned from them now that I'm home again. I have tried to be honest about my attempts (which have not always been successful) at reordering my priorities and energies to reflect what the sisters have taught me.

Living with them has underscored the importance of cultivating an *interior* life of prayer and reflection in order to guide the choices and behaviors of my *exterior* life. I believe all of us are called to the spiritual life regardless of whether or not we have taken religious vows. It is up to each of us to seek whatever guidance we may need to help us respond to that call and find our way to God. For me, the sisters at Mississippi Abbey have been role models as well as teachers and I will be forever grateful to them. This book is an attempt to explain why.

LEARNING TO LIVE IN COMMUNITY

It is the following to whom you should associate yourself: to blessed people, godlike men and women who have committed their whole selves to our Lord. Let people who have grown old in religious life be your neighbors, let them be your source of advice; attach yourself to them and love them. And if you have your abode among such people, then emulate their way of life and become such as they. Do not separate yourself from them by your actions lest you become like lupine seeds strung together amid strings of pearls.[1]

> Babai, in *The Syriac Fathers on
> Prayer and the Spiritual Life*

Silence as a Communal Effort

January 21

Sister Louise has just left me here in the cozy little room that will be home for the next three months. She was all smiles and exuberance when she came over this morning shortly after Terce to pick me up at the retreat house and help me get moved in. Louise is to be my guide during my stay and already she's done a terrific job making me feel welcome. Like all the sisters around here, she's got an energy about her that makes me wonder just what her secret is. (Maybe I'll discover it during the next three months!) She spent several hours helping me settle in and find my way from place to place, pointing out where things are and how things are done. There are only a few

---

1. Sebastian Brock, trans., *The Syriac Fathers on Prayer and the Spiritual Life*, Cistercian Studies Series 101 (Kalamazoo, Michigan: Cistercian Publications, 1987) 159.

house rules and they all have to do with keeping things quiet in order to avoid disturbing those nearby. No hair dryers or vacuum cleaning in the dorm area during great silence, meridian,[2] and other times the sisters are likely to be in their rooms studying or praying. And I must remember not to run the water in my sink after 8 p.m. until 6 a.m. and during the afternoon meridian because the pipes are so noisy. Shower rooms are downstairs but I'm still not certain about when we can use them—probably not during meridian or great silence because of the noise they make.

During the first few weeks I lived with the sisters, much of my energy was spent trying to avoid making noise. The intensity of the silence inside the monastic enclosure amazed me, even though since Denny and I are the only two people living in our house I'm used to things being pretty quiet at home. That might be why it was easy to adjust to an environment where maintaining silence is the norm rather than the exception. I grew accustomed to feeling like I was completely engulfed in stillness. It seemed to hang in the air just like the faint fragrance of incense that lingered in the church after a Sunday liturgy.

Because silence was such a natural part of the environment, anything that made noise sounded like it had been amplified to sound even louder. The deafening screech of the buzzer that went off each morning at 3:30 to awaken the sisters for Vigils was a case in point. On my first morning in the monastery my sleep was shattered by what can only be described as a cross between an air-raid siren and a fire alarm. The fact that it was making such a racket inside the normally quiet and tranquil environment of a monastery made it even worse because it seemed so out of place. I never did get used to it in the weeks that followed and I wondered why the sisters didn't use something a tad *gentler* for their early morning wake-up call. I found out later that there was a very good reason: expense! They had looked into a system that used chimes but found that it was far too costly to install.

---

2. The word *meridian* derives from the Latin word for midday. It is used in monasteries to refer to the short rest period between the noon meal and the Office of None.

Getting up in the middle of the night for Vigils was not easy at first. I was always tempted to ignore the ear-splitting intrusion of that obnoxious buzzer and go back to sleep, and there were a couple of times I did. But it didn't happen very often because once I was up, I was glad I'd decided not to stay in bed. Having resisted the temptation to go back to sleep, I would dress quickly and hurry down the hall to the church. There was always a night-light outside the door and a candle burning in the sanctuary, which softened the darkness and provided just enough light to keep us from tripping all over one another as we made our way to our places in choir.

Wearing long white cowls that took on the color of candle-light, the sisters slipped in so quietly that it was almost impossible to hear them coming. Monday, Wednesday, and Friday mornings the lights were kept off and instead of singing or reciting together from our Psalters, we all listened to two sisters alternate reading that morning's psalms, prayers, and readings from the lectern near the altar, using only a simple spotlight for illumination. Afterwards, the sisters used the interval between the end of Vigils until the beginning of Lauds for their own personal prayer and meditation. I soon discovered that this was a favorite time of the day. There was always something very rich and soulful about the combination of silence and darkness that seemed such a perfect backdrop for prayer. No matter how much I tried to capture that feeling at other times of the day, it was never quite the same.

It is one thing to relish the kind of silence that happens in periods of prayerful solitude, but it is another thing entirely to get used to being completely silent in the company of other people when they are doing things that in my experience always called for conversation . . . having dinner, for example!

It took awhile to get comfortable eating with the community in the refectory and at first, my main criterion for choosing what I was going to put on my plate was whether or not I would be able to eat it without making any noise. That meant a couple of weeks without fresh vegetables or fruit for fear of creating what might sound like an intolerable racket. I also noticed that the silence in the dining room seemed to amplify the sound of my coffee cup whenever I set it down on the table. I became acutely aware of how loud knives and forks can be when they come in contact with each other on a dinner plate. But after a couple of weeks, it began to dawn on me that the sisters did not seem to have any such scruples. They munched serenely on crisp carrot sticks, or tranquilly crunched on their morning cornflakes, and didn't seem the slightest bit worried about coffee cups or flatware. Once I got over my initial discomfort, I began to view eating in silence in a different light. Mealtime became another example of what it means to approach an everyday experience with reverence, and to recognize the goodness of something we otherwise tend to take for granted—like the taste, texture, and fragrance of ordinary fruits and vegetables.

The sisters are vegetarians. They also are terrific cooks who do amazing things with potatoes, beans, tomatoes, broccoli, squash, fish, cheese, and eggs; and a person could probably live quite happily on nothing but the fresh bread and homemade soups that come from their kitchen each week. I had not anticipated that it would be so easy for me to get along without meat. And yet one taste of Suz's tomato and cheese lasagna or Martha's herb baked salmon was enough to convince me otherwise. Eating with the sisters was a real treat. Not only was the food great but once I got used to eating in silence, I quickly discovered that it's a good way to slow down and enjoy the meal without hurrying through it.

Dinner is served at noon. While the rest of the community is at Midday Prayer, those who have been assigned to cook for that day are busy setting out the food they've prepared that morning. By the time the *Angelus* bell rings, everything has been carefully and efficiently arranged buffet-style on the big counter in the center of the kitchen. The dining room is right next door. It contains long tables arranged in a hollow square around the sides of the room with a bench at each sister's place. The abbess and prioress are usually first to enter, taking their places at the table nearest the entrance. Once everyone is present, the abbess rings a tiny bell and the chantress begins the prayer before the meal with the words "Let us bless the Lord." The community responds: "His love is everlasting. Praise the Father, the Giver of

Life; Praise the Son, the Bread of Life; Praise the Holy Spirit, Living Water, who makes us one in Christ." Then the kitchen doors are opened for the sisters to go through the buffet line.

Even though I came to appreciate the value of dining in silence, I was always a little uncomfortable eating in the refectory with the sisters. It felt odd not being able to turn to one of them and strike up a conversation about whatever came to mind. This was especially frustrating because there were things it would have been nice to be able to talk about with the sisters who were seated on either side of me. I had already gotten to know Kate, who sat on my left, through her involvement as a monastic liaison to the Associates of the Iowa Cistercians. Everyone in the AIC loved her and so did I, which made it all the more frustrating not to be able to talk to her even though we sat next to each other day after day in the refectory.

I wasn't nearly as well acquainted with Suz, the sister who sat on my right. We seldom saw each other outside of the refectory because she worked in the office with the computer end of the candy business. I was itching for a chance to get to know her a little better because the few times I did run into her, she was always smiling and laughing. She seemed like so much fun. And she was an artist too! I had seen some of her icons and would have loved to learn more about them. But even though we sat next to each other every day for three months, the strict silence of the refectory made it impossible to take advantage of the chance I had to talk to her. It often struck me while sharing a silent meal with so many other women that Jesus himself might have preferred a little conversation had he been there. In view of the value he placed on table fellowship and the importance of using mealtime as a chance to come together in friendship and unity, he might not have been too keen about having to refrain from talking to his friends while eating with them.

While I would have preferred a little quiet conversation during dinner, I gradually began to realize that there's a big difference between refraining from speech and refusing to talk. The latter is essentially self-centered; a passive-aggressive attempt to communicate displeasure or disregard of another person. That is not the reason the sisters eat in silence. For them, refraining from speech during mealtime is something positive and communal because silence does not happen without the combined efforts of everyone involved. It needs to be cultivated and protected. Being silent is not a solitary and selfish activity. It is something the sisters do together to create an atmosphere where each of them is able to pray quietly. Eating with the sisters taught me that the silence that is such a distinctive feature of life inside a monastic enclosure is a communal effort, something each sister has to work at, for the good of all.

While the sisters do not make a vow of silence, they are careful not to disturb others by the things they say. This can be interpreted several ways. On the one hand, the sisters take the Rule of St. Benedict very seriously—including his comments about the restraint of speech. Referring to Proverbs 10:19, Benedict advises monks to give careful thought to the way they use the gift of speech (RB 7.56-60). In particular he cautions against gossip, idle or argumentative talk, and the use of inappropriate or offensive humor. It is good advice for us all, but for the sisters it provides the backdrop for the way they live and interact with one another.

In addition to paying attention to what they say and how they say it, the sisters are also careful about *where* they speak. They never go into one another's rooms, and rarely, if ever, do they talk in the hallways of the dormitory. (Only once did I detect the sound of voices near my room and they were so faint that it was impossible to hear what was being said.) They never speak in the scriptorium, unless taking part in a class or discussion that is going on there. They are silent even when they work together—preparing meals, washing windows, tending the gardens, or teaming up on the candy line—and they avoid falling into casual conversation when they are together at other times and in other places as well. But this does not mean they avoid one another! I found them to be a warm and open community of women who obviously care very much about each other. I would often see two sisters out walking together, deep in conversation, or laughing over something that must have amused them both. But always they would be careful to have these kinds of conversations in places where they would not be disturbing the silence for the other sisters. Interestingly, one of the few bits of Trappist sign language I picked up was this one: to let a sister know you needed to speak to her, you simply caught her eye, quickly tapped your own and then pointed at her. It's the sign for "can I see you?" That way the two of you could meet at a spot where you would be able to speak freely without disturbing the others.

Silence at Home

Those of us who do not live in monasteries spend our waking hours up to our ears in sounds—a fair amount of which probably are not worth listening to. It is typical for families to own several television sets, which often are blaring continually throughout the day along with stereos, radios, cell phones, and assorted electronic gadgetry. We have grown quite accustomed to all this noise, and the thought of turning it off and being left with *nothing* blaring away in the background can seem unnatural. And yet throughout the ages, contemplative men and women of all the world's great religions have reminded us that it is in periods of silence and stillness that we are more apt to glimpse the transcendent dimension of life.

More often than not, we must create this kind of silence for ourselves. That's not such an easy thing to do in a world where many of us have a tendency to hurl ourselves through the events and circumstances of daily living. Yet, people who live and work in hectic, clamorous environments often find that seeking out a quiet spot to get away from all that noise and confusion for even a few minutes helps clear their minds and replenish their energy supplies. Those who are accustomed to solitary hikes through parks or along winding country roads often fall naturally into a more reflective frame of mind. Stillness and solitude can sharpen our focus, leaving us much more attuned to the beauty of the natural world. Finding ourselves in a quiet place often soothes our spirits, and it is during times like these that we may be more likely to open our hearts and senses to the luminous world of the Spirit. Silence can lead us deeper into ourselves—and the sisters would say that this can be a place of encounter with God. My own experience has taught me that sometimes—not always, but sometimes—it is from that silent space within me that my most personal and creative prayer arises.

Finding silent places in our noisy world is a challenge—even for those of us who live relatively quiet lives. And yet it is not as impossible as it might seem. It is primarily a matter of carving out little slivers of silence in order to go there, with some regularity, at certain times during the day. The most obvious times are in the morning or the evening and involve either getting up before everyone else does, or waiting until the house settles down at night. It is also helpful to seek out places where silence occurs naturally—churches, for example—and make it a point to stop by on a regular basis when nobody else is around. The natural world is another good place to look for opportunities to savor a few moments of silence. And it does not always have to involve going very far to find it. I've discovered that some of the most beautiful places are right outside my front steps either at the beginning or the ending of the day.

Silence can slow me down and help me pay closer attention to the changing cycle of the seasons and the rhythm and pace of the natural world. Sunrises, sunsets, starry skies, moonlight, as well as morning mist, falling snow, leaves drifting off trees, and fireflies flickering in the dusky shadows of a summer evening— all speak to me in the eloquent language of silence, inviting me to take notice of what is being communicated. In the words of Annie Dillard:

> You say to the woods, to the sea, to the mountains, the world, now I am ready. Now I will stop and be wholly attentive. . . . You feel the world's word as a tension, a hum . . . . This is it: this hum is the silence. The world and its noise are out of sight and far away. Forest and field, sun and wind and sky, earth and water, all speak the same silent language.[3]

But there is also value in getting into the habit of being silent in the company of other people—especially when we find our-

3. Annie Dillard, *Teaching a Stone to Talk* (New York: Harper Colophon Books, 1983) 71–72.

selves about to say something we will only end up regretting later. The monastic way of dealing with this is by practicing restraint of speech, and I cannot help wondering how different it would be if the rest of the world did likewise. One of the hardest things to get used to once I had left the monastery was listening to the abusive way people speak to one another. I suppose it was especially noticeable having just come from an environment where nobody spoke that way. Amazingly, I had actually gone for three straight months without once hearing the f-word! Suddenly I was back where it's hard to go for even three hours without hearing it somewhere. I suspect that many people have become so accustomed to hearing rude, offensive, and downright vulgar language that they don't even notice it anymore. What used to be considered inappropriate and offensive language seems to have become the norm for persons of all ages. I have heard a few elderly people, for example, toss off words and phrases they would never have used when they were younger.

But having discovered what a difference restraint of speech can make, I find I am much more sensitive to the words I hear people using, especially on television and in the movies. It has made me recognize how easy it is for that kind of language to creep into a person's everyday speech and to pay closer attention to my own. And I am not the only one trying to do that. An architect friend of mine makes a point of deliberately not using profanity even on job sites, where that kind of language seems to come naturally. He says it often has an interesting effect on contractors and construction crews—particularly when something has gone wrong and he feels as frustrated and upset as everyone else on the job site. The fact that he is able to express his frustration without resorting to profanity usually has a much more positive effect than had he let loose with a stream of four-letter words.

But there is more to restraint of speech than avoiding profanity. The Rule of St. Benedict advises monks to pay attention to the things they say, by speaking "gently and without laughter, seriously and with becoming modesty, briefly and reasonably, but without raising [the] voice" (RB 7.60). That does not mean there is anything wrong with laughing and having a good time, but I can't help thinking that much of what passes for humor in our culture is not really so amusing because there is nothing very funny about coarse, malicious, and demeaning jokes that belittle and embarrass others.

Monastic restraint of speech gives the sisters access to a place of quiet within themselves in order to listen to the voice of God. I've found that it has another benefit as well. It can help me remember that words have a powerful impact—they can nurture and encourage and motivate us, but they can also be used as weapons for unleashing our anger or as tools for criticizing, blaming, or humiliating one another.

Restraint of speech is a powerful concept because it emphasizes the fact that when all is said and done, there is a lot more to communication than what we are trying to say. The most important part of the process usually involves maintaining an interior silence so we can quiet down and listen to what someone else is trying to tell us.

During the time I lived with the sisters I began to realize the importance of cultivating interior silence. Spending long periods of the day without talking meant learning to get comfortable with that place within me—wherever it is—where I am most able to be who I really am. I think that is one of the benefits of silence. Out of it can come a deeper recognition of our own individual identity, as well as a greater awareness of those around us. I believe there is value to the monastic way of doing things together, but in silence. It is a way of honoring the worth and dignity of others without constantly trying to impose our own expectations on them.

Since coming home again, I seem to require more silence in my life—and fortunately I'm married to someone who has similar needs. We have fallen quite easily into the monastic way of being companionably silent together and often spend large periods of our day that way. We are comfortable sharing the same space together without having to fill it up with chatter or with the intrusive blare of a television set or stereo in the background.

I think that sharing silence is a form of intimacy. It helps us honor the interior life of another person. For Denny and me, silence is not the result of having nothing to say to one another. In fact I suspect that it has actually enhanced the way we communicate because it has helped us become more responsive and attentive when we do have things to talk over and share.

Monastic Decorum

January 22

The sisters move through the halls without making any noise at all—even when they're walking over the spot in the floor that always creaks and groans whenever I step on it (no matter how careful I am). They know how to open and close the doors to their rooms so carefully that it's impossible for their neighbors to hear them coming and going. And once they're inside, you'd never know it—except for an occasional cough next door or the muffled sound of footsteps overhead. I think they've figured out one of the secrets to living together —and it has to do with trying not to bother anyone else.

What is now Mississippi Abbey was once a private country home and when the sisters acquired the property, they had to remodel the main house and build a substantial addition in order to make room for a chapel, sleeping quarters, library, and refectory. They have done a lovely job, but even so, for over twenty women to live that close together in such a small amount of space calls for special effort. The fact that they are able to do it so gracefully has a lot to do with "monastic decorum."

Cistercian monk Charles Cummings says that monastic decorum is all about the way people conduct themselves. It has to do with everything they say and do, and for Cummings it is "the spontaneous expression of an interior harmony, the exterior reverberation of an inner gracefulness and dignity. When we are being ourselves, our graced selves, we will radiate a certain charm, attractiveness, and kindness both in speech and deeds, and we will have an instinctive feeling for the right thing at the right time."[4]

4. Charles Cummings, ocso, *Monastic Practices* (Kalamazoo, Michigan: Cistercian Publications, 1986) 86.

That was the way it felt living with the sisters because they seemed to know intuitively when to do or say the right thing. Often that meant knowing when not to say anything at all. That was definitely the case when they were together in church. It was tacitly understood that once someone slipped quietly into her choir stall or settled herself on her prayer bench, she was not to be disturbed. It's a no-no to speak (even in a whisper) to someone in choir, unless it is absolutely necessary, and the sisters take care not to distract one another in other ways as well. Not only are they adept at slipping in and out of their choir stalls so quietly that it is practically impossible to know they are there but they have also figured out how to flip back and forth among the pages of their Psalters and hymnals with barely a rustle. The absence of these kinds of distractions helps create a more prayerful environment in which to stay focused on interior prayer. This is why the sisters make a practice of respecting one another's personal space when they are all together in choir. And they do that primarily by practicing what is known in monastic circles as "custody of the eyes." Simply translated, it means "don't stare at other people." It's the kind of thing our mothers used to tell us and like so many other things they told us, it makes a lot of sense—especially in the monastic choir, where the sisters are seated in stalls that face each other across the open expanse of their church. There wouldn't be much privacy if you had the feeling that everyone seated across the room was looking straight at you. But because everyone on the other side is practicing custody of the eyes, you need not worry. Of course what you do have to do is make darn sure you avoid sneaking a little peek at what everyone else is up to over on their side of the choir! It works both ways. And that is what makes it such a remarkable system for creating personal space and respecting another person's privacy.

Custody of the eyes isn't just for the times the sisters are together in choir. It comes in handy just about everywhere in the monastery—eating across from one another in the silence of the refectory, sitting at the same reading table in the scriptorium, working quietly together in the candy house—whenever a sister needs to be mindful of the importance of not intruding on someone else. I have to admit that it took me awhile to get accustomed to being with another person without needing to do something to acknowledge her presence. Eventually I caught on to the fact that when I met a sister who was avoiding eye contact it did not mean she was being unfriendly. It was actually just the opposite: she was respecting my privacy and assuming I was doing the same for her.

As important as it is not to intrude on another person's silence or solitude, monastic decorum also involves knowing when and how to be present to others. Once the afternoon work period ended each day, different pairs of sisters would soon be seen outside. Bundled up against the cold, they would head off together along the long, winding road that led past the stone retreat house and out across the rolling farm fields. I used to watch them disappear down the road, with their heads bent companionably toward each other, moving their hands this way and that way as if to emphasize what they were saying.

The sisters invest a lot of energy into the relational side of their communal life. They put a heavy emphasis on taking the time to listen to and support one another, and no one worked harder at it than the abbess. Mother Gail, who was abbess during the time I was there, was a busy woman with a lot on her mind, but she always seemed to have the time to listen when one of the sisters needed her ear. Nowhere was this more apparent than in her custom of scheduling "see time" with each of the sisters on a regular basis. She posted a calendar in the common room with specific times each week when any sister could schedule a personal visit to talk over whatever happened to be on her mind. Gail even set up her office space with "see time" in mind. Next to a bright and sunny window two comfortable rocking chairs face each other across a simple braided rug. Off to the side is a small table with a Bible and a votive candle. It's a welcoming space—perfect for sitting down with a steaming cup of tea on a winter's morning, knowing you have the full attention of someone who will listen carefully to whatever it is you have to say.

Monastic decorum often involves making the effort to do something that will make life a little easier or more convenient for someone else. For example, singing the Divine Office in choir seven times a day involves finding one's way through what can seem like an impossible variety of books—all of which need to be arranged in a certain order so that the proper psalms, antiphons, responses, and hymns are readily accessible. At first I was worried I would never be able to get myself organized so I could flip back and forth without getting helplessly lost in the process. What a relief it was to arrive at my place in choir and discover that all the books had been set out in front of me, conveniently opened to exactly the right spot for that particular Office! I assumed either Sister Kathy or Sister Ciarin (my choir stall neighbors to the right and the left) was looking out for me because I was the new kid on the block. But then I discovered that I was not the only one to arrive in choir and find the books neatly arranged and ready to go. It is customary that once a sister has arranged her own books on the ledge in front of her choir stall, she will reach over and get things set up for her neighbor if that sister has not arrived yet. It is just one of the many little things sisters do for one another simply for the sake of being helpful.

They also take advantage of any opportunity that arises to let someone know she's being thought of, prayed for, or noticed in a loving way. The morning I moved into my room inside the enclosure the first things to catch my eye were a vase of dried flowers on my bureau and half a dozen or so notes and handmade cards that had been propped up on the bed, the desk, the bureau, and even next to the sink. At my place in the refectory was a hand-lettered name card and a tiny arrangement of dried flowers. During the next three months I loved coming back to my room to discover that a handmade card or note, artfully decorated with recycled illustrations from greeting cards and calendars, had been slipped under my door. I quickly discovered that this is something the sisters do for each other as well—especially on birthdays, anniversaries, feast days, solemnities, and other special occasions. It's all a part of monastic decorum.

For the sisters, monastic decorum is a matter of working out the details of daily life in a gentle and nurturing way. There is more to it than simply avoiding behaviors that will be offensive and intrusive to others. It is equally important to bring a little more beauty, joy, and harmony into what it means to live together on a daily basis. This is a shared responsibility that the sisters take very seriously. But they are also quick to show their appreciation and gratitude for one another's efforts, as was evident each time I noticed a sister bring her hand to her mouth while making eye contact with another sister. That's the monastic sign for "thank you."

Domestic Decorum

I am often struck by the lack of "decorum" in our world outside the monastery where people do not always remember to pay attention to the effect they have on others. It's unpleasant enough to run into rude and discourteous strangers at shopping malls, movie theaters, and other public places. But what is even more disheartening is that we are often to blame for not paying more attention to our own behavior. And perhaps nowhere are we more in need of "decorum" than in our own families. For some strange reason we often act as if there is no need to be careful of what we say and do when we are in our own homes. It's easy to ignore the impact our words and actions can have on the people who are closest to us even though we can be quick to take offense when the tables are turned. Three months of living with the sisters opened my eyes to the importance of paying closer attention to these kinds of things.

For me, "domestic decorum" means reminding myself that I am not the only person in this house, and now that both Denny and I are retired that has become even more important. It has meant taking a look at what is involved in being together all the time—and how that affects the way we treat each other.

Domestic decorum includes doing what we can to maintain a comfortable and pleasant living environment. Personally, I have tried to be more honest with myself about my tendency to conveniently overlook all those little things I hope Denny will take care of so I don't have to (replacing burnt-out lightbulbs; refilling the gas tank). And I have really tried (not always successfully) to get in the habit of putting things away after I have used them so they will be there the next time he goes looking for them.

True, they're all just little things, but so is the way the sisters arrange one another's choir books. It's such a simple favor and it hardly takes any effort. I keep reminding myself that I can take the same approach right here at home by doing a few little favors for Denny now and then—without having to be asked first. Why not take out the garbage or tie up the newspapers for the recycling bin when he is busy doing something else, or take the car in for an oil change if I am going right past the service station—even though I really wouldn't have to.

The other side of domestic decorum has to do with the importance of respecting one another's need for privacy—something that is not always easy for people to do when they have been living together for nearly forty years. We tend to forget there is value in treating each other with some of the same courtesy we commonly extend to guests. We end up ignoring closed doors and may even act surprised or affronted when the other person complains that we could have at least taken the trouble to knock first! We grow accustomed to interrupting each other with the expectation that the other person will immediately drop everything in order to pay attention to what we came barging in for. Now that I am retired I have found it is more important than ever to recognize Denny's need for personal space, and to remember that there are definitely times when one of the nicest things I can do for him is to leave him alone for a while.

On the other hand, one of the benefits of being retired is the opportunity it provides the two of us to be together again—the way it used to be before there were so many family and work responsibilities to juggle. Unfortunately, I've discovered it's just as easy to get wrapped up in the projects and activities that occupy my time now that I no longer work outside the home as it was when I did. Nevertheless, family specialists and marriage counselors say relationships suffer when people are too busy to pay attention to one another. I suspect that happens in marriages when people grow so accustomed to living together that they simply stop noticing each other. As a newlywed I used to watch how bored older couples looked when they were together and wonder what it was that made them seem so indifferent to each other. Now that Denny and I have reached that age I think I know the answer. Marriage takes people in many different directions and unless we are careful, we can lose sight of the other person, even though we sleep in the same bed night after night. To avoid turning into another bored and indifferent old married couple, I think we need to make a point of being present to one another. Sister Gail's "see time" custom has been a good reminder of how important it is to break out of our individual routines long enough to pay attention to each other for a little while. Sometimes all it takes is spending half an hour or so together after our morning coffee to talk over our plans and priorities for the day and catch up on what is going on in the other person's mind. But we have also found it important to create opportunities to get out and have fun together—just as we used to do in those long-ago days before we were married. We have learned to take advantage of the freedom that comes with no longer having to trudge off to work on Monday mornings by taking off occasionally on spur-of-the-moment trips to wherever we can get to without needing to be gone more than a day. Given how quickly our calendars fill up with things that take us *away* from each other, it makes sense to look for opportunities that will bring us back together again.

I have found that when I get all caught up in the details and routines of my life as it unfolds from day to day, I can lose sight of the persons who are such an essential part of it. Living with the sisters affirmed what I have known for a long time: it is not enough simply to assume people will automatically know how I feel about them. Domestic decorum reminds me that it is important to pay attention to what it means to share my life with the people who matter the most to me and to do what I can to make life a little more pleasant for them.

The Sacredness of Others

March 31

Today I was in the wardrobe helping several of the sisters iron the beautiful, long white cowls they wear in choir when one of the sisters suddenly burst into the room, visibly upset, because the car she needed was missing. She had a doctor's appointment in half an hour and afterwards she needed to be at a meeting. But in the meantime, someone else had taken the car—along with a box

*of materials she had already loaded in the back seat—even though
she had signed it out well in advance.*

*Everyone commiserated with her but no one had the slightest
idea who had taken the car. After she had left (even more upset
than when she had arrived), one of the sisters remarked that she
didn't blame her sister for being angry, even though it wasn't a
very saintly way to behave. To which I said it was hard to imagine
that saints never got frustrated, but maybe they just knew how
to handle it a little better. At which point, Sister Mary Ann of the
soft voice and sweet smile replied, "And most likely that's one of
the reasons they ended up being saints."*

A big misconception people have about monastic life is that
it is all a matter of silence and solitude. People who live in monasteries are not there to live a life of prayer all by themselves.
True, they seek God in the depths of their hearts—but they do it
together, in community, and that complicates the picture consid-
erably. It is one thing to talk about living together in harmony
and love, and it is truly a noble thing to remind ourselves that
we have all been created in the image and likeness of God. But
when it is a matter of putting up with people who are hard to
get along with, the last thing I am likely to be thinking is that
there is something sacred about them. However, I got the feeling
the sisters really do make a conscious effort to keep that in mind.
While they are no more immune to anger and frustration than
anyone else, they seem to have a different way of dealing with
it than many of us do. In her book, *Seasons of Grace*, Gail suggests,
"Let's not miss the goodness of the ever-present Lord in others
because of some quirk that makes someone irritating or even
obnoxious. . . . Let's feast one another with the sacred bread of
kindness."[5] Kindness isn't all that easy to put into practice. That's
why one of the things that stands out about the sisters is their
kindness toward one another—especially when you consider
that living together in community isn't all sweetness and light.

---

5. Gail Fitzpatrick, ocso, *Seasons of Grace* (Chicago: Acta Publications, 2000)
105–6.

One of the things I had been most curious about was how on earth so many women could live in such close proximity without getting on each other's nerves. What I found out is that they *do* get on each other's nerves. Even though much of their day is spent in silence, and regardless of the fact that they value and respect one another's privacy, the reality is that the sisters are *together* much of the time. They pray together, work together, eat together, and come together frequently for community meetings and presentations. What's more, because they have few personal possessions, they share almost everything. That means that if someone takes a book out of the library, or the car from the garage, or the key to one of the hermitages without signing it out first, the next person who wants it won't know where to look. It means that if a sister uses up all the glue in the craft room and does not make a note of it so it can be replenished from the housekeeper's supply, the next sister who wants to work on a project is going to be out of luck. It means that if a sister breaks something, or misplaces something, or does not get around to returning something to its rightful place, most likely somebody else is going to be inconvenienced. And when that happens, you can bet that somebody is going to be irritated.

So it is impossible for the sisters to live together that closely and intimately without getting upset with one another on occasion, just like other people. The difference is that they seem to be more aware of their own faults and are more likely to try to correct them—especially when their actions have offended or hurt someone else.

For example, one of the most startling things that happened the first day I spent inside the monastic enclosure had to do with the sisters' openness to accepting responsibility for the way their actions affect others. At dinner that first day, as everyone stood quietly at their places before praying grace, the silence was broken by one of the sisters, who said, "I apologize to my sisters for not getting the sidewalk shoveled before Lauds." After a short pause, someone else spoke up: "I apologize to my sisters for breaking the lamp in the common room." There was another short pause, followed by the prayer before meals, and that was that.

There were few days that went by without this same little ritual being repeated before the noon meal. It always left a deep impression on me, and no wonder. Ours is a culture where people are quick to look around for someone to blame rather than accept responsibility for their actions, or to staunchly defend what they have done in an attempt to exonerate themselves. But at Mississippi Abbey the sister who apologized for not shoveling the sidewalk did not try to pass it off as someone else's responsibility in the first place; and the sister who broke the lamp did not remind everyone that it was really an accident and she certainly did not mean to do it. They simply apologized for what they had done. Period. They did not offer any explanations. (I forgot it was my turn to shovel the walk. The lamp was in the way and I didn't see it.) No excuses, no explanations, no further comment. Just an apology that acknowledged the fact that the sister herself took responsibility for what had happened.

Living in community the way the sisters do would probably become intolerable were it not for the fact that they pay attention to what is involved in dealing with things that can be sources of irritation and conflict. And I got the impression that there was more to it than what I as an outsider was able to observe. It happened occasionally that a note would go up on the bulletin board outside the dining room calling the sisters together at such and such a time for dialogue. The first time this happened, I assumed that since I was always invited to join the sisters when they got together for chapter talks, discussions, and other get-togethers, I was supposed to come along for this meeting too. But then Louise pulled me aside and tactfully explained that this time the sisters were going to be having a community-only meeting and that they would be talking about things that wouldn't be relevant for me. What a polite way to say, this is personal and it's really none of your business! From then on I always checked with Louise first every time one of those little notes appeared on the bulletin board.

I found out later that when the community gets together for dialogue it does not necessarily mean there is a problem. In fact usually it's because there is something the abbess needs to report to the community in order to keep them informed or to gather their input. Whenever a decision needs to be made that affects the entire community, everyone takes part in a discernment process that makes prayer—alone and as a community—a central factor in arriving at a course of action. So most of those little notes that appeared on the bulletin board had to do with things that simply needed to be brought to the sisters' attention, or with a discernment process that was taking place.

I was curious about those meetings and yet I never had any reason to suspect that what went on during them was particularly problematic. I watched the sisters breeze down to the chapter room and emerge half an hour to forty-five minutes later without the faintest hint that there was a problem brewing. If any of the sisters were upset with one another, you would think I would have been able to pick up on it because it is usually impossible to cover up the kind of tension that hangs in the air when something upsetting is going on.

That is not to say it never happened. As I got to know the community and feel more at home, it did not take long to notice when there were strained expressions on the faces of normally upbeat sisters and to wonder about other nonverbal clues as well. Now and then while out walking I would come across pairs of visibly upset sisters who were clearly in the midst of a heated discussion—until I showed up. And once I glanced out the window while sweeping the scriptorium during the morning work period and noticed two sisters standing outside arguing with each other. Even though they were too far away for anyone to hear what they were saying, it was obvious from their body language that they were not out there having a friendly little chat.

What I discovered is that just because the sisters are committed to living together in charity, charity is not always going to be hassle free. But it's charity that compels the sisters to do something about hassles when they do occur. It is expected that sisters will deal with the problems and conflicts that arise between them instead of ignoring them until they spill over and affect the entire community.

While it rarely happened, occasionally I would get a strong sense that the whole community was on edge, and once I stumbled across a situation where it was obvious something very uncomfortable was going on. I must have missed the note that had gone up earlier because I was not aware the sisters would be gathering in the chapter room that afternoon right around the same time I usually checked my mailbox. Space is at a premium at Mississippi Abbey, and the common room—where the mailboxes are— is located right next to the chapter room with only a flimsy little accordion door separating the two. When I went breezing in to check my mail, I could hear something I was definitely not used to hearing at Mississippi Abbey—voices that were bristling with tension and thick with frustration. I was horribly uncomfortable about being close enough to hear what was being said and wished I had waited until that evening to check my mail.

Even though I did not stick around that day to eavesdrop on what was going on, I have to admit I was awfully curious. Here was a side to monastic life that the rest of us never get to see—a chance to discover what goes on behind their closed doors when there are conflicts in the community. I had come to Mississippi Abbey with some pretty unrealistic notions of the way I thought the sisters behaved toward each other. I knew they couldn't always be as tranquil as they looked when they were all together in choir—sitting there in their white cowls, eyes closed, hands folded in their laps, the picture of serenity—and yet somehow I had always resisted the idea of them getting really angry with each other. Sure, I could understand how they might get upset, frustrated, and out of sorts with one another. But *angry* is something else entirely. As I hurried out of the mailroom that day, trying not to listen to what those raised voices were saying, part of me wanted to stay behind and find out. Just how upset *do* they get with one another? What kinds of things do they argue about? Do they have trouble controlling their tempers? Do they say things they wish they would not have said? Do they lose their cool? Do they sometimes get so infuriated that they end up bursting into angry tears like so many other women do? Why should I think it is any different for them than it is for the rest of us when we find ourselves burning with anger, resentment, and hostility—all those feelings that can be so hard to handle?

Whenever people with different personality styles and temperaments get together for long periods of time, there are bound to be some clashes. It is hard enough living with one person when his or her rough edges start to show. I cannot imagine what it must be like living with twenty. What intrigued me was the way the sisters go about doing it. And one of the more startling discoveries I made was that they really do try to remind themselves that despite whatever it is that is upsetting them about the other person, there is something sacred inside her. Such a mindset is bound to influence the approach they take when conflicts arise and probably explains why they try to deal constructively and charitably with the things that upset them rather than harboring grudges and building up resentments. I got the impression they are much more likely to confront any tensions and conflicts that arise within the community than to ignore them, and judging from what I could observe, the same thing is true of their approach to interpersonal conflicts as well. With the one exception of the two sisters who were arguing outside the refectory door that day, I never saw any evidence that there were problems brewing between sisters, but I know it happens because occasionally the subject came up during conversations and discussions I had with various members of the community.

They never seemed the slightest bit uncomfortable talking with me about the challenges involved in living with one another. Sometimes during a conversation someone would allude to the fact that she had had an argument with "one of the sisters," or that she was feeling frustrated about something "one of the sisters" had said or done. Names were never mentioned, nor did they ever say much more about the matter other than to express how they were feeling about it. But to hear them talk about it gave them an added dimension of credibility because it proved they are just as likely as I am to feel irritated and upset with other people. It also gave me a chance to discover that they have some pretty healthy approaches to handling those kinds of feelings when they arise.

The subject came up one day when I met with a small group of sisters who were discussing a sermon St. Bernard had written about how to handle problems that often erupted between the monks in his monastery. I had never thought about those medieval monasteries being anything but pictures of tranquility and I found it fascinating to discover that those ancient monks were just as likely to get irritated and upset about other people as the rest of us are. But it was even more interesting to listen to what the sisters had to say about the issue. It gave me a chance to see a side of their life that is not usually visible to outsiders and it confirmed what I had suspected all along, namely, that for the sisters conflict is a normal part of community life. They see it as something to be accepted and resolved rather than allowed to fester and grow. They are intent on resolving interpersonal problems in a spirit of charity, always mindful of their own character flaws and shortcomings.

One sister told me she has noticed the things that upset her most about someone else's behavior are often associated with something about herself that is problematic. She explained that it drives her crazy when some of the sisters appear to be so poorly organized. But on closer examination she has come to see the problem has less to do with the other sisters' laid-back approach to things and more with her own tendency to be overly meticulous and fussy.

It is also obvious that prayer is an essential part of their approach to conflict resolution. The sisters pray for themselves, asking for guidance in identifying the true nature of the problem and for help in choosing the words to say when trying to talk about it. They pray for the other sister, praying that she will be able to hear what is being said and understand that it is being spoken out of charity rather than animosity. And they pray for the grace to be open to whatever God is about to reveal to them through the other person.

One of the sisters told me that when she has a problem with someone, she tries to remind herself of that sister's inherent goodness; and before talking to her about the problem, she identifies one or two of that sister's positive qualities. She reminds herself that both of them are children of God, created to reflect something of his goodness and love. And so she makes an effort to look at her sister as if she were looking through the eyes of God at the goodness that is there in this person who has offended her. To be able to see this sacred dimension in others is what it means to "feast on the sacred bread of kindness." It is a great grace, and we would all do well to pray for it.

The Sacredness of Others at Home

Living in the midst of a culture that places a high priority on the ambitions, desires, and achievements of the individual rather than on the needs and concerns of others has serious consequences when it comes to relationships. When rights outweigh responsibilities and control is more important than cooperation, it is no surprise that we see so little compassion, tolerance, and generosity in the way people treat one another. Sometimes it's easier to feast on power and self-gratification rather than "the sacred bread of kindness" Sister Gail so lovingly describes. To be a kind and gentle person probably is not high on the list if you're keen on living in the fast lane, intent on getting ahead and making a name for yourself. Chances are that even those who are not on the fast track end up putting their own needs first when push comes to shove.

Actually, pushing and shoving are good metaphors for the way we often treat other people: we push aside their needs and shove our own demands onto them instead; we push our expectations for how they ought to behave and shove aside the things they need from us; we push our ideas, opinions, and critical observations about their behavior and shove aside the things they try telling us about our own. We push against them with our anger and resentment and shove aside the need to forgive.

At the same time we know the Gospels are based on a radically different approach to others. What Jesus teaches about love, forgiveness, compassion, generosity, and service can have a powerful impact on our lives in terms of the way we relate to people in our families, neighborhoods, faith communities, and workplaces. Unfortunately, the process of getting from the message to the impact of the message is often an uncomfortable one, probably because we have picked up some inaccurate notions of what love entails.

In our culture, *love* is often equated with the way we *feel*—feeling good, feeling happy, feeling loved in return. Much of what passes for love stems from our own needs and desires. I want to feel good about myself, to be cherished and affirmed, to be accepted and valued. And so I can end up confusing what it means to love someone with how I want that person to make me feel.

But the kind of love that is involved in recognizing the sacredness of others has less to do with the way I feel and more to do with the choices I make to behave or not to behave in a certain way. Perhaps in the long run it is more an act of the will than a matter of the heart. Certainly this is the case when I am called upon to do the loving thing even though my heart may be heavy with the weight of anger, resentment, or even ambivalence. And yet I have been called to love in spite of the fact that people can be unreasonable, self-centered, demanding, and ill-tempered; arrogant, argumentative, self-righteous, and rude; selfish, greedy, and mean-spirited. I have a lot to learn about how to recognize what is sacred about them (especially since I'm so adept at complaining about them). But Gail would say I must be willing to share the bread of kindness with everyone at the table. In other words, be kind to people regardless of what they do or how they behave, not because of how they make me feel but in spite of it.

Come to think of it, sometimes I have a hard enough time being kind to the people in my life who are lovable: those persons who are nearest and dearest to me, the very ones who do love me in return. It is so easy to let closeness to the people I cherish cloud my vision. I know it is a dreadful mistake to assume that since they know how much I love them, this somehow excuses me from having to pay attention to the things I say and do (or don't say and do). I can end up taking them for granted, ignoring the things they need from me, and refusing to acknowledge the hurtful impact my actions and words can have on them.

So it seems to me that one of the lessons monastic people have to teach me has to do with what it really means to be a loving person. It is so much harder than it sounds, especially when I find myself struggling to deal with people who frustrate and upset me. But observing the sisters at Mississippi Abbey has given me some fresh insights into what that involves.

For starters I have tried to be more honest about confronting things I would rather overlook about myself when it comes to the way I feel about those people who "push my hot buttons" and trigger all sorts of unpleasant thoughts inside me. I don't like admitting it, but I have come to recognize that I am simply not the epitome of tolerance I would like to think I am when it comes to getting along with people whose opinions and ideas are at odds with my own. While I may try fooling myself into thinking I am a pretty tolerant and nonjudgmental person, the fact is I can be terribly critical of the faults and limitations of others. Even though I am usually (but definitely not always) able to refrain from outwardly carrying on about other people's behavior, inwardly I tend to let myself dwell in great detail on everything about them that upsets me.

It is always easier to justify the way I feel rather than to look at what I need to do about it, and nowhere is this more obvious than with my tendency to have very high—and frequently unrealistic—expectations of other people. Often the reason I feel disappointed or frustrated by others has more to do with me than with them. I have preconceived ideas about the way I expect them to respond to me, and when they do not, I feel that they have let me down. My tendency is to tell myself that I am perfectly justified in expecting the other person to behave according to my wishes, or see things my way. Since it makes perfect sense to me, why can't he or she see it that way too?

It is one thing to recognize all this about myself. Changing it is another story. It is a lot like exercise. My sister Marti's healthy lifestyle (not to mention her trim figure) is a good reminder of how beneficial it is to work out on a regular basis. But I keep coming up with excuses for not following her example. It comes down to the fact that so often the things I ought to be working the hardest at are usually the very things I am most likely not to want to do. The same thing is definitely true when it comes to changing the way I respond to people in my life who frustrate and upset me. It means learning to concentrate on recognizing the needs and concerns of others rather than acting as if mine should always come first.

But it also means learning how to handle one of the hardest things about conflict—the anger that it often generates. I think it is safe to say that many of us (especially those of us who are women) do not handle conflict very well because we don't know what to do with the anger that usually goes along with it. Either we shy away from it completely—which leaves us especially vulnerable—or else we give in and let our tempers take over. Both are no-win scenarios that usually leave us feeling bad about what has happened. Meanwhile the problem itself remains unresolved and ready to fester until the next spark of dissension sets it off again.

I remember reading once that one of the most important things we can teach our children is how to deal constructively with problems, especially the kinds of problems that crop up between people. It makes a lot of sense when you consider how hard it is for people to get along in this world. Yet we surely are not doing much to show our kids that there are alternatives to the steady stream of violence and aggression they see modeled all around them. And it's not just children who are at risk. While the entertainment industry claims it is only responding to what the public wants to see, I find it disturbing that so many adults seem to enjoy watching quarrelsome, belligerent, and abusive people confront one another with such malice. I can't help but wonder whether a steady diet of media violence colors the way we deal with our own anger by reinforcing destructive behaviors that do nothing to resolve problems that need to be addressed. It surely doesn't do much to help us recognize that there are alternatives to that kind of behavior, and that those alternatives are much more effective.

We all need positive role models to show us how to handle our anger so we can address the problems that lead to it. Some of the best lessons I've learned about that come from the monastery. Perhaps it's because the sisters' life of prayer strengthens their resolve to take seriously what the Gospels say about forgiveness and love.

The point is not to stifle anger but rather to stop dwelling on it, because if I allow it to escalate, chances are my anger will only become harder to handle. It takes a tremendous amount of discipline to keep that from happening. Truth be told, when I am angry I have a tendency to indulge myself in spelling out in great detail all the many reasons I have for feeling that way. Obviously this only fuels the fire and the more I think about it, the worse I feel. It's far better to catch myself in the act and simply refuse to go any further. But that means being willing to give up that strangely sweet pleasure that goes along with thinking about how miserable I am.

Recently I saw a woman wearing a T-shirt that said, "Put on your big girl panties and deal with it." That is a good thing to keep in mind in order to avoid being consumed by anger. Pretending that I do not feel angry will not help at all. But concentrating on how upset I am only makes it worse. The sooner I'm able to catch myself in the process of mulling over how furious I am, the sooner I'll be able to control what I say or do about it. That way I stand a better chance of finding a constructive way to deal with the problem.

Developing a constructive approach to conflict requires effort on the part of both parties involved. Sometimes I think the most difficult relationships are those where one person is committed to working hard at it and the other person is unwilling to cooperate. I often think of Christ's words about reconciling your grievance against your brother before offering your gifts at the altar. But what if the brother isn't willing to do his share of what needs to be done to rebuild the relationship? What if he is so consumed by his own anger that his only stance is one of aggression? What if he couldn't care less about reconciliation and is only interested in confrontation? It's hard enough trying to deal with conflict when both parties are working at it, but when one of them is too stubborn, resentful, or self-centered to even try, it puts a dreadful burden on the other one. I wonder how many marriages come apart for that very reason, and I feel blessed to be married to someone who is willing to help resolve the inevitable conflicts that occur between us rather than give in to the kind of anger that can cripple a relationship.

Over the years we have found out a thing or two about handling these kinds of situations. We have learned that concentrating on how right we are and how wrong the other person is only leads to defensiveness and inflexibility. We have discovered that instead of spending our emotional energies thinking about how justified we are in being angry, it is far better to make an effort to get to the bottom of whatever it is that's bothering us. And experience has taught us that it definitely is not a good idea to try talking about the problem when we are both so mad we can barely think straight. It's far better to agree on a neutral time to sit down together and take an honest look at what happened without having to worry about being blinded by the anger that went along with it. As Benedictine Sister Mary Margaret Funk explains in her book *Thoughts Matter*, the insidious thing about anger is that regardless of the severity of the incident that caused it, it can get ugly in a hurry if we're not careful about how we handle it. She points out that anger "causes distraction and misguided actions. When I am angry both my own soul and that of another person are equally inaccessible."[6] That explains why anger makes it so difficult to deal effectively with conflict. When we are angry we become inaccessible to one another. Once that happens it becomes impossible for any real communication to take place between us, because in order to communicate we must be willing to listen. It is hard enough to do that under the best of conditions, but it's even trickier when there are sensitive issues to be discussed, and it's next to impossible when we are consumed with the kind of anger that makes us inaccessible to each other. But listening is how we gain access to the hearts of others. It helps us understand the world as it appears to them, gives us insights into why they behave the way they do, and helps us recognize what they need from us.

It occurs to me that at the core of the sisters' approach to conflict is a strong commitment to making sure that anger does not keep them from being accessible to one another. It is based on the importance of communication and the recognition that anger impedes it. It is why the sisters meet for "community dialogues" to address problems as they arise, and it makes a lot of sense for the rest of us to follow their example. The point is to set a neutral time to discuss problems instead of simply stewing about the angry feelings they create. That way there will be a better chance of getting to the bottom of whatever was going on in order to find a workable solution.

6. Mary Margaret Funk, osb, *Thoughts Matter* (New York: Continuum, 1998) 70.

Someone who should have known better once told me that it's idealistic to expect people to be willing to approach conflict constructively. "That's not the way it is in real life," he said. "We all get mad and say and do things we shouldn't but nothing can be done about it except to try to forget it happened." It is unfortunate that for so many people "real life" is such a bleak and negative business, as if the normal state of affairs consists of being unhappy with ourselves and continually at odds with everyone around us. And my friend of the dismal outlook seems to be oblivious to the fact that some of the things we say and do can hurt others deeply, leaving behind wounds that sometimes never heal.

Our lives are constantly entwined with the lives of others. Complex bonds connect us, adding depth, purpose, and joy to our lives, and yet the weight of those bonds can fall heavily upon our hearts. The relationships we have with the people we care about are often as fragile as they are strong, and sometimes it is difficult to know how we are to go about loving others as we should. I think it has a lot to do with remembering that there is something sacred about each one of us, even the most mean-spirited, cantankerous, and obnoxious of us. I read somewhere that we would all be a lot better off if we could only remember that there is always more good in a person than his or her own worst act. I think that says a lot about what it means to reverence what is sacred in others.

Times of Celebration and Times of Solitude

January 31

Gail's birthday celebration was today! The festivities began with a coffee break in the refectory following Mass and it felt strange to be talking in that room now that I've finally started getting used to the strict silence the sisters maintain during meals. This morning, however, everyone was laughing and talking while they congregated around the coffeepot and a tray of Hanne Maria's homemade biscotti. But the real celebration came right after Midday Prayer. We gathered in the scriptorium, which had undergone quite a transformation. The heavy bookshelves in the center of the

room had been lugged off to the reading porch and the sturdy
reading tables had been pushed to the sides of the room and covered
with white tablecloths, candles, and centerpieces. The cooks had
outdone themselves and we oohed and aahed our way through
treat after treat from the appetizers right on through to the dessert
course. Then the tables were cleared and we all sat back for the
program, presented by an energetic team of sisters who had put a
note up earlier that week requesting volunteers. There was a wide
and eclectic range of talent that came forward. Everything from
a violin solo to an audience participation number in which our
part was to add appropriate vocal punctuation marks to the bal-
cony scene from Romeo and Juliet. It was a hard act to follow, but
Louise and Kate pulled it off with their dance routine—a lively
jitterbug—which brought down the house possibly because in
their bobby socks and ponytails the two of them looked like they
had stepped straight out of the fifties.

The idea of going to parties inside a monastery probably
sounds like an oxymoron to some people. A friend of mine re-
acted in horror when I told her I was planning to live with the
sisters for three months. "Does that sound like *fun* to you?" she
asked with a horrified look on her face. I suppose like many
people who don't know much about monasteries she assumes
they are pretty glum places. But that is definitely not the way it
is at Mississippi Abbey, where the sisters are so good at recognizing the importance of celebrations and so clever at finding creative ways to have *fun*.

Looking back, I think I probably did more partying during
those three months I lived with the sisters than I would have
done had I stayed home. But they were not ordinary parties. They
were celebrations and one of my favorites was Mardi Gras, held
the afternoon before Ash Wednesday. The heavy, gray storm
clouds that accompany a major winter storm had been rolling in
all during the morning and by the time we gathered in the chapter room for the party, it had already begun to snow. We were all
in a festive mood and while the storm raged outside we helped
ourselves to candy, popcorn, and soda before settling down to
watch a movie. Although the sisters have a television, the only
times it is used are when there's a national crisis or emergency—

and even then the reception is so poor that it's hardly worth the effort. But they do have a VCR and several times a year the community gathers for a movie. When I was there, the movie of choice (everyone gets a chance to vote) was *My Big Fat Greek Wedding*. And what a hoot it was! We laughed all the way through it, enjoying the movie immensely—even the sister who had voted for something different and had told us she was only coming for the party food and planned to leave as soon as the movie started. She enjoyed it as much as the other sisters did, and it occurred to me that it had probably been a long time since she—or any of the others for that matter—had even been to a wedding. I couldn't help wondering whether the movie caused anyone regrets about what she had given up by choosing to live as a cloistered nun instead of wife and mother. It certainly didn't seem that way judging by the fun the sisters were having. Everything about the party was a great success, including the "wedding cake" on the snack table and the little white napkins with gold wedding bells printed on the corners.

There was always a generous array of good food on hand whenever the sisters got together to celebrate. And for the really grand occasions there was wine as well. But what made the various treats that showed up at parties taste even better was the very fact that we didn't have them every day. And that was definitely the case at the Mardi Gras party, since we all knew that Lent was starting the next day!

Mardi Gras was just one of many celebrations I was able to get in on while I lived with the sisters because they have a knack for tuning in to what is significant about a given day or a particular occasion. I think that's the difference between merely getting together for a party and gathering together to celebrate. It has to do with centering in on why there is a cause for celebration in the first place.

Take feast days and solemnities, for example. In the monastery, where the year unfolds according to the liturgical calendar, there is not a month that goes by without something to celebrate. To begin with, the events that mark what is most significant about our faith—the incarnation, Easter, the resurrection, and Pentecost—form the framework for an annual cycle of celebrations that focuses on God's action in the world. Celebrating these mysteries means entering into the realm of the sacred, and that's what liturgy and ritual can do for us. They help us articulate the profound nature of what we believe even though we are at a loss to comprehend it. We need a way to bridge the gap between what is ordinary and routine about our lives, and the fact that we sense a deeper meaning beneath it all. Liturgy and ritual take us beyond the surface of our lives into the depths of our hearts and give us a vocabulary of the spirit to express what we find there. The rituals and symbols that play a part in our liturgical celebrations enable us to respond to what is most significant about our faith and join with one another in affirming it. I've always known that. But I haven't always experienced it. Living with the sisters gave me a chance to do both. And so after a while I began to look forward to celebrating the various feast days, solemnities, and other special occasions that showed up on the liturgical calendar.

The first one that occurred while I was there was on February 2, the feast of the Presentation, also known as Candlemas. The liturgical readings for that day are filled with references to light and remind us to be patient and persevere in hopeful trust that goodness and love will overcome the darkness of our world. "Master, now you are dismissing your servant in peace, according to your word; for my eyes have seen your salvation, which you have prepared in the presence of all peoples, a light for revelation to the Gentiles and for glory to your people Israel" (Luke 2:29-32).

We're used to using light imagery all the time to describe what it means to look for something and then have it suddenly show up right there before our eyes. We talk about needing to "shed a little light on the subject" and we agree that it's helpful to "look at things in a new light." When "a light goes off" in our heads it is because all of a sudden we have been given a new *insight*. Some people call it an "aha moment." The Church calls it revelation. But regardless of what it is called, it always involves discovery and illumination, and it's certainly worth celebrating when it happens.

And so just before dawn on the morning of the feast of the Presentation, we gathered in the dimly lit scriptorium. Each of us was given a lighted candle in a little glass container to carry with us as we processed into the darkened church for Mass. Right before the reading of the Gospel, with its emphasis on the themes of light, hope, and recognition, we rose from our choir stalls and took our candles up to the altar. There they remained, flickering brightly throughout the rest of the day, symbols of the light of Christ and the part each of us plays in bringing his message of peace, compassion, and love into the lives of others. They were still there that night when we gathered for Compline, a reminder of the beauty of belonging to a community of people who have been touched by Christ and are committed to living accordingly.

The Candlemas procession at Mississippi Abbey was the first of many special rituals in which I was able to participate while I lived with the sisters. I had scheduled myself to be in the monastery for Lent and Easter, and if ever there is a time for recognizing the significance of liturgy, symbol, and ritual in our lives, this is definitely it! Lent began at Mississippi Abbey, as it does everywhere in the Church, with the distribution of ashes on Ash Wednesday, a potent reminder of our fragility and mortality. But in the monastery we did not simply file up to the altar to have our foreheads smudged with soot. We removed our shoes and socks first and then we walked up to the altar barefoot. Why? All kinds of reasons come to mind. My first thought as I sat in my choir stall taking off my shoes and stockings was the passage from Exodus where Moses is commanded to remove his sandals because the place he was standing was sacred ground. And so are our churches and holy places, which is why it is appropriate to treat them with respect. Approaching the altar in bare feet is also a sign of humility and poverty. It is a reminder that when you get right down to it, we human creatures are not as grandly in control of our world as we might like to think we are. On the other hand, walking barefoot across a cold floor is also an interesting sensation in itself. It is an earthy kind of feeling, and it reminded me of the way it used to feel on a summer day when I was a child running through the grass "foot naked," as my own son once called it many years later. It's similar to what Thomas Merton said about the tradition of going barefoot to receive the ashes on Ash Wednesday: "Going bare-foot is a joyous thing. It is good to feel the floor of the earth under your feet. It is good when the whole church is silent, filled with the hush of people walking without shoes. One wonders why we wear such things as shoes anyway. Prayer is so much more meaningful without them. It would be good to take them off in church all the time."[7]

Despite the fact that it would be impractical to go sockless and shoeless to church on a regular basis, I'm glad I was able to do it that Ash Wednesday morning at Mississippi Abbey. Merton was right—praying was so much more meaningful that day. And perhaps that is another reason why I need liturgical celebrations. They give me words and actions to express what I am unable to articulate any other way, and rituals that enable me to participate in something I know to be sacred even though it lies beyond my comprehension.

The yearning to be able to believe what is difficult for me to believe has been a driving force within me for as long as I can remember. I keep wanting clarity and conviction, but for me, faith has always meant putting up with the ambiguity and un-certainty that surrounds my yearning for it. And so in order for me to be faithful, I have had to get used to the darkness that goes along with it because searching and struggling with my questions and doubts is one of the ways I encounter the mystery of God. Good liturgy invites me to step out of that darkness for a while in order to encounter what is mysterious without trying so hard to understand it. Liturgy helps me recognize that mystery is something to be welcomed and embraced rather than rejected and run from.

No wonder the liturgy of the Paschal Triduum, beginning on Holy Thursday and ending with the Easter Vigil at midnight on Holy Saturday, spoke so powerfully to me while I was living with the sisters. We began our Triduum observance with an early dinner on Holy Thursday afternoon. The tables had been deco-

---

7. Thomas Merton quoted in J. Robert Baker et al., eds., *A Lent Sourcebook: The Forty Days* (Chicago: Liturgy Training Publications, 1990) 23.

rated with wild plum blossoms, daffodils, and branches from the tulip trees just coming into bloom. There were candles, wine, and a simple meal of seafood quiche, fresh fruits, and homemade bread. As usual we ate in silence but this time, as soon as Gail had finished saying grace, one of the sisters turned on the CD player and the room was filled with the music of traditional Jewish folk songs. It was a poignant reminder of the ethnicity of that Passover meal Christ celebrated with his companions on Holy Thursday night.

After we had finished the meal and pitched in to help with the clean-up chores, we took our refectory benches upstairs and placed them in the hall outside the chapel so we could retrieve them for the mandatum, the footwashing ritual that is such a significant part of the Holy Thursday liturgy. I've seen this performed many times at parishes, and have sometimes heard people object to the time it takes or question the reason for doing it in the first place. But I suspect even the staunchest skeptic would have been touched by what took place that evening at Mississippi Abbey.

At the appropriate time, we brought in our benches and took our places around the altar. We removed our shoes and stockings as Gail, Emma, and Anne Elizabeth entered from the sacristy, wearing white aprons and carrying pitchers of warm water, basins, and towels. Starting at separate sections of the circle we had formed, they moved among us, kneeling down to wash, dry, and kiss our feet. I have to admit the prospect of having someone else wash, dry, and *kiss* my bare feet left me wishing I could somehow ask to be excused. Obviously that was completely out of the question. I won't pretend it wasn't uncomfortable. For one wild moment I even found myself wishing I could have managed to sneak into Dubuque ahead of time for a pedicure. The very idea of the abbess *kissing* my feet still makes me squirm whenever I think about it. But that's the whole point. It's why Peter was aghast when he figured out what Jesus was intending to do. "Oh, no you don't," said Peter in words to that effect. He couldn't stand the thought of letting the man he loved and revered perform such a messy and menial task. That's the point of the Gospel story and the ritual that enacts it. It's a lesson in the humility that goes along with service and the vulnerability that is often a part of accepting it.

What took place that Holy Thursday was the beginning of a series of liturgical celebrations that center around the mystery of Christ and why he is the answer to the darkness, pain, and yearning at the heart of our desire for God. Traditionally, on Good Friday we are faced with the difficult challenge of coming face-to-face with the passion and death of Jesus and what that means for all of us who must live in a world where suffering is an unavoidable reality.

The monastery was a somber place to be that Friday. The tone had been set with Vigils, which took place entirely in darkness with the psalms being read by individual sisters instead of sung by the community. The mood intensified as the day progressed. Even though silence is the norm at the abbey, that day it seemed to grow even quieter from noon until five minutes to three in the afternoon when we assembled in the chapel, having been summoned there by the clacking noise of the wooden clapper that takes the place of bells from Holy Thursday until the Easter Vigil.

For me, the most awesome part of Good Friday has always been the veneration of the cross—despite the fact that most years I tell myself I'm not going to go through with it because of all the perplexing questions about Christ that keep plaguing me. Each year as I listen to the passion being read on Good Friday, I spend most of my time trying to decide whether or not to stay seated while the rest of the congregation processes to the altar to kiss the cross. And each year, by the time the rest of the congregation has started to move forward, I've always made up my mind to join them. I've never understood why. On that particular Good Friday at Mississippi Abbey there was absolutely no doubt in my mind that I'd be joining the sisters for the veneration of the cross. It was because I could sense that the liturgy that day was touching me in a way that was much more powerful than my most troubling uncertainties.

We approached the cross in single file beginning in the back of the church, moving slowly down the center aisle. But we didn't simply walk up to the sanctuary, where two sisters stood holding a large cross between them. Instead we began with a bow at the back of the church and then stopped to perform two separate prostrations along the way. Kathleen had given me a quick demonstration ahead of time. First came what's called a "knuckle prostration," performed by kneeling down, placing the knuckles to the floor, and leaning forward in a solemn bow. Then you rise, take a few steps forward, and kneel again—this time going all the way to the floor in a full prostration, arms folded, hands crossed, palms down with your head resting on top of them. After a few moments you rise again and step up into the sanctuary. You kneel, kiss the base of the cross, rise, and return to your place in choir. I have to confess that Good Friday's veneration of the cross was one time I just couldn't force myself to observe custody of the eyes. Once I got back to my place I couldn't resist watching the rest of the sisters as they approached the altar. It was like a wave of reverence that had been perfectly choreographed to flow from the back of the church to the sanctuary because just as one sister began with a bow at the back of the church, another was already on her knees, while another had just sunk to the floor in a full prostration, while another was kneeling to kiss the cross in the sanctuary. Not only was it was absolutely beautiful but it was also another example of why I need liturgy. In this case it was the prostrations—sinking to my knees and then stretching out face first, feeling the floor beneath me— that did it. I'd never before been so keenly aware of the difference between the *human-ness* of being a man or woman and the *God-ness* of what is sacred. As I participated in the liturgy that Good Friday, I knew I was being caught up in the mystery of an incomprehensible God who shares our vulnerability and our weakness—never mind the fact that I cannot comprehend how this can be so. It was hard to imagine that anything could be more profound.

And then came Holy Saturday. Even though Gail had reminded us that it would be a good idea to spend the day quietly and prayerfully, it wasn't until the Easter Vigil later that evening that things began to calm down enough for that to happen. The monastery was humming, quite literally, with last-minute preparations, almost all of which revolved around the liturgical celebrations that were to come. Much of it involved music.

The sisters give a lot of careful attention to the music that's part of their prayer lives. This is true even for ordinary Sundays as well as for the psalmody that is sung throughout the week. They have choir practice each Saturday afternoon and unless a sister has a very pressing reason for missing it, she's expected to be there. So on that particular Saturday, with the Great Easter Vigil approaching to be followed by Easter Sunday Mass the next day, there was a lot of practicing going on. Even I had been given a part to sing along with Chris and Colum during the Easter Vigil, which began at 3:30 a.m. on Easter morning.

Fire, water, darkness, and light are elemental and earthy symbols that speak to us as nothing else can. They each play a crucial role in the Easter Vigil, which begins in complete darkness, a reminder of what it is like to find ourselves lost and alone, fearful of dangers that threaten to overwhelm us. Due to wet and stormy winds coupled with the threat of worse weather to come, we didn't get to light the Easter fire outside that year. Instead we assembled in the scriptorium and stood there in complete darkness while Julie attempted to start a fire the ancient way, with a flint and rock. Once it began to blaze, its flame was used to light the tall Paschal Candle, symbol of the risen Christ, which one of the sisters held aloft as she led us through the darkened hall and into the church—a potent reminder that Jesus has broken into the darkness of our world to be a lamp for our steps and light for our path. At this point, Gail touched a taper to the newly ignited Paschal Candle in order to pass its flame to four other sisters, who quickly circulated among the rest of us to light the candles we held in our hands. This is one of my favorite parts of the Easter Vigil because it demonstrates how much we need others to bring the light of Christ into our lives. They are the ones who show us mercy, kindness, and compassion, who teach us the power of forgiveness and help us to live lives of peace. In the same way we ourselves are called to be lantern bearers carrying Christ-light into the world.

The glow of those flickering candles is made even more luminous by the words "I am the light of the world. Whoever follows me will never walk in darkness but will have the light of life" (John 8:12). It's appropriate that as we process to the altar, we stop three times along the way to sing, each time on a slightly higher pitch, *Lumen Christi! Deo gratias*—"Light of Christ! Thanks be to God."

Still holding our candles, we took our places around the altar and the Easter Vigil liturgy continued with the gloriously exultant and aptly named *Exsultet*, which takes its name from the Latin word for "rejoice." It must surely be one of the most sublime pieces of music in our tradition, dating back to the seventh century when it was sung in Latin. The year I was at Mississippi Abbey it was beautifully sung in English, without instrumental accompaniment, by Chris and Kathleen. "Rejoice now all you heavenly throngs of angels, rejoice you servants of God most high . . . rejoice, O earth . . . all of creation is illumined, tasting its freedom from the cloud of darkness . . . this is the night Christ burst the bonds of death . . . O unthinkable predilection of love divine . . . O happy fault that merited such and so great a redeemer . . ."

Following the *Exsultet*, the lights were turned on inside the church as the Gloria was sung, and outside the abbey bells began to ring again for the first time since Holy Thursday. Then it was time to settle down and listen to the history of salvation unfold in a series of Scripture readings beginning with the creation story in Genesis, the covenant agreement with Abraham, and the exodus story. The lessons continued with readings from Isaiah, Baruch, and Ezekiel, which described the tenderness and mercy of God and reminded us that we have been given laws to guide us in his ways. The final reading was from St. Paul—a reminder that we have been baptized into the death and resurrection of Christ. Then it was time to hear the central Easter message of Christ's resurrection as recorded in the Gospel.

The Easter Vigil continued with the blessing of the baptismal water and the renewal of baptismal vows. Water is another potent symbol—the stuff of creation and the primal element that sustains all of life. Scripture abounds with watery references that speak of its power to cleanse and sanctify, and to participate in the ritual of baptism by renewing our baptismal vows is to be reminded of our call to holiness.

The Easter Vigil drew to a close with the celebration of the Eucharist and by the time the closing hymn reached its triumphant ending (it sounded like Kathleen had pulled out all the stops on the organ), all of us felt like we were flying pretty high. But the liturgy on Easter Sunday morning has a serene and peaceful feel to it, almost as though we are being invited to reflect and savor the significance of what we celebrated with such intensity the night before. Once again I was reminded of the power liturgy has to awaken within me such a profound response to mystery. Father Tom McCarty touched upon it in his Easter homily when he began by commenting that the phrase "seeing is believing" isn't so accurate after all. Seeing is knowing, said Fr. Tom, and believing is something entirely different since it requires openness to the sacred dimension of life and a willingness to trust what our experiences tell us of our God who dwells there. That's why liturgy is so important. It helps us do that.

As far as I was concerned, there was nothing to compare with how profoundly moving it was to participate in the Triduum liturgies at Mississippi Abbey. But the liturgical calendar is filled with countless opportunities for us to enter into the realm of the sacred as we move through the seasons of the year. These include a number of special times that have been set aside to celebrate the eminent position Mary holds in the teachings of the Church, as well as other days that have been scheduled to help us remember and honor the "superstars" of our faith—that dazzling array of saints whose wisdom, teachings, and examples have left us with such a rich heritage of insight into the spiritual life.

A saint's feast day is especially significant for a sister who has taken that particular name for her own when she received the monastic habit. In fact, a sister's feast day is every bit as important as her birthday. All day long she'll be the recipient of special greetings, notes, and remembrances intended to let her know that her sisters are thinking and praying for her on her special day. The sisters also celebrate anniversaries that are particularly meaningful for them individually or as a community—for example, the anniversary of the founding of their own monastery, as well as the annual feast day in honor of Saints Robert, Alberic, and Stephen Harding, the three founders of the Cistercian order. And for each sister, the dates that mark when she entered the monastery, received the habit, or made solemn profession are every bit as important as wedding anniversaries are to those of us whose vocation it is to be married.

Pivotal events in the life of a sister are always causes for celebration within the community. This is especially true of the day a sister makes her solemn profession. It is an occasion of much rejoicing and festivity both in terms of the special liturgy she plans as well as the gala reception and festive dinner that always follow.

But as important as celebrations and community traditions are, much of the sisters' life is centered on the importance of paying attention to what can only be discovered in solitude. The word "monastic" has its origins in the Greek word *monos*, meaning "one." And while monastic people live together communally, a central aspect of their communal life revolves around the importance of having opportunities to be alone. The sisters are respectful of one another's need for personal space—on a physical as well as a spiritual level. Each sister has her own sparsely furnished room, or cell, with a narrow bed, desk and chair, sink, small chest, and tiny closet for storing the few personal items she needs. Her room is the one place in the monastery where she knows she will not be disturbed and there aren't a lot of other places in the crowded abbey where she can go and be certain she will be alone. She might slip into the church, but someone else might already be there, if not for prayer then to practice the organ. She might go out for a walk across the fields, down to the pond or into the woods, but that's no guarantee that another sister has not had the same idea. At first glance the scriptorium might seem like a good spot for a little solitude, except that there is always a good chance a few other sisters have already made themselves comfortable at one of the heavy library tables. So the only sure bet if a sister wants to be guaranteed she'll be alone is her own room. And I had the feeling that for most of them, the best time of the day for being there is during the early morning hours between Vigils and Lauds. At least it was for me. There was something energizing about being awake at that hour. The interplay between silence and darkness often left me with the impression that I was living on the boundary between the world of dreams and the world of wakefulness, aware that both of them have much to reveal about God.

In addition to the privacy of the monastic cell, each sister has the opportunity to take a "hermit day" once a month. A calendar is posted next to the work chart in the library annex with dates for the sisters to reserve a day and a space in one of the facilities ordinarily used by guests and retreatants, provided it's available. There is a duplex on monastery grounds that serves on one side as a guesthouse for visiting relatives and friends, and a retreat house on the other side. Not far away, nestled up against the woods, is a small cabin with a tiny kitchen and cozy bedroom. Down the twisting road that leads to the fields and gardens below the abbey is an old two-story, stone farmhouse with three bedrooms upstairs, and a bathroom, kitchen, living room, and an old-fashioned porch below. If no guests or retreatants are scheduled to use one of these spaces, the guest mistress makes it available as a hermit destination. Otherwise a sister can choose to spend the day in one of the monastery hermitages or in her own cell.

A hermit day gives a sister a much-needed chance to be truly alone for a little while. She takes along what she will need to prepare her own meals (often consisting of leftovers scrounged together from the kitchen the night before) because aside from joining the community for Mass, the rest of her day is hers alone. In addition to using part of that time for personal prayer and meditation, she may choose to read, write, paint, draw, or work on a craft project. There is a CD player handy for her to use if she would like, and the chance to go for a long walk without needing to hurry back when the bell rings.

In addition to individual hermit days, every so often the sisters take a community hermit day. Except for Vigils, Lauds, Mass, and Vespers, the Liturgy of the Hours is prayed privately on those days, and the sisters are free to use the rest of the day however they wish as long as they are careful not to disturb or infringe on the solitude of someone else. I remember one community hermit day in particular. It was in the middle of February and it snowed the entire day—one of those gentle winter snowstorms that fall softly and steadily for hours on end. The sky was thick with it and every time I looked out it was blowing in gentle drifts across the ground, and swirling through the stark winter branches of the big crab apple tree outside my window. This went on all throughout the day and later, before going to bed, I stood outside the chapel for a few moments peering out into a night that was heavy with snow that could no longer even be seen because of the darkness. Although I had not spoken to any of the sisters that day, I felt especially close to all of them. We had shared a day of companionable solitude, alone together while the snow fell on and on, hour after hour, in its own solitary way. Much later when I got up for Vigils, the church was drenched with light from a perfectly full moon. The snow had stopped falling and lay glittering in great silvery blue mounds outside the abbey. It was one of those indescribably beautiful moments that are over far too quickly, but while it lasted I remember thinking about grace. It's another one of those words we use to express the inexpressible—in this case an attempt to describe the mysterious way God works in our lives. Just what does it mean to be "in a state of grace"? It is a phrase I had never really understood back in the days when I was required to memorize all the answers in the Baltimore Catechism. But that winter morning at Vigils I finally had an image for it. Perhaps the grace of God is like snow that falls gently and silently into our world; it is lovely and ephemeral, but it has the power to transform even what is broken into something beautiful. It seems to me that one of the gifts of solitude is this heightened sense of what it means to live in a world where God is present in so many different ways. Such a recognition must surely be a grace itself, as well as a cause for celebration.

Times of Celebration at Home

When our sons were little boys Denny and I used to take turns scheduling "hooky days" with each of them. One of us would take a day off work, and call the school to say that Casey or Brendan would be absent that day. We even had a name for it. We called it "going on the run" because we were able to get away for a little while without any interruptions. It was a chance to create a special occasion all our own by spending an entire day together, even if what we ended up doing was not all that exciting. It wasn't what we did—a trip to the zoo, an afternoon matinee, lunch at McDonald's, exploring in the woods—that mattered so much. Just being together for the whole day with no one else to interfere was more important than whatever we ended up doing. Now that I think of it, "going on the run" was a way of celebrating what I loved about my children and the experience of being a mother.

Having spent some time with the sisters, I have come to the conclusion that when it comes to celebrations it is not simply a matter of what we *do* to celebrate as much as why we are doing it that is significant. And yet all too often it's the *doing* that seems to be the only thing that matters. What happens during the secular Christmas season is a good example because it bears little resemblance to what I've been told goes on inside monasteries during the liturgical seasons of Advent and Christmas.

For monastic people Advent is a time to be vigilant and patient, a time to prepare oneself interiorly by pondering the great mysteries of our Christian faith. Then beginning on Christmas Eve comes the Christmas season itself, a time to rejoice and marvel at the gift of God's presence in our world. I'm told that at Mississippi Abbey the sisters don't do any holiday decorating until the day before Christmas Eve. That's when the tree goes up and ornaments get unpacked and, with the exception of the crèche in the chapel, all decorations are expected to be in place by Vespers on December 23.

In the secular world it's very different. Once Halloween is over, ads and TV commercials show up, featuring people having fun eating, drinking, partying, and exchanging expensive gifts. Christmas parties and get-togethers get started shortly after Thanksgiving and many people don't have a clue that there even is such a thing as Advent.

During this time the emphasis is on getting together to party and have fun, and there is certainly nothing wrong with that. It's just that getting together for a party isn't necessarily the same thing as getting together for a celebration. I think the difference has to do with the reason for getting together in the first place. That is probably why so many people hate office Christmas parties and similar gatherings that take place during the holidays.

It is because they feel obligated to attend even though they feel there is no compelling reason for doing so.

That might also explain why many people say they hate everything about the "Christmas season." It's because from their perspective there is no real reason for celebration. For millions of others Christmas means rushing through November and December feeling stressed and irritable because there is not enough time for everything they think they need to be doing. People tend to be more impatient and out of sorts than usual; tempers flare and feelings get hurt. Schedules need to be arranged and rearranged so that extended families, blended families, and miscellaneous assortments of relatives who often haven't spoken to each other all year (and in some cases can't stand to be together anyway) can assemble for a few hours of what often turns out to be extreme discomfort, usually revolving around the exchange of presents that were purchased in a hurry, wrapped at the last minute, and often destined to be returned the day after Christmas on what the retail industry acknowledges is one of the busiest days of the year. Google the words "holiday stress" on the internet and you will find scores of web sites with tips and suggestions for coping with the tension, anxiety, and depression that are so prevalent during this time of year. No wonder some people don't feel like celebrating when December 25th arrives. It's because Christmas has no *meaning* for them.

But for the sisters Christmas is a time for focusing on their belief in a God who cares enough about humankind to have entered into the reality of what it means to be one of us. It's a pretty mind-boggling thing to celebrate and helps explain why the rituals and traditions surrounding Advent and Christmastime are so significant.

My own definition of a tradition is any activity or event that occurs with some regularity and holds special meaning for those who observe it. In a changing world, traditions provide a sense of continuity and cohesiveness, especially when passed from generation to generation and valued as a link to the past. Traditions have a lot to do with what it means to belong—to a group, or community, or family—because they help us affirm and express something about what binds us to one another. When we get right down to it, much of what is most significant about these kinds of things cannot even be put into words. That's why it is good to be able to rely on rituals and symbols to help us.

I have always been drawn to the rich symbolism of ritual and ceremony, and so it came as no surprise to find myself reacting so enthusiastically to the opportunity to participate in the various liturgical celebrations that occurred during the three months I spent with the sisters. Now that I'm home again I realize that I've always needed to recognize the spiritual significance of certain things about my life and the way I relate to the people I love. I need to do this prayerfully, even though saying the words of formal prayers doesn't always capture what I'm trying to express. But certain traditions do—in fact, sometimes they even function in much the same way as liturgy and ritual. During Advent, for example, Denny and I light the candles on our Advent wreath and share some special readings, prayers, and poems gathered over the years from a rather eclectic variety of sources. We listen to some music that's been cued up in advance on our CD player and then sit together for a while in silence before blowing out the candles. It is one of my all-time favorite family traditions and always has been—even back in the days when our sons were little boys and it used to be such a hassle trying to get them to cooperate (especially during the quiet parts). Now I would not trade those memories for anything, even though at the time I sometimes used to wonder whether it was worth the effort, since inevitably there would be scuffles and arguments about whose turn it was to blow out the candles. Perhaps it's the poignancy of these kinds of memories that makes traditions so meaningful.

I feel the same way about many of the significant transitions that occur during the course of a lifetime. In planning my parents' fiftieth wedding anniversary, for example, my five siblings and I wanted to make it a celebration of the things that had been important to Mother and Dad throughout the years of their marriage. We sorted through boxes and boxes of old photos and arranged them into a series of displays documenting our parents' lives. We put together a special program featuring a slide/tape presentation that told the story of their courtship, wartime marriage, and the years they spent raising their family. And then came the most exciting part of the evening. The lights were dimmed and the deejay we had hired for the night put on a recording of the "special song" Mother and Dad had danced to during the days of their courtship. Down the aisle came a grandson, looking spiffy in Dad's dress-white naval uniform and a granddaughter looking beautiful in Mother's wedding gown and veil. I'll never forget the look in my parents' eyes as they watched their two grandchildren walk up to them. And when Erik and Karah took their grandparents by the hand and led them out onto the dance floor, there was no doubt in anyone's mind about what was happening. It was not just a celebration. It was a sacred moment, filled with grace and blessing, because it gave us a chance to recognize and be grateful for all the strength and love that has gone into my parents' life together.

Times of Solitude at Home

Like many people who grew up in a large family, I had to get used to doing without much personal space. I can remember how envious I was of my friends who had bedrooms all to themselves and even during my college years there was always a part of me that resented having to share my dorm room with a roommate. Since I was married a week after graduating, it wasn't until I got to Mississippi Abbey that I finally ended up with a room of my own. I loved the sense of privacy—during the entire time I was there no one else set foot inside that room—and I loved the solitude.

But some of my friends who live alone have reminded me that not everyone agrees solitude is such a blessing. For many people it can mean spending long and dreary hours feeling bored and restless, or possibly even depressed. Loneliness can be a very real problem for those who live alone. Without the warmth and companionship of others to relate to and love, life becomes empty and difficult to endure. On the other hand, it is good for us to have opportunities to be alone now and then—not because we have no need for other people but because there is value in getting to know and become comfortable with ourselves as well.

Many of us tend to concern ourselves with the image we present to others, hoping it does the trick and they'll end up believing we're the kind of persons we want them to think we are. And we often measure our worth according to external criteria and standards that don't necessarily reflect what's in our hearts. It's the old story of the person who has climbed the ladder of success only to discover it was propped up against the wrong wall. Carving out an identity based on career recognition, status, prestige, and whether or not we are making a favorable impression on others is ultimately a pretty superficial way of defining who we are as people. That's why all the great spiritual teachers have always placed such a strong emphasis on the importance of coming to the truth of who we are at a deeper, more interior level:

> Begin to recognize yourself, to love and possess yourself, to be kind to yourself, and you will be happy. If you desire to know yourself and to possess yourself, go into yourself, and do not search for yourself outside. Distinguish between what is around you, what belongs to you, and your self! The world surrounds you, your body belongs to you, and you yourself are within, made to the image and likeness of God. Return then, transgressor, to your heart, within, where you are truly yourself.[8]

We need times and places of solitude so that we can get to know ourselves as we really are. We need space—emotional as well as physical space—in order to turn aside from the outside world and pay attention to what is going on inside us. A certain amount of introspection is a healthy thing because without it we run the risk of skimming across the surface of life, missing out on what is to be found by going a little deeper. That's why we need moments of solitude. They give us a chance to imagine and create, to ponder and reflect, to struggle with our demons and draw upon our strengths.

---

8. Isaac of Stella, "Sermons on the Christian Year," quoted in Edith Scholl, ocso, ed., *In the School of Love: An Anthology of Early Cistercian Texts* (Kalamazoo, Michigan: Cistercian Publications, 2000) 56.

As important as solitude is, you would think we might be more careful about fitting it into our lives. Instead, there is a tendency to do just the opposite by filling up our days and weeks with all sorts of things that leave no room for being alone. As a matter of fact, I think somewhere along the line we have picked up the attitude that there is actually something wrong with wanting to go off by ourselves for a little while. It's what Anne Morrow Lindbergh was getting at when she wrote:

> If one sets aside time for a business engagement, a trip to the hairdressers, a social engagement, or a shopping expedition, that time is accepted as inviolable. But if one says: I cannot come because that is my hour to be alone, one is considered rude, egotistical or strange. What a commentary on our civilization, when being alone is considered suspect; when one has to apologize for it, make excuses, hide the fact that one practices it, like a secret vice.[9]

I did not have to feel that way during the time I was living with the sisters, but it's probably because they know that, as important as solitude is for our emotional and psychological well-being, there's a lot more at stake. We need opportunities to be alone because they provide an environment in which we can listen more attentively to what is in our hearts and pray in the language we find there. Solitude invites us to devote our time and energies to what the abbot of New Melleray Abbey calls our "God Awareness." For me that's not always been such an easy thing to do. To be honest, it's something I might avoid altogether were it not for what I've learned from my monastic brothers and sisters about the importance of making it a priority, because quite frankly it often raises questions that are difficult for me to confront—questions that have to do squarely with issues of faith and doubt.

I've never been able to simply take what others have told me about God and hang onto it without a great deal of scrutiny. At the same time, I sense that knowing all about the canons of

9. Anne Morrow Lindbergh, *Gift From The Sea* (New York: Pantheon Books, 1955) 47–48.

our faith isn't necessarily the same as coming to know what we can about the God who dwells within us. I realize that faith is not a matter of what my mind can comprehend because God cannot be researched, measured, analyzed, and defined once and for all the way our twenty-first-century minds would like so very much to be able to do. Nevertheless, I still find myself struggling to make sense of doctrines, dogmas, and teachings that raise so many questions about what theoretical knowledge will never be able to explain.

The author of the book of Hebrews sums it up by pointing out that "faith is the assurance of things hoped for, the conviction of things not seen" (Heb 11:1). But he didn't say it would be easy and it certainly hasn't been for me. I suspect I will struggle with these questions all my life because the path I am following to God isn't as well marked as I'd like it to be. In fact, it's led me into some pretty dark and dismal places. But I sense that this is a journey that really matters and I am beginning to suspect that struggling with the questions I have about God is probably as important as being able to believe I have found the answers. After all, even St. Augustine once said that *if you think you understand God, then it is not God.*

Among the many insights I've brought home with me from the monastery is the importance of remembering that faith depends much more on trust than on intellectual proof. I may not be able to understand what I've been told to believe about a God who is completely beyond my powers of comprehension, but I can learn to trust what my deepest intuition tells me. I sense that there is another way of knowing. It belongs to the realm of the heart and solitude calls me to go there.

When I left the monastery I came home to a husband who understands how important this is. We both know that just as marriage requires a commitment to share ourselves with each other, it also means learning to respect one another's need for solitude. In fact, I think that making sure we each have opportunities to be alone now and then is one of the nicer gifts we can give one another, especially now that we're retired. So it occurred to me that some of what the sisters do to ensure one another's solitude might work equally well at home, in particular the hermit day idea. We have been experimenting by occasionally giving one another the gift of an entire day to spend alone at home free to do—or not do—whatever he or she wishes. It means one of us has to vacate the premises and come up with somewhere else to go for the day so the other one can stay home. Depending on where that person ends up, it usually turns out to be just as much of an opportunity for solitude for the non-hermit as for the hermit!

Occasional hermit days are nice, but they are no substitute for what we need to be doing on a daily basis simply by trying to respect one another's need for a little privacy. It is not so much an issue of physical privacy (I'm reminded of how astonished I was to learn that my grandparents lived together over fifty years and never saw each other naked) as it is a matter of honoring that place inside us that is inaccessible to the other. We must take care not to intrude on the interior space each of us requires in order to educate our hearts and listen to the lessons we learn there. Respecting that space takes many forms. At its simplest it means trying not to interrupt Denny when he is involved in something that is occupying all his concentration. Likewise, it means learning not to make unreasonable and inappropriate demands on his time or expect him to be available to drop whatever he is doing whenever I need him to do something for me. But just as importantly, it means recognizing that there are places deep within him that must remain inaccessible to me because they shelter the mystery of who he is. To respect his solitude enables me to honor what is sacred about him. It is an act of trust and expression of love.

LEARNING TO PRAY

Insignificant man, escape from your everyday business for a short while, hide for a moment from your restless thoughts. Break off from your cares and troubles and be less concerned about your tasks and labors. Make a little time for God and rest a while in him. Enter into your mind's inner chamber. Shut out everything but God and whatever helps you to seek him; and when you have shut the door, look for him. Speak now to God and say with your whole heart: I seek your face; your face, Lord, I desire.[1]

Saint Anselm
The Proslogion

The Liturgy of the Hours

February 26

I wonder if I'll get used to that ear-splitting buzzer that goes off like a fire alarm every morning at 3:30 a.m. to wake everyone up for Vigils. On the other hand, it definitely achieves its purpose, which is to make it next to impossible not to wake up. But it's not waking up that's the problem. It's getting out of bed at that hour of the night when my first inclination is to burrow back down under the blankets for a few more hours of sleep.

In Cistercian monasteries the day unfolds around the Liturgy of the Hours, seven distinct periods when monks or nuns gather together to pray the ancient psalms that have become the

---

1. Saint Anselm, The Proslogion, *The Liturgy of the Hours* (New York: Catholic Book Publishing Corporation, 1975) 184.

universal prayers of the Church. ("Seven times a day I praise you for your just decrees" [Ps 118:164].) Also known as the Divine Office, this is a central part of the sisters' life because it's the *Opus Dei*, the Work of God, and to pray it daily is their main "work." This ancient form of communal prayer takes place in much the same way in monasteries all throughout the world, just as it has for centuries.

The Liturgy of the Hours consists of psalms and prayers that are usually chanted by two choirs of sisters sitting across from each other in the abbey church. The psalms reflect our human condition. They express our anger and insecurity in the face of cruelty and injustice as well as our yearning for goodness and peace, our fears and pain as well as our happiness and wonder, our tendency to grumble and complain as well as our expressions of praise and gratitude. Since there are one hundred and fifty psalms in the Psalter, it takes two weeks to pray all of them in turn according to a pattern that corresponds to the challenges, struggles, sorrows, and joys that are often encountered at various times throughout the day.

Vigils

The day gets started at 3:45 a.m. with the Office of Vigils. It may seem like a ridiculously early hour to be up and about, yet most every monastic person I've ever known has been quick to agree that it's one of the best times of the day for prayer. "Better than the day, then, is the night, since night conceals a man from the disturbances to which the day exposes him," said Gilbert of Hoyland, a twelfth-century Cistercian monk. "Good then is the night which in discreet forgetfulness disguises all things ephemeral, scheduling a time and providing an occasion to seek him who is eternal."[2]

Getting up for Vigils was never easy, but it was always worth the effort. Sometimes on clear nights I could look out the big picture window behind the altar and see the stars and the dim

2. Gilbert of Hoyland, *Sermons on the Song of Songs*, Cistercian Fathers Series 14 (Kalamazoo, Michigan: Cistercian Publications, 1978) 47–48.

shapes of trees against a moonlit sky. Inside, the candle burning
in its stand next to the tabernacle seemed an appropriate metaphor for the prayer that arises within the stillness of our hearts
to illumine the darkness we sometimes find there. I think Vigils
is meant to evoke these kinds of feelings because it's a time for
being watchful and attentive to the things of the spirit. Within
this setting we pray: "O come, bless the Lord, all you who serve
the Lord, who stand in the house of the Lord, in the courts of the
house of our God. Lift up your hands to the holy place and bless
the Lord through the night. May the Lord bless you from Zion,
he who made both heaven and earth" (Ps 133:1-3).

The psalms that are prayed during Vigils reflect some of the
most intense and visceral of human emotions, running the gamut
from alienation and loss, abandonment and desolation, fear and
longing, to bitterness and anger. This is no accident. Who has not
awakened in the night feeling alone and weighted down by an
ominous sense of being frightened and vulnerable in a hostile
world? The depths of the night conjure up dangerous images in
our minds. We instinctively dread the thought of being out by
ourselves at such an hour, having heard too many stories of terrible
acts of violence and horror that take place under cover of night.
This is the time to pray for ourselves and for our world, that we be
protected against the force of darkness and destruction that lurks
outside us as well as from the dark side of what lies buried within
our own natures. The heavy burden of our humanity is contained
in the psalms we pray during Vigils: "In my anguish I called to the
Lord; I cried to my God for help" (Ps 17:7). "See how many are my
foes, how violent their hatred for me" (Ps 24:19). "Why do you hide
your face and forget our oppression and misery?" (Ps 43:25).

The Office of Vigils is divided into two segments or "noc-
turnes" of three psalms each. Following the first nocturne, one
of the sisters steps to the lectern to read a selection from Scripture;
this is followed by a short period of silent prayer. After the second
nocturne of psalms is read, another reader steps to the lectern to
read a short excerpt from various sources, including contemporary authors or from the early days of both the Eastern and the
Western churches. After several short closing prayers, the sisters
stand quietly for a few moments in darkness.

Vigils usually lasts about forty minutes and afterwards some sisters stay behind in the darkened church, while others head downstairs to the kitchen for a cup of coffee and a light breakfast before returning to their rooms and their own private prayer practices.

I rarely went back to bed even though it was still the middle of the night as far as I was concerned. I liked the heightened sense of solitude and the companionable feeling of knowing that everyone else was up alone at that hour too. And I loved the stillness that hung in the air. For some reason it sounded quieter than it did at any other time, possibly because silence loses some of its potency when it's punctuated by the familiar sounds of a busy day.

Toward dawn my favorite place to be was at the big window in the narrow corridor that connects the chapel and dormitory wing to the rest of the house. It was only a matter of time before the sisters would be gathering for Lauds and the abbey would start coming to life again. Usually I wasn't gutsy enough to brave Iowa's subzero winter temperatures, but if it was not too cold I'd step outside for a few moments to watch the sky as it began to change from darkness into the first faint traces of morning. Sometimes I'd take along my camera, hoping to catch that elusive moment in between night and day. But I never did.

Lauds

By around 6:30 a.m. the morning was always well under way and the sisters were scurrying back and forth because there were always early morning chores that needed to be done—shoveling sidewalks if it had snowed the night before, throwing a load of laundry into the big washing machine downstairs, getting the kitchen ready for the day's baking, or possibly just catching up on a little last-minute studying before a class that was going to be held that day. But for me those few minutes before the bell rang were among the most tranquil of my day. I loved standing by the window to watch the little gray and white juncos dart about the ground beneath the bird feeder on cold winter mornings when the sky was gray or thick with snow. So I was usually in exactly the right mood for Lauds, because the very word itself is all about praise. Appropriately enough we begin with: "O praise the Lord, all you nations, acclaim him all you peoples! Strong is his love for us; he is faithful for ever" (Ps 116:1-2).

Mornings are good times for noticing how lovely the world can be. Even if it turns gloomy and dismal in the end, there's still something fresh and hopeful about the beginning of the day. It is a time for paying attention to the importance of gratitude. So it should come as no surprise that the psalms prayed during Lauds are full of praise and thanksgiving. "Let everything that lives and that breathes give praise to the Lord" (Ps 150:6).

On five days of the week Lauds concluded with Mass. I have always heard it said that there is something about daily reception of the Eucharist that nourishes us in a way nothing else can. But until I actually experienced it I never really understood it. Belief has never come easy for me anyway, and I have spent my adult life grappling with questions and doubts that have never been resolved. The mystery of the Eucharist is right up there at the top of the list, which might explain why I have never gotten into the habit of attending daily Mass. But to miss it while I was at Mississippi Abbey would have been unthinkable. It was something I was rather ambivalent about in the beginning. There were so many other things about monastic life that were new and intriguing. I had been going to Sunday Mass for most of my life and so part of me was tempted to dismiss the whole thing as just another case of "been there, done that." What changed my attitude was the fact that the sisters didn't go to Mass. They were a part of it. They were fully engaged and present in every aspect of what was taking place, approaching it with a reverence born of the absolute conviction that there was something sacred going on. Even though they stood in the same spot every day and participated in the same rituals and ceremonies—chanting the same prayers, eating the bread and drinking the wine—each time I watched them as they did it, I had a feeling something very profound and significant was happening for the very first time.

It was that sense of the profound and the significant that struck me about participating in daily Mass at Mississippi Abbey. This is the most important part of the sisters' day because of their deep belief in what it means to be given the Body and Blood of Jesus through the sacrament of the Eucharist. But this kind of belief has never been easy for me. I am still just as mystified as I have always been when I try to comprehend what it all means. Yet I can no longer deny that somewhere deep inside me I recognize that what is happening—incomprehensible as it may be—is more important than I can ever know. Participating in daily Mass helped me better understand another aspect of the Eucharist: the communal nature of it all. How many homilies have I heard on that subject? How many articles have I read about table fellowship and the banquet of the Lord? How many times have I mouthed the words of hymns that sing cheerily of our connection to one another through our participation in the Eucharist? I guess it never really sank in until I found myself doing it day after day with the sisters as we sat together to listen to the readings, joined hands for the Lord's Prayer, turned to embrace one another for the kiss of peace, and approached the altar to bow before being offered the bread, and again before reaching for the cup containing the wine. For the first time I began to sense what it really means to be connected to other people this way. It means that regardless of things that are different about each one of us—our personalities, our temperaments, the way we behave, the way we pray, and the doctrines we believe or disbelieve—we have this one very important thing in common: we are all caught up in the mystery of our faith, whether or not we even realize it or give it a moment's thought. It means that even though I am struggling with my own personal doubts, or preoccupied with the details of my life or whatever may be troubling me, as I approach the altar I am being swept along by something that is much greater than myself. And it is this that sustains me and supports me and carries me along when I am unable to go there on my own. It's as if I am a migrating bird flying with the flock, or a tiny part of the ocean surging along to the shore.

The Little Hours

Cistercian monasteries set aside time throughout the day for monks and nuns to gather together to pray Terce, Sext, and None. They're called the "Little Hours" because of their brevity when compared to the lengthier Offices of Vigils, Lauds, and Vespers; and they consist of a series of short psalms and prayers that help keep the burdens, tensions, and challenges of the day in a more prayerful perspective.

During the morning work period the sisters gather in small groups to pray at their work sites. Mississippi Abbey's candy house is probably one of the very few "factories" in the country that actually has a chapel on the premises. It's a simple, brightly lit little room, with benches along three sides and a small crucifix on the wall. It was designed for no other purpose than to allow the sisters a space to gather for Terce (mid Morning Prayer) when the bell summoning them to come together for that purpose rings. Meanwhile, those who have work to do outside the candy house get together wherever they happen to be—in the kitchen, the liturgy office, the library, or possibly outside working in the fields—to pray with two or three others who are in the vicinity.

It took me awhile to get used to having my work interrupted to go pray Terce. But no matter how busily engrossed the sisters were in their tasks, everything stopped when the bell rang. I often wished I could have ignored it and kept right on working instead of having to leave whatever I was doing and come back to it later. But after awhile I began to see the value in deliberately slowing down to focus on prayer instead of giving in to the notion that nothing mattered except the task at hand.

The morning work period ended at 11:30, giving the sisters thirty minutes to clean up and take a short break before gathering back in the church for Midday Prayer (Sext and None combined) at 12:00. By that time I was usually tired after my morning's work and it felt good to get back to my place in choir and rest a bit. It also helped me stay focused and after a few weeks it dawned on me that praying the Little Hours was a good way to keep work itself in perspective. The psalms and prayers that comprise Terce, Sext, and None reflect the burden of labor and remind us that there are more important things than the plans we have made for whatever it is we hope to accomplish during the day: "To the Lord in the hour of my distress I call and he answers me" (Ps 119:1). "If the Lord does not build the house, in vain do its build-ers labor" (Ps 126:1). " O blessed are you who fear the Lord and walk in his ways! By the labor of your hands you shall eat. You will be happy and prosper" (Ps 127:1-2).

Vespers

For me, the word *vespers* belongs with words like *twilight* and *eventide*, words that aren't used to describe either the afternoon or the evening but rather that period in between. It is a pleasant time, especially during the winter months when the sun slips closer to the horizon and the light that falls across the trees and valleys is tinged with gold. It's one of my favorite times of the day and I suspect other people feel that way too, even though those of us who do not live in monasteries are likely to miss out on it entirely. Hurrying home through rush hour traffic, scurrying around the kitchen to fix a quick supper, caught up in the stress of juggling a busy family's multiple schedules, many of us are just too busy to stop long enough to pay attention to this loveliest time of day. But those who pray the Liturgy of the Hours are more likely to notice it because they are accustomed to following schedules that are in sync with the natural flow of time as it swings from darkness into daylight and then back again.

As is the custom in all Cistercian monasteries, the sisters gather for Vespers when late afternoon begins to fade into early evening. It is one of the most tranquil and restful of all the liturgical hours, a time for looking back on the day and giving thanks for having had another opportunity to be there for it, regardless of what it has involved. The hymns, psalms, and prayers that are sung during Vespers speak of God's goodness, praising him for the beauty of creation and the many gifts he has given us: "Let the sea and all within it, thunder; the world, and all its peoples. Let the rivers clap their hands and the hills ring out their joy. . ." (Ps 97:7-8).

Sitting in choir at the end of the day while the sun was setting, I often felt a warm and comfortable drowsiness come over me and sometimes I had to struggle to keep my eyes open. It would have been pleasant enough to drift off to sleep then and there, accompanied by the soft sound of the sisters' singing. In fact I used to wonder if any of them had the same problem, especially since they had been up since 3:30 a.m. and had worked much harder than I had all day. If anyone did nod off, nobody else paid any attention. After all, practicing *custody of the eyes* means learning to resist the temptation to check out whether or not any of the sisters sitting across from you are struggling to stay awake!

Compline

It was dark by 7:00 p.m. on wintry evenings when the sisters gathered for Compline, a word that has its origins in a Latin term meaning "to complete." During the week we stood in the dimly lit church to chant Psalms 4 and 90, but Mississippi Abbey is blessed with a talented harpist and so on the weekends we were always accompanied by the "murmuring sound of the harp" (Ps 91:4).

Like most everyone who has ever prayed Compline in a Cistercian monastery, I loved this last Office of the day. It was a perfect ending, a beautiful reminder that all will be well because we are being held in the tender hands of a loving God. "You will not fear the terror of the night nor the arrow that flies by day, nor the plague that prowls in the darkness nor the scourge that lays waste at noon. . . . When he calls I shall answer: 'I am with you.' I will save him in distress and give him glory" (Ps 90:5-6, 15).

I've always thought that Compline is the most feminine of all the liturgical hours. To begin with, it's one of those times when traditional images of God as a stern and decidedly masculine authority figure completely break down. Instead, the Compline psalms speak of the gentleness of a God who watches over her children with a mother's nurturing love—a love that is both tenderhearted yet fiercely protective. Psalms 4 and 90 have a lullaby-like feel to them and there's something about Compline itself that reminds me of a mother preparing her children for bed. "I will lie down in peace and sleep comes at once for you alone, Lord, make me dwell in safety" (Ps 4:9).

After the two Compline psalms are sung, the sisters recite several short prayers asking for God's protection through the night. Then they chant the lovely canticle from Luke 2:29-32 in which Simeon thanks the Lord for having kept his promise and asks to be dismissed in peace.

There are few embellishments in Cistercian churches. The architecture is simple and aside from a crucifix there are no statues or artistic representations. The sole exception is an icon of Mary located near the altar. As Compline draws to a close the church is darkened, save for a single lamp left burning in front of the icon while the sisters sing the *Salve Regina* (in Latin one week and in English the next). This beautiful hymn in honor of Mary has been sung in Cistercian monasteries at Compline since the thirteenth century.

Compline ends with the sisters kneeling silently in the darkness to prayerfully review the day and reflect on what they have done or not done to live according to Christian values and practices. After a few moments the last *Angelus* bell is rung and the sisters come forward in pairs to bow before the abbess and receive her blessing before retiring for the night. Now begins the great silence—the custom of maintaining strict silence until Lauds the following morning. The sisters have completed another round in the sequence of prayers that make up the Liturgy of the Hours. Following Compline, and on through the early hours of dawn, no one will speak or engage in any activity that is likely to disturb the deep stillness of the night.

Once during a presentation to the Associates of the Iowa Cistercians, Fr. Brendan Freeman, the abbot of New Melleray Abbey, remarked that the Liturgy of the Hours takes us into a different kind of time zone. We enter through doors that have been hung on the great hinges of the day, dawn and dusk. Lauds and Vespers are the gateways into a continuous cycle of prayer that is in harmony with the rhythms of the day and of the night. It is how we participate in the sanctification of time, says Abbot Brendan.

It's one thing to pray the Liturgy of the Hours each day for three months. But what must it be like to fit an entire lifetime around such a tightly structured framework? After a few years of faithfully showing up to pray seven times a day I would probably begin to lose my initial enthusiasm about doing it. I imagine I'd start to find the whole thing rather tedious and even a bit boring, especially since the very same prayers, hymns, and psalms are used over and over and over again. I know for certain I wouldn't appreciate being interrupted to go pray just as I was getting into the swing of doing something else. Maybe I would go reluctantly and end up spending the whole time preoccupied with thoughts about what I had been doing before the bell rang. I'm guessing my mind would wander off in all sorts of directions and many of them would not be very prayerful. So I couldn't help but wonder whether the sisters ever feel that way about needing to structure their lives around the Liturgy of the Hours.

I'm betting the answer is yes. I've been told that yes, they do get distracted in choir while they're reciting or singing words they have sung numerous times before. And yes, it is inconvenient if the bell rings while they are right in the middle of something they wish they could stay behind and finish. And yes, there are times they would like to be able to stay right where they are instead of joining their sisters in choir. So the question inevitably arises: what keeps them going back?

To begin with, although the Liturgy of the Hours nourishes the spiritual lives of monks and nuns, that is not their sole reason for praying it so faithfully. It is probably more accurate to say that through the Liturgy of the Hours, which is actually the prayer of the whole Church, monks and nuns pray for and with the people of God. It has been a vital part of the spiritual lives of men and women throughout the ages, and because it is composed primarily of the same psalms that Jesus prayed all throughout his life, it is his prayer as well as ours. Monks and nuns tell us that when they show up day after day for the Liturgy of the Hours, they are not simply mouthing empty words. They are repeating the prayers Christ prayed and in doing so they are giving voice to his voice speaking within them.

There is another reason for the sisters' fidelity to the highly structured Liturgy of the Hours even when it seems inconvenient or burdensome. It is because prayer is their life's work. It is their way of being of service to others. It is what would be outlined in their job descriptions, if they had such things. Come to think of it, they do and it's probably one of the oldest ones around, since it was put together in the sixth century when St. Benedict devoted twelve chapters of his Rule to what he termed the *Opus Dei*, or the Work of God. He summed up the principal occupation of a monk by noting that nothing else is as important as that kind of work.[3] That is why the sisters get together to pray the same

3. See RB 43.3.

psalms each day, week after week, month after month, year after year, even though sometimes they are tired and distracted. It is because they are serious about their work.

The Liturgy of the Hours at Home

While the Liturgy of the Hours is not the exclusive prayer of monks, nuns, priests, and other members of the clergy, they are the ones who are most familiar with it. Even though technically it is the prayer of the entire Church, it is probably safe to say that many of her members haven't got the slightest idea how to go about praying it.

There are indications, however, that more and more laypeople are learning. Many Catholic and non-Catholic churches now offer opportunities for members of their parishes and congregations to participate in regular Morning and Evening Prayer based on the Liturgy of the Hours. In addition, there are a number of excellent books available for those who want to learn how to make it a part of their own prayer lives. There are even some web sites, such as universalis.com, that make it possible for people to pray Morning, Midday, and Evening Prayer right at their computers.

It is also worth noting that in recent years greater numbers of laypersons are turning to monasteries to help them deepen and nurture their spiritual lives. Following the tradition of monastic hospitality, most monasteries have guest facilities with rooms available for personal retreats, and people who come are always invited to participate in the daily Liturgy of the Hours. In addition, Cistercian and Benedictine monasteries have opened their doors to growing numbers of people eager to join other like-minded men and women in order to learn and support one another in applying monastic wisdom to their lives. Currently there are hundreds of Benedictine oblates and Cistercian lay associates who meet regularly at monasteries throughout the world. One thing these groups have in common is that all of them pray a portion of the Liturgy of the Hours when they gather for their meetings, as well as when they are apart.

As members of the Associates of the Iowa Cistercians (AIC), my husband and I belong to a group of over fifty men and women who meet regularly at Mississippi Abbey or nearby New Melleray. Our monthly meetings take place during the day and are scheduled around the Little Hours of Terce, Sext, and None, which we pray together with our monastic brothers and sisters. During the rest of the month we strive to incorporate what we can of the Liturgy of the Hours into our daily schedules at home. Some are more successful at this than others.

A few associates incorporate the Little Hours of Terce, Sext, and None into their daily routines even though they are still working at jobs and careers outside the privacy of their own homes. As one busy professional man has pointed out, it's perfectly appropriate to take coffee breaks in the morning and again in the afternoon in addition to having a lunch hour, so why not use some of that time to pray the Little Hours?

We know a few others in the AIC who actually pray Vigils in the middle of the night. Perhaps they are night owls who just happen to be awake at that hour, or maybe they're insomniacs who have trouble getting to sleep. On the other hand, it is possible they have gotten into the habit of starting the day at 3:30 a.m. Since that's way too early for us, we do not have much experience praying Vigils on a regular basis at home. Occasionally I have awakened in the middle of the night and been unable to get back to sleep, so I've gotten up to pray Vigils. It's comforting to know that the sisters are doing the same thing at Mississippi Abbey, just as hundreds of other Cistercian men and women are doing all throughout the world. Even though we are miles and miles apart, the fact that we are all up during this dark time of the night praying these same prayers has linked us together into one vast spiritual network.

When I came home from the monastery I was full of good intentions regarding the Liturgy of the Hours. I told myself that since I was retired there was no reason I couldn't try to make them a regular part of each day's schedule. In reality it has been easy to come up with lots of excuses for not doing it. Probably the biggest explanation is that I simply have not been willing to structure my days around the well-ordered uniformity that the Liturgy of the Hours demands. Now that I don't have to go trudging off to work each morning, I love the flexibility of being more spontaneous about what I do each day.

But even though we never pray the Little Hours and have only on the rarest of occasions gotten up together for Vigils, Denny and I do make an effort to incorporate some of the other liturgical hours into our daily schedule. During Advent and Lent we try to say Compline together, and less frequently Vespers as well. But almost always we begin each day by praying Lauds together. Before we retired, we used the thirty minutes or so it took us to drive to work together to pray Morning Prayer. Now we meet each morning in the living room to pray our version of Lauds while the coffee is brewing.

In the monastery, Lauds begins with a hymn and includes a reading from Scripture. We've taken some liberties and replaced the hymn with a poem, and added an additional reading we've selected ourselves. Sometimes both the poem and the reading deal with religious themes. But just as often I select pieces from some of my favorite poets and nature writers whose work speaks eloquently of the presence of God. Recently we've added another innovation to our homegrown version of Lauds by ending with the appropriate entry for the day from the beautifully illustrated book of astronomical photographs *The Universe: 365 Days*.[4] The dazzling photos of such things as newly formed stars, nebulae, meteor storms, spiral galaxies, and so forth, are awesome reminders that to praise God for the wonders of creation is to acknowledge that it is still going on.

We've been praying Lauds long enough to catch on to how monotonous it can be to recite the familiar words of the same psalms over and over again. That's why it has been important for us to remember that we're not doing it in order to be spiritually enlightened. We pray Lauds together for the same reason everyone else does: to participate in the Church's prayer. We are not praying for ourselves alone but also for the sake of others.

I have always been vaguely uncomfortable praying for other people, not because I haven't cared about their well-being but rather because like so many other things about the spiritual life, I

---

4. Robert J. Nemiroff and Jerry T. Bonnell, *The Universe: 365 Days* (New York: Harry N. Abrams, 2003).

have more questions than answers about what it involves. Part of the problem stems from notions I've grown up with. As a child I think I picked up the idea that prayers were a bit like supernatural prescriptions to be sent away to some sort of heavenly pharmacist in order to be filled. True, Christ himself told us that we shouldn't shy away from prayers of petition. But what about some of the extremes people go to just to make sure those prayers are heard? I imagine Jesus would have rolled his eyes in utter astonishment had he been told that someday people would bury cheap plastic statues of St. Joseph upside down in the dirt hoping to bring about the speedy sale of their houses. That comes a little too close to superstition for me and I have no problem putting it in the same category as knocking on wood or carrying a lucky rabbit's foot.

It's the bigger questions about prayer that plague me: questions that have to do with why there is so much suffering and violence in the world in spite of all the prayers that have begged for an end to it, questions that cause me to wonder about our tendency to behave as if our trivial needs are at the very center of this vast and mysterious cosmos, questions that bubble up from the murky pools of uncertainty to muddy my mind with doubts.

And yet even though I do not understand it, in my heart I cannot deny that prayer is something very real and very necessary. Regardless of whether or not I can explain it, the reality is I need to pray. And I need to pray for others. That's one reason I am drawn to the Liturgy of the Hours. It helps me do that. It also explains why I bristle whenever I hear people criticize the sisters for not being useful members of society. Their work is to pray on behalf of others throughout the world, and God knows the world is in need of it. It seems like a pretty "useful" occupation to me, especially when you consider that the world is full of people who make a living for themselves engaged in occupations whose "usefulness" we might well question.

The service the sisters provide through prayer is not confined to the Liturgy of the Hours. Twice a day—at Mass and again at Vespers—they have a time for spontaneous prayers that encompass a wide range of needs: they pray that those in leadership roles exercise their authority with wisdom; for an end to violence in war-torn countries; that the children of the world grow up safely, surrounded by caring and supportive adults; for the sick, the lonely, and the dying; for those who live on the fringes of society, alone and forgotten; and for numerous other intentions that reflect the needs of a broken and suffering world.

The sisters also pray for the specific needs of people for whom they have promised to pray. On a bulletin board inside the main door are posted the numerous requests that come in each week from people (most of whom the sisters will never meet) who have asked for their prayers. Many of these persons are trying to cope with tragedy and heartbreak in their families: a daughter-in-law who is pregnant and has just been diagnosed with leukemia, a husband who has taken his own life, a parent who is suffering from Alzheimer's, a grandchild who was killed in an automobile accident. Others are struggling with personal crises of their own: chemical dependency, loss of employment, divorce, cancer, family problems. They all know the community will indeed pray for them because the sisters are deeply committed to their vocation of prayer.

Observing the depth of this commitment has made me much more aware of what I am doing each time I tell someone, "you are in my prayers." It's a way of letting that person know that I recognize the depth of his or her pain and distress and I want to share the burden of it. To hold someone in prayer is to name what it is we want for that person—peace of mind and heart, an end to suffering, a successful resolution to a difficult problem—and to believe, in the face of all our doubts, that it is possible for God to make it so.

Praying from the Heart

February 21

I've been here nearly a month already and the days are going by so quickly. Yes, I love it here but it would be a mistake to say it's all serenity and peacefulness. Even though things seem blissfully tranquil on the outside, it troubles me that I'm having such a hard time trying to pray. Prayer has often been a problem for me, but I had thought that it might be different here.

Following Vespers each evening it was the sisters' custom to spend an additional fifteen minutes in silent prayer. By this time the last of the daylight had faded and the church was dark except for the candle flickering in front of the tabernacle. It was a perfect setting for prayer. Except prayer never came easy for me. I'd close my eyes and try my hardest to let go of all my thoughts and calm my mind, but most of the time my attempts at prayer opened up a deluge of thoughts and distractions that were anything but prayerful. On a few occasions what I hoped would turn into prayer turned into sleep instead and I would jerk awake with a start when the bell chimed and the sisters rose to leave the church and head downstairs for a light supper. It was distressing to find this happening night after night as I sat there surrounded by all those women who, as far as I could tell, were not having the same problem. Now and then I'd open my eyes and take a quick peek around me. Some sisters were sitting quietly in their choir stalls while others had settled down lotus fashion or on prayer benches where they sat with their eyes closed and their hands in their laps. What was going on inside them was anyone's guess, but from the outside they certainly *looked* prayerful.

The fact that Cistercians are a contemplative religious order can lead to the mistaken notion that the way they pray is pretty much beyond the reach of most of us. In fact the very term "contemplative" is easily misunderstood, conjuring up images of people with nothing else to do for hours on end but sit around in the lotus position having sublime religious experiences. But from what I have been able to figure out based on living with the sisters, the purpose of contemplative prayer is not to have a sublime religious experience. It's a mistake to think that contemplative people have their heads in the clouds, when in reality they are firmly grounded in paying attention to the presence of God in the here and now of their lives. Contemplative prayer does not require special skills or techniques but rather a willingness to slow down and attempt to quiet the noise that is constantly going on inside us. But for me, that was always terribly hard to do.

That I need to pray seems to be a given. I need it in the same way I need to believe in something outside of myself that is larger than my own limited and self-focused worldview. From my conviction that there is something that transcends what can be explained and comprehended arises a great yearning to connect with it even though it is far, far beyond me. Or, in the words of Psalm 138, "Too wonderful for me, this knowledge, too high, beyond my reach" (v. 6). In other words, we're not going to get very far finding definitive answers to the really big God questions. "If you think you know something about God and describe it in words," says Meister Eckhart, "the God you have described is not God. God is greater than your terminology. God is far greater than your language. He is inexpressible."[5]

I find a certain amount of comfort in those words because they seem to suggest that to comprehend the mystery of God is beyond the efforts and abilities of even the most articulate among us. On the other hand, where does that leave the rest of us? How are we to respond with reverence and gratitude for the many wonders that are part of life if what we think we know about its source falls far short of the mark? How do we reach out for consolation, solace, and help for ourselves and others when our very images and perceptions of the God we are petitioning are so hazy? How can we ever hope to transcend the limits of what it means to be human and connect with what it means to be divine? Our Christian tradition asserts that the answers are to be found in the reality of Christ, but to take any comfort in that answer requires another profound leap of faith.

Perhaps that's what prayer is: yet another way to make that leap that takes us beyond what cannot be comprehended into what we must learn to accept as mystery. I wish I knew why that is so terribly hard for me to do when other people seem to have far less trouble with it. I have a feeling it has to do with the images I'm carrying around in my head about God, and it reminds me of a talk I heard by Fr. Thomas Davis, a Cistercian abbot from the Abbey of New Clairvaux in Vina, California, who came to Mississippi Abbey to direct the sisters' annual retreat. (Instead

---

5. Meister Eckhart as quoted in Bernard Bangley, ed., *Nearer to the Heart of God: Daily Readings with the Christian Mystics* (Brewster, Massachusetts: Paraclete Press, 2005) 85.

of going away on retreat, Cistercians reverse the process by simply bringing the retreat director to them for a week.) Father Thomas pointed out that much of the spiritual life has to do with examining our personal images of God. Since each of us approaches God through a labyrinth of experiences and perceptions it's important for us to recognize what they are and how they fit into our prayer lives. The way to do this is to search our hearts and pay attention to what we find there.

If the heart is where authentic prayer begins, each of us must find the path that will lead us there. But for some reason it is not an easy journey for me, and it was especially unsettling to discover that even within the deeply contemplative environment of the monastery I was still having trouble with it. I had expected it to be easier there and so I was distressed by the paradox of it all: on the one hand I was caught up in the desire for prayer and yet most of the time it felt like I was getting nowhere with my attempts at actually praying.

I was curious to talk to the sisters about this. Fortunately I was able to seek out Kathleen, who was acting as my main spiritual "coach" during the time I was living there, along with Gail, Louise, Martha, and Emma. Each of them said pretty much the same thing: the expectations, images, and perceptions I had about what prayer ought to be were probably keeping me from being open to what it really was. The desire to pray is in itself a kind of prayer and Thomas Merton cautions us against ruining it:

> We ruin our life of prayer if we are constantly examining our prayer and seeking the fruit of prayer in a peace that is nothing more than a psychological process. The only thing to seek in contemplative prayer is God; and we seek him successfully when we realize that we cannot find him unless he shows himself to us, and yet at the same time he would not have inspired us to seek him unless we had already found him.[6]

I knew I needed to let go of my expectations in order to discover my own path to authentic interior prayer. But it did not

6. Thomas Merton, *Thoughts in Solitude* (Boston: Shambhala, 1993) 51–52.

come easily. Often the harder I tried to tell myself to be open to wherever my prayer was taking me, the more overcome I would be by distractions that seemed to lead me away from it.

It usually happened during the quarter hour of quiet prayer that followed Vespers. Before I knew it I'd be thinking about those persons I am closest to in my family—wondering how they were and what was going on at home, worrying about whether everything was OK, thinking about things I wanted to be sure to tell them the next time I wrote or telephoned, carrying on all kinds of conversations with them in my mind. Or I'd end up thinking about people I have the most trouble relating to—those who are hard to get along with, whose words and behaviors have offended others and who continue to be a source of friction and dissension among us. Then suddenly I'd remember that I had started out trying to pray, and had once again wandered far off the mark. When I asked Kathleen for some tips on what to do about these kinds of distractions, she suggested that perhaps the very fact I was so distracted by thoughts of my family was a pretty good indication that I *needed* to spend that time simply letting myself hold them in my heart. Maybe simply being troubled and concerned can itself be a form of prayer.

The sisters' insights taught me to stop fretting about how to pray and simply let prayer unfold in its own fashion, even when I felt distracted and distressed. It reminded me of something Gail had said in one of her talks to the Associates of the Iowa Cistercians. Commenting on the old maxim that advises us to pray as we can and not as we can't, she emphasized that all of us are called to pray because we have a great capacity for it. However, each of us will respond in our own unique way according to our individual natures and personalities. Gail told the AIC that any form of prayer can be contemplative prayer if it is truly our own.

Henri Nouwen, who has written frequently about the importance of searching for our own heart's prayer, makes a similar point: "Just as there are many ways to be hospitable," he writes, "there are many ways to pray. When we are serious about prayer and no longer consider it one of the many things people do in their life, but rather, the basic receptive attitude out of which all of life can receive new vitality, we will, sooner or later, raise the question: 'What is my way to pray, what is the prayer of my heart?'"[7]

The sisters seem to instinctively understand why it is important to find the prayer of the heart and remain faithful to it. This is why in addition to praying together as a community, each of them spends a significant portion of the day praying privately. Aside from liturgical prayer as a community, the sisters do not all share the same prayer practices. Some of them are drawn to more devotional kinds of prayers (e.g., the Stations of the Cross) while others have found ways to adapt Eastern meditation techniques into their Christian contemplative practice. Several sisters use specific postures extensively in their prayer—sitting on prayer mats or benches, for a specific length of time. Some use rosaries or prayer beads. One sister was rarely seen without the well-worn bracelet of prayer beads she made from macramé yarn. I used to see her quietly going about her work, or out for a walk, while she fingered the knotted beads she'd wound loosely around her wrist. She used them to say the Jesus Prayer over and over throughout the course of her day, repeating to herself the words, "Lord Jesus Christ, Son of God, have mercy on me, a sinner."

There was never the slightest indication that any one way of prayer was better than another. It was implicitly understood that each sister was free to pray in her own way rather than somebody else's. The diversity in prayer practices among the sisters helped me appreciate the value of being open to the great variety of prayer methods and techniques that have evolved throughout the ages. Prayer helps bridge the gap between our humanness and our yearning to connect with whatever our hearts reveal of God. Prayer is how we acknowledge the significance of what lies beyond us by listening to what lies within. It is central to all the world's religions and wisdom traditions, and I think we have much to gain by being open to what we can learn from them.

7. Henri Nouwen, *Reaching Out: The Three Movements of the Spiritual Life* (Garden City, New York: Doubleday, 1975) 133.

For example, Buddhist meditation practices include a variety of methods intended to quiet the mind by focusing on one's breathing. Since that's equally important while praying, several of the sisters use these techniques to complement their own meditation practices. Once I began letting go of my preconceived notions about what I thought I needed to be doing in order to pray, I began experimenting with some of the Buddhist meditation techniques I had heard about, adapting embellishments of my own that were major departures from Buddhism. Because I am drawn to scriptural images and metaphors, I have tried to combine them with my breathing in much the same way that mantras or special words are used as centering techniques. For example, I find the image of Jesus going out to a deserted place to pray especially appealing. As an introvert I can understand the urge to slip away from the crowd now and then just to be alone. And I'm partial to the various scriptural passages that describe Christ as a praying person. By combining those images with my breathing I am sometimes able to settle more comfortably into prayer. I try to picture a footpath that leads to a secluded place and then I try to imagine that I can follow it simply by breathing slowly in and out. With each inhalation and exhalation I concentrate on moving farther and farther away from the noisy crowd, closer and closer to the quiet place where Christ is praying.

While I lived at the abbey I was constantly coming across scriptural images and metaphors that spoke to me. There is one in particular that has stayed with me because it is closely linked to one of my earliest memories. The scriptural image comes from the tenth chapter of Mark—that endearing story of Jesus and the little children. It was the Gospel reading one morning at Mass and that day Msgr. James Barta of the Dubuque Archdiocese was presiding. During his homily he pointed out that there is a difference between being childish and being childlike in the way we live out our faith. The former is an immature approach to the spiritual life based on a simplistic belief system that may have been appropriate for young children but is no longer adequate for adults. The latter has to do with certain qualities and characteristics of young children that adults would be well advised to emulate in order to nurture their faith. According to Msgr. Barta, Christ probably was not suggesting we go back to our childish notions of heaven. Rather, by trying to recapture some of the exuberance and trust we once possessed as children, we may be able to listen and respond more eagerly to the Gospel.

It got me thinking back to my own childhood and in the process a distant memory emerged that must surely be one of my very earliest. I couldn't have been much more than three years old at the time, young enough still to fit easily on the lap of whatever willing adult happened to be handy. In this particular case it was some long-forgotten, cigar-smoking great-uncle, whose name and identity have totally escaped me. But I can distinctly remember being scooped up into his arms and snuggling down next to his extremely ample belly. I also remember the pungent smell of his cigar and the way his wool vest scratched against my cheek. But most of all I remember how good it felt to be held there in his lap listening to the steady thump of his heart and the sound of his voice as he sat there talking and laughing with all the other grown-ups that long-ago evening.

The reason I mention all this is because I often turn to that memory, together with Msgr. Barta's homily on Mark's Gospel account of Jesus and the little children, when I get impossibly distracted during prayer. I like to bring back that little three-year-old self and put her in the group of children that the disciples tried to shoo away from Jesus. I wonder what it would have been like to be so trusting—so willing to be scooped up in the arms of that strange man; so comfortable nestling down in his lap; so content to inhale the faint smell of wood shavings, fishing boats, and oil-burning lamps that probably clung to his clothing. I try to imagine laying my cheek next to the scratchy fabric of his shirt to listen to the thump of his heart and the sound of his voice as he talked on and on to all the grown-ups who had come to see him. Sometimes I can stay there long enough for the experience itself to turn into a prayer. But not always. Sometimes the distractions come crowding back in on me and that three-year-old self simply will not stay put any longer. She starts fidgeting and squirming until the only thing is to let her get down and scamper away.

Looking back at how frustrated I used to be those evenings after Vespers when it felt like I wasn't praying, I can see now that I was actually discovering a great deal about my own particular approach to prayer. I have come to realize that the call to prayer comes from the depths of my own heart and I need to rely on my own instincts and inclinations in order to answer it in my own voice. I have learned to recognize that my way of praying doesn't need to be the same as other people's. Nor does it depend so much on what I say but rather in finding a way to express what is in my heart in a language that does not always need to be put into words.

Praying from the Heart at Home

I left the monastery with some valuable insights into making prayer a more natural part of daily living. But it has required a fair amount of discipline because it's easy to get so immersed in the way my life is unfolding that I forget all about making it the entry point into prayer. I have had to learn to be just as concerned about fitting prayer into my schedule as I am about all the other priorities that occupy my time and energy. As with other attempts at incorporating something new and important into my lifestyle, I have had to turn it into a habit. That has meant making time for it, and creating an environment that is conducive to it. But it has also meant remaining alert to moments and experiences that function as pathways to prayer, and recognizing that many of them include the arts.

Making Time for Prayer

The most practical suggestion I have ever heard about how to cultivate a prayer life came from an old monk who, when asked for his thoughts on the matter, replied, "just show up for it." It's good advice because on any given day I can think of all kinds of reasons why I don't have time to pray and so unless I'm in the habit of "showing up for it" there's a good chance I won't get around to doing it at all.

One of the benefits of living in the monastery is that it makes showing up for prayer a very high priority. But here at home, the freedom I have to pray whenever I choose as opposed to specific times during the day makes it convenient to choose not to pray at all. If I am busy with other activities or have a lot on my mind, it's far too easy to tell myself that I'm really not in the mood to pray and so there's no sense in even trying.

I discovered I had to get into the habit of praying by setting aside time on a regular basis to show up and do it. My preferred time is right away in the morning—fairly early because I am a morning person anyway. I like to get up around 5:30. In the winter it's still dark and I like being able to watch the sky gradually lighten as dawn approaches, and in the summer the sunlight is already filtering through the curtains and the birds outside the window are in full song.

I have grown accustomed to starting my day in the little room across from our bedroom, the room we euphemistically call "the library" because it has comfortable chairs for reading, a little writing desk in front of one of the windows, and book-shelves against every wall. It's quiet and peaceful there, especially at 5:30 in the morning.

But just because I get up to pray every morning does not automatically guarantee that it comes easily. Sometimes about all I can say for the time I've spent is that at least I showed up. Now and then I find myself feeling the same frustration I used to feel while sitting in the darkened church at Mississippi Abbey after Vespers, trying to pray, but troubled because it didn't seem like I could. If I can catch myself soon enough when I start feeling that way, I try to pull myself out of it by remembering what the sisters taught me about the importance of simply letting go of my expectations. It means learning to wait in patience and trust, willing to go wherever my prayer ends up taking me.

Creating an Environment for Prayer

"Simply put, we are formed by our surroundings," said medieval architectural historian Terryl N. Kinder, in an interview with the former editor of *National Catholic Reporter*. For Kinder, who has written and lectured extensively on the subject of Cistercian architecture, St. Benedict's rules about silence have to do with visual ambience as well as the absence of sound. She says it's difficult to listen with the ears of the heart if the rest of the senses are on overload. But we live in environments that bombard us with heavy doses of sensory stimulation and there aren't many places we can go to escape. So it is no coincidence that we feel a deep sense of peace and serenity visiting Cistercian monasteries. Because Cistercians do not want to be distracted from the peace they seek within, they have traditionally built simple, uncluttered monasteries designed to blend in harmoniously with their natural surroundings. "If you want a simple life," says Kinder, "you have to be free of clutter; the ambience around you is key."[8]

Even though Mississippi Abbey is not a magnificent thirteenth-century stone structure like many of those that appear in Terryl Kinder's beautifully illustrated book *Cistercian Europe*,[9] the sisters have taken great care to make their monastery a place of beauty and tranquility in keeping with their Cistercian heritage. It is located in the midst of America's heartland, surrounded by woods, pastures, and rolling farmlands high atop a bluff overlooking the Mississippi River. The sisters have a huge vegetable garden and they do much of their own farmwork, raising crops of organic soybeans, corn, and oats. The original buildings that the sisters acquired when they purchased the property have been meticulously maintained, and the remodeling they have done, as well as the new candy house they've recently built, reflect their preference for keeping things simple and unadorned. Inside, even on cloudy days, there is a warm and sunlit feeling that fills the various rooms of the abbey, and it's especially obvious in the church, which is always filled with light during the daytime hours because of the huge south window directly behind the altar. With the exception of an icon of Mary and a simple crucifix, there are none of the usual statues and religious ornamentation found in many Catholic churches. The only adornments are natural ones—

8. Thomas C. Fox, "The Architecture of Simplicity," *National Catholic Reporter* 43 (January 26, 2007) 13–14.
9. Terryl N. Kinder, *Cistercian Europe: Architecture of Contemplation* (Grand Rapids, Michigan: Wm. B. Eerdmans Publishing Company, 2001).

vases of fresh flowers and herbs from the sisters' gardens in the spring and summer months, arrangements of dried gourds and autumn foliage in the fall, baskets of evergreens and pinecones in the winter. The loveliness that is so visible at Mississippi Abbey speaks of the care the sisters have taken to make sure their external surroundings are in sync with the interior landscape of prayer. All of this made a big impression on me—just as it has on guests and retreatants who frequently use the term "sacred space" to describe what they experience there.

For me the word "sacred" has to do with what is intangible and transcendent about life. It is not so much a matter of doctrines, creeds, and religions (helpful as they can be to some people) as it is with my ability to trust what my instincts and experiences tell me about the presence of God in my life. There are some places where I'm much more likely to do that, and Mississippi Abbey is definitely one of those places. But there are others as well and I have discovered that of all of them, the place I call home is by far the most important because it's where I am most engaged in the everyday business of living my life.

I think there is a connection between the physical place where I live and the interior place where my prayer begins. The house, after all, is a symbol for the self. In fact, some psychologists tell us that when we dream about houses or rooms in houses we are actually dreaming about various aspects of ourselves: our emotions, attitudes, past experiences, aspirations, memories, etc. But houses are more than symbols. They are also expressions of who we are and what we value.

It reminds me of a book written by Anthony Lawlor, an architect with a keen interest in the connection between spirituality and architecture. His book takes the reader through each room of the house, describing what can be done to turn a living space into a place of inspiration and tranquility. He believes that our homes can reflect a sense of the sacred and help us be more attentive to what is significant and meaningful about the various tasks and activities that are a part of our everyday lives. Bringing in pots of geraniums to bloom through the winter on a sunny windowsill, folding freshly laundered towels and tucking them away in the linen closet, lighting candles at the dinner table even though there's nothing special going on, falling asleep to the fragrance of lily-of-the-valley on the nightstand in the spring, or opening the windows to the sound and the fragrance of summer rain . . . these are all part of what Anthony Lawlor calls "the here and now of daily life."[10] All of it can be sacred. All of it can lead us into prayer.

Obviously, our prayer lives do not depend on our decorating and landscaping skills. Nevertheless, living with the sisters made me more aware that there definitely is a connection between what we see around us and what is going on within us. For example, some people have a greater intolerance for clutter and mayhem than others. My mother tells the story about her German grandma, a true neatnik, who spotted a cobweb on the ceiling as she lay on her deathbed. It bothered her so much she informed one of her daughters that unless it was swept down immediately she herself would get up to do it. Evidently even death had to wait until my great-grandma felt the room was tidy enough to leave behind. While I am hardly the housekeeper she was, I have noticed that when everything around me is in a state of disarray I'm likely to end up feeling that way too. So one thing I have done to focus on my prayer life has been to try creating a more prayerful environment within the sacred space of my home.

It's been helpful to have a specific place I associate primarily with prayer and for me it's my little "library" room. I will admit it does not measure up to the monastic standard of simplicity because in addition to the many books Denny and I have accumulated, the room is full of all sorts of other things: a little round table his parents were given as a wedding gift from their parents; an old armchair that belonged to my grandmother; my mother's high school graduation photo; the flag that was draped on the casket of Denny's father, who was killed in the Second World War; a scrapbook filled with pictures and mementoes of our family over the years; a dusty bouquet of dried flowers from our twenty-fifth wedding anniversary. The room is filled with re-

---

10. Anthony Lawlor, *A Home for the Soul: A Guide for Dwelling with Spirit and Imagination* (New York: Clarkson Potter, 1997) 36.

minders of so much that is important to me, and so it has become my favorite place to go to read, or write letters, or make journal entries.

And because that's where I go in the mornings to pray, I have discovered that when I walk into that room at other times of the day I tend to associate it with prayer, regardless of what I went there to do. It has become more and more of a "sacred space" to me, the one room in the house that I try the hardest to keep looking neat and clutter free. I wouldn't dream of using my little writing desk for anything as stressful as trying to balance my checkbook, for the same reason that I make sure Denny and I find a different place to have our arguments. On the other hand, there is something warm and intimate about sharing my sacred space with another person. I remember getting up once and finding my sister Mary in the room. She was visiting for the weekend and had gotten up early that morning to do a little reading. It was too good of an opportunity to pass up. She put down her book, I decided to skip my regular routine, and for the next few hours we sat there talking quietly until our husbands came knocking at the door wondering where on earth we had been.

Remaining Open to Moments of Prayer

As important as it's been for me to make prayer a priority by setting aside times and places for it, living with the sisters taught me that it's a mistake to assume I need only pray during the times I've made a point of fitting it into my schedule. Since coming home I've learned that some of my most prayerful moments occur while I'm doing other things.

It reminds me of what happens when Harry Potter uses a portkey to travel back and forth from the land of magic to the non-magic kingdom. For those Muggles who've never opened any of J. K. Rowling's books about what goes on at Hogwarts, a word of explanation will be necessary. In Harry Potter's world, a portkey is a transportation vehicle for traveling from one location to the other. It's always a very ordinary object (an old boot, a flower pot, a photograph) that has had an enchantment placed upon it so it has the power to take a person somewhere else in the blink of an eye.

Similarly, I have found that in my own everyday world there are many ordinary things that catch my attention and for some reason I don't fully understand, they take my breath away. They are like portkeys—portals into a more prayerful way of experiencing things. It can happen when I stand outside under a full moon, or get up early in the morning to work in the garden after it has rained all night. Suddenly I notice what I may have seen countless times before, but this time there's something sacred about it simply because of the way I respond to it.

Sometimes people have the same effect on me. As I get older I find that I am often deeply moved watching young parents and their little children. It's not simply being around them that does it. (Being seated in a restaurant next to a table of misbehaving children whose parents don't seem to have noticed that they're wreaking havoc all around them has a decidedly unprayerful effect on me.) What I'm talking about are those moments of pure tenderness that happen between parents and their children when it's actually possible to catch a glimpse of what an awesome thing it is to be a mother or a father. Watching a woman reach down and take a small child's hand before crossing a street, noticing a man stroke his finger across the cheek of the sleeping baby in his arms—moments like these are prayer portals for me. In the space of a heartbeat I feel once again the intensity of what it means to love a small child with a parent's fiercely tender love.

For that matter, I believe there is something prayerful about all of my most cherished relationships. We have been told that "God is love, and those who abide in love abide in God, and God abides in them" (1 John 4:16). So there is a sacred dimension to what it means to love another person deeply and be assured that he or she loves me as well. In my heart I can sense that it is a blessing and that is why I feel there is something prayerful about the gratitude I feel simply knowing that certain beloved people are part of my life.

Prayer portals also open up through sensory experiences and for me they frequently appear in the form of fragrances. I've heard that the part of the brain where memories are stored is close to the part of the brain that processes olfactory stimuli. So that might explain why I can suddenly be reminded of something

I haven't remembered for years all because of a particular scent that has caught my attention.

Not long ago I walked into an elevator in a large parking ramp and was immediately overcome by memories of my grandfather, who has been dead for over thirty years. There was something about the way the elevator smelled that instantly took me back to Grandpa's basement workroom and the way I would bury my face in his ratty, old cardigan sweater when he reached down to put his arms around me. That day I rode the elevator all the way up to the top of the parking ramp and back down again and still I didn't want to get off, because it would mean losing my beloved Grandpa all over again. But then it occurred to me that no, that wasn't quite true. Somehow that elevator ride had taken me into a place where all the love I have felt for my Grandpa suddenly came bubbling out of wherever it has been all these years. It was a sign that everything he has ever meant to me will always be there locked away in the memories I cherish about him. For me, it was a vivid reminder that the immensity of the love I feel for another person can be a prayer in itself, and so can the sudden realization of what it means to be loved in return.

Those kinds of experiences have shown me that my path to prayer is an experiential one. And thanks to what I have learned from the sisters, I've finally learned to accept it as a gift instead of worrying about whether or not I ought to be trying to find a more traditional way to pray. The sisters helped me realize that our lived experiences form the bedrock of our prayer because it is precisely within the context of our lives that we learn to recognize what is in our hearts.

The Arts as Paths to Prayer

"[A]ttend . . . with the ear of your heart," says St. Benedict in the prologue to his Rule,[11] and I find it interesting that implanted within the word "heart" are three other important words: "hear," "ear," and "art." The *arts* enable us to listen to

11. See RB Prol. 1.

what we *hear* in our *hearts* and that is why in my view they are an essential component of the spiritual life. There is something innately contemplative about the way we respond to the arts that can lead us to a deeper awareness of the sacred dimension of life. Art opens us to a new understanding of reality, drawing upon our emotions and our imaginations to take us where our intellects often fail to go. Like contemplative prayer, it beckons us to move into our interior world and pay attention to what we find there.

For me there is an especially strong link between poetry and prayer. In fact I've found that reading a poem is a lot like doing *lectio divina*, the monastic practice of reading the Scriptures slowly and reflectively, because poetry can be read the same way. It is an invitation to look beneath the surface of words, to ponder them and reflect on why some of them touch me or disturb me or set off bursts of recognition within me. Like *lectio divina*, poetry requires a willingness to spend some time with it, or as poet W. S. Merwin has observed, "you've got to stop what you're doing, what you're thinking, and what you're expecting and just be there for the poem for however long it takes."[12]

For Esther de Waal, poems are to be savored and lingered over in order to pay attention to certain words or phrases that have captured our attention. She writes: "I like to remind myself of Mary pondering in her heart what she did not immediately understand—the Latin *pondus*, weight, giving us the clue: to hold something precious like a stone in the hand, feeling its weight, letting it communicate its essence to us."[13]

Perhaps one reason there is so much weight to a poem is because poets use words much more intentionally than other people do, paying careful attention to the layers and layers of meaning they contain. Poems use the lush language of metaphor and symbol to express what would be difficult to explain any other way, and so I need to trust my feelings, perceptions, and

12. Quoted in Bill Moyers, *The Language of Life: A Festival of Poets* (New York: Doubleday, 1995) 2.
13. Esther de Waal, *Lost in Wonder: Rediscovering the Spiritual Art of Attentiveness* (Collegeville, Minnesota: Liturgical Press, 2003) 28.

intuitions in order to understand them. Luci Shaw reminds us that this is the same language that is so frequently found in the Bible, which is "the teaching tool on which God has set the imprint of approval, by constant use."[14]

Reading poetry requires that I use my imagination, something my head isn't always inclined to do. It means being willing to be perplexed and bewildered, because reading a poem can be frustrating when I do not completely understand what it means. Sometimes poems leave me searching for answers to questions I haven't considered before, but just as frequently they provide fresh insights that prompt me to think about things from a different perspective. Over and over again the luminous language of poetry expresses something I know to be sacred but have never been able to put into words of my own. Like *lectio divina*, poetry can point to what my own life is revealing about God, and help me find a language in which to speak of it.

This is true of all the visual arts as well. From earliest times sketches, symbols, drawings, and carvings have been a part of religious ritual and celebration. And some of the world's greatest works of art, sculpture, and architecture have been created in order to express the glory of God. From the rich iconography of the Eastern Church, to the ancient stone crosses of Celtic Christianity, to the elaborately illuminated pages of medieval manuscripts, to the magnificent frescoes, altar pieces, stained glass windows and paintings of the high Renaissance, art has been used throughout the ages to instruct, inspire, and invite the faithful into prayer.

Like most people, I haven't been able to spend a lot of time praying in medieval cathedrals, and the art galleries I have visited over the years have not been particularly conducive to prayer. Nevertheless, I have access to many great works of art simply by browsing through bookstores and libraries, and thanks to technology I'm even able to visit a number of the world's great art museums online in order to take virtual tours of some of their

14. Luci Shaw, "Art and Christian Spirituality: Companions in the Way," *Direction* 27, no. 2 (1998), http://www.directionjournal.org/article/?980.

finest collections. While there is no comparison between an original and a reproduction, all this has given me an opportunity to respond to what a painting can reveal about the world of the spirit, because as Dorothy Sayers has said, "The words of creeds come before our eyes and ears as pictures."[15]

Not surprisingly, it was one of the sisters who introduced me to the practice of using art in this way. On Saturday evenings, several sisters were in the habit of meeting informally to share their thoughts about the next morning's Mass readings. They took turns preparing questions in advance and facilitating the session, often incorporating some of their own personal prayer practices. One evening Emma used a variety of icons to lead us into a discussion of the Gospel account of the transfiguration. She instructed each of us to select an icon and then look at it carefully while listening to her read the Gospel aloud. Then we were invited to spend a few moments in silence with the icon we'd chosen in order to hear what it was revealing about the passage we had just heard.

Since then I've discovered that color reproductions of great masterpieces of religious art can be used the same way and that often they become visual pathways to prayer. It's easy to obtain books containing full-page color reproductions of these beautiful paintings and sculptures, most of which were originally intended to be used in spiritual contexts. Theirs is a visual language that blends color, shape, and texture with religious imagery and symbolism to express some of Christianity's most profound beliefs. Taking the time to "read" a painting closely can be like doing *lectio divina* visually. I find it particularly fruitful to use art reproductions this way during the liturgical seasons of Lent, Advent, and Christmas because so much great art focuses on the life and death of Christ.

Giovanni Bellini's fifteenth-century *Pietà* is one of many examples of paintings that can be used for *lectio divina* on Good Friday. It's a particularly poignant depiction of the dead Christ as he is being taken to the tomb, supported by his mother and

---

15. Dorothy Sayers, *The Mind of the Maker* (London: Methuen, 1942) 161.

John the beloved apostle. There is an unmistakable feeling of anguish that pervades this painting. It is obvious in the grief-stricken face of John, who has turned slightly away from Christ as if the horror of what has happened is too much for him to bear. But there is also a heartbreaking sense of tenderness that makes it impossible not to be emotionally drawn into this painting. Mary has pulled Christ's lifeless body close to hers so that their faces are touching. Her chin rests on his shoulder as she looks directly at him through eyes that are swollen with sorrow. She has taken his lifeless right hand in hers and is pressing it firmly over his heart, as if willing it to start beating once more. It is a gesture that speaks volumes about the indescribable grief of mothers who must bury their children. Focusing on the images and the emotions depicted in this painting is, for me, an invitation to ponder one of the most fundamental cornerstones of Christianity—the impenetrable mystery of why the divine should choose to enter so completely into all the pain of what it means to be human.

But of all the arts, I feel that music is the most elevating. And no wonder. Consider that in the sixth century BC, Pythagorus, the father of geometry, believed the planets moved in harmony with the "music of the spheres." It's also interesting to note that ancient Hindu sacred texts taught that celestial melodies influence the movement of the planets, making music one of the highest forms of worship.

It's probably safe to say that from earliest times music has had a central role in the religious customs of all cultures and that throughout history people have consistently linked music to the sacred. Thomas Carlyle believed that since music is the speech of angels nothing else brings us closer to God, a notion that is still shared by many people in our own day. Once while attending a concert in a large city I noticed the following graffiti scrawled outside the concert hall: "Bach gave us God's word. Mozart gave us God's laughter. Beethoven gave us God's fire. God gave us music that we might pray without words."

The idea that God himself has given us music is reflected in the fact that much of it has been inspired by scriptural texts and written specifically for religious use. Palestrina alone wrote over

a hundred Masses and hundreds of other hymns and composi-
tions based on Scripture. Some composers, like Handel, who
believed that *the Messiah* had been directly revealed to him by
God, claimed that their music was divinely inspired. It's said that
Robert Schumann used to say angels had dictated his music to
him. Regardless of its source there's no denying that music uses
a language of its own and to understand it we need to rely on
our emotions as much as our intellects. Perhaps that's why
Beethoven wrote, "from the heart; may it go to the heart" on the
dedication page of his ninth symphony.

This may explain why I respond so powerfully to all kinds of
beautiful music, especially sacred music from the age of polyphony
as well as the great choral masterpieces of Bach, Mozart, and
Brahms. Listening awakens something within me—something
that speaks to my heart and touches my spirit. The Church has
always used music as a gateway to prayer, and I've found that
thanks to the recorded music industry it's easy to gain entrance.

I once asked Kathleen, Mississippi Abbey's organist, to recommend some of her favorite pieces of music for "sacred listening." She promptly provided me with an impressive list beginning
in the fifteenth century with Josquin des Prez right on through
the twentieth-century work of Messiaen. Later I added a few of
my own favorites going back a few more hundred years to include eleventh-century Hildegard of Bingen as well as a variety
of Gregorian chants from the twelfth and thirteenth centuries.
And to round things out I've included the very contemporary
but beautiful music of Estonian Arvo Pärt to my collection of
CDs. Along with Kathleen's list came some advice about how to
listen to music prayerfully. She recommends approaching it the
same way I would as if I were about to read a passage from Scripture. In other words, give it my full attention rather than use it
as a background for doing something else. Usually there are liner
notes along with the CDs that include translations of choral settings of the Psalms and other scriptural texts that are being sung
in Latin or German, but Kathleen also suggests keeping a Bible
handy to look up the passages and read along.

I have found that her advice about listening attentively
makes a lot of sense. A few years ago I decided to listen to Bach's

"St. Matthew Passion" on Good Friday and discovered that it's the kind of work that demands an entire afternoon or evening of careful attention. The liner notes to the CD contain a complete translation of all the additional texts—including the betrayal of Judas, Peter's denial, and others—that are part of the work. Used in conjunction with Matthew's passion narrative, there is much opportunity for personal reflection and prayer.

Because the arts have become an important part of my prayer life, I tend to use them in much the same way as others use prayer books, rosary beads, and similar items. I keep art books and volumes of poetry right there next to all my other spiritual reading along with my CD collection. I've also found the internet is an amazing resource for finding visual images that can be used prayerfully.[16]

Recently a friend helped me put together a PowerPoint presentation using artwork downloaded from the internet in combination with a sound track I recorded separately using music, poetry, and scriptural references. The process of putting it together was just as much a part of my prayer as was viewing the finished product. It was a chance to trust the response I have to certain poems, paintings, and pieces of music that move me, and to recognize that they carry within them the seeds of prayer.

The Wisdom Books: Scripture, Nature, Experience

February 20

> *I feel like I'm in a different world and it's not just because of the silence, the slower pace, and the strenuous monastic prayer schedule. There's a whole different mind-set here . . . and it all has to do with the way the sisters' lives are shaped and formed by their desire to discover what it is that can be revealed to them about God. They have figured out how to make that an everyday priority by looking for opportunities to grow in wisdom and insight. I keep thinking it should be everyone's top priority.*

16. A few good sources of sacred art on the internet include: http://artcyclopedia.com, http://virtualuffizi.com, http://abcgallery.com.

"Wisdom is radiant and unfading," says the author of the book of Wisdom, "and she is easily discerned by those who love her, and is found by those who seek her" (Wis 6:12). For the sisters, seeking wisdom is not the same thing as acquiring information or accumulating knowledge. It is something else entirely, as Raimon Panikkar says in his book *A Dwelling Place for Wisdom*:

> Wisdom is not complicated; it is not the sum total of many facets of knowledge, not even of multitudinous experiences. One cannot pile up and accumulate wisdom. . . . Wisdom is free; it is a present, a pure gift. Our readiness for wisdom is an end in itself, not a means by which to acquire wisdom. . . . We only have to care about not putting any obstacles in the way.[17]

In this sense I think wisdom is much like grace. It is a gift and a blessing that can help us in our attempts to unravel the mysteries that confound us about life. And though we may seek wisdom and long for what it can teach us, it's not something we can set out to find in the same way we go looking for information. Wisdom has more to do with what is revealed to us, which is why it's important to be open to opportunities where that is likely to happen. Living with the sisters taught me that there are quite a few ways to do that but three of them stand out as important sources of revelation into the mysteries of God. They are the Book of Scripture, the Book of Nature, and the Book of Experience.

The Book of Scripture

I was raised in a Catholic family during the fifties. It was the era of "the family that prays together, stays together" and pray we did. We prayed the rosary regularly as a family, attended Mass faithfully, and participated in First Friday devotions, novenas, forty hours of adoration, May crownings, and parish missions. I went to confession every Saturday, and whenever I think

---

17. Raimon Panikkar, *A Dwelling Place for Wisdom* (Louisville, Kentucky: Westminster John Knox Press, 1993) 10, 14, 21.

back to those days I'm reminded of the afternoon I took my preschool-aged brother along with me and told him to sit quietly in the back of the church until I was finished. Back then it wasn't unusual for churches to be filled with people waiting their turn to enter the ornately carved and heavily curtained cubicle that had a light on the outside when occupied. That afternoon there was an unusually long line of people who apparently had committed a number of pretty hefty sins, judging from the length of time they were inside the confessional. After sitting quietly for as long as he could manage, John's impatience got the best of him. Marching over to where I stood in line, he demanded for everyone to hear, "how much longer do you have to wait before it's your turn to use the bathroom?"

I imagine most everyone who grew up in the pre–Vatican II Church can tell a story or two like that one. Once after my brother Ray and I had seen a movie about Our Lady of Fatima, I woke up in the middle of the night convinced that the Blessed Virgin intended to appear to the two of us as well. Ever the bossy big sister, I dragged my sleepy brother out of his bed, handed him a rosary, and made him kneel down with me in the living room awaiting the mother of God's arrival. We waited and waited and waited. And when morning finally came, the worst part of the whole affair was how embarrassing it was hearing my little brother point out that he had known all along that the Blessed Virgin wasn't going to show up because she didn't visit people in their own houses.

These kinds of stories evoke a great deal of nostalgia. To a child there was a strong aura of mystery and excitement about what it meant to be a Catholic. But there was something missing. I had memorized all the answers in the Baltimore Catechism, read stories about the saints, and collected holy cards, scapulars, and medals. But the only time I ever heard anyone other than a priest read from the Scriptures was when I visited my Protestant grandparents. I used to come downstairs in the mornings and find them at the breakfast table with their well-worn Bible open in front of them. They always closed it in a hurry when I appeared, as if they had been doing something I wasn't supposed to see. As a result I grew up thinking the Bible was only for

Protestants—sort of a consolation prize for those who weren't born into the "one true faith." Much later I realized the Bible belongs to all of us, but it wasn't until I started hanging around monasteries that I began to catch on to the value of reading it regularly.

Scripture is a prominent part of the sisters' life. There is not a day that goes by without paying careful attention to what is to be found there, not only through the Mass readings and the Liturgy of the Hours but also because of the ancient tradition of *lectio divina*. One of many monastic practices readily accessible to laypersons, *lectio divina*, or sacred reading, involves reading only a short segment of text slowly and deliberately in order for the words to find their way to the heart. Reading is only part of what's involved in *lectio*, because the real focus is on listening prayerfully to what the words are saying. This involves using the heart as well as the mind in order to notice what might otherwise be overlooked. It is something that cannot be done in a hurry. Perhaps that's one reason it does not come easily to those of us who are used to doing whatever needs to be done quickly and efficiently so that we can move on and get busy doing something else.

I had been introduced to *lectio* through my involvement with the Associates of the Iowa Cistercians. As much as I liked the idea, the actual practice proved to be a lot more difficult. Part of the problem was that I was putting far too much emphasis on technique, assuming that there was a specific method I needed to learn in order to "do it" properly. These days there are no small number of books, pamphlets, and other resources available on the subject and many of them are most instructive. For all the underlining and highlighting I have done in the various books I've accumulated, you'd think I would have figured out how to make *lectio* a regular part of each day long before arriving at the monastery. But learning about *lectio divina* is not the same thing as doing it. (Just as reading about prayer is not the same as praying.) My problem was that as much as I wanted to, I just couldn't seem to get into the habit of doing it on a regular basis.

All that changed once I got into the swing of things at Mississippi Abbey. Suddenly I had entered an environment where taking the time for *lectio* was the norm. In fact it's important enough to warrant designating Wednesday and Friday afternoons as *"lectio* afternoons." Instead of being given afternoon work assignments, the sisters are free to use that time for *lectio*, in addition to whatever time they ordinarily take for that purpose.

I decided to follow their example and after a few weeks of wondering whether I was doing it the "right way," it occurred to me that there probably wasn't a "right way" in the first place. What mattered was taking time to read a particular Scripture passage and reflect on what it was saying to me. *Lectio divina* invites me to be open to what images, symbols, and metaphors can reveal. With some particularly evocative scriptural passages, for example, Matthew 4:18-22, I like to let myself enter the scene and wander around for a while: a warm day, a calm lake shimmering beneath a blue sky, a long stretch of sandy shore where clusters of grubby fishermen sit propped against their boats mending nets, anxious to be back out on the lake again. Here comes someone else, kicking up little wisps of sand as he walks, bending down to pick up a few flat stones and toss them one by one into the lake. Maybe they land with a little plop next to one of the boats. "Follow me," says this solitary man without so much as a greeting, and amazingly enough, four of the fishermen drop everything and take off after him as if they had nothing else to do that day anyway. Or maybe having heard about him through the grapevine, they had been standing around all morning hoping he would wander by so they could size him up for themselves. *Lectio* invites me to indulge my imagination for a little while in order to consider any number of possibilities and then draw my own conclusions about all of them. But there is a lot more to *lectio* than simply having fun picturing scenes and making up dialogue. The prayerful part comes from looking beneath the images for clues about what they mean. And it is not always a comfortable process.

Lectio can raise some sticky questions. The passage from Matthew is full of them, as far as I am concerned. First there is the matter of how quickly Simon, Andrew, James, and John answered the call to follow Jesus, without even needing to think it over first. Not me. As much as I would like to say I have no qualms about answering the call to follow the Lord, I know in my heart it's not true. Because I have fretted over issues of faith and belief for most of my adult life, brooding over doubts and misgivings that have plagued me for years, I am afraid that had I been part of that Gospel scenario, I would have wanted a little information before answering the call to discipleship: Can you tell me where we're headed? How many other people are coming along? What am I supposed to do when we get there? Do you have any references? Give me a few days to think this over and I'll get back to you.

The most troubling part of the deceptively pleasant little scene from the fourth chapter of Matthew's Gospel has to do with the fact that I know the rest of the story. It wasn't just a case of following along for a while and then dropping back into business as usual once the novelty wore off. Those four guys were in it for the long haul—and as it turned out it was anything but a lark. Their decision led to a firm commitment to stick with the program regardless of what it entailed. I simply have not been able to do the same thing when it comes to matters of faith. There has always been a hesitancy on my part, an indecisiveness that has kept me from letting go of my uncertainties in order to surrender myself to genuine discipleship. I don't like admitting this about myself because I do not like being so riddled with doubts about my faith. But that's the thorny side of doing *lectio*. It can lead me to places I would rather not have to go and this is definitely one of them.

But *lectio* doesn't always lead to such heavy soul searching, nor does it need to involve a lengthy scriptural passage. Another approach is to read a short segment of text slowly several times until drawn to a particular word or phrase in order to ponder the various meanings it evokes. Then by paying attention to any thoughts or feelings that arise, it is possible to go deeper and explore the significance of that particular word or phrase as it relates to my life. Listening and responding to what is being revealed is how *lectio* leads to prayer. Once while reading a short passage from the book of Tobit, my attention kept coming back to the line "Prayer with fasting is good, but better than both is almsgiving with righteousness" (Tob 12:8). It was the word *alms-giving* that jumped out at me and so it became the focus of my *lectio* that day. I began by defining the word almsgiving: an act of charity, something given to help provide for the needs of the poor and the disadvantaged, in order to help alleviate some of their suffering. But what occurred to me was that as important as it is to donate food and money to those who are literally poor and hungry, almsgiving doesn't end there. I know quite a few people who are poor and needy in other ways and I have just as many opportunities, if not more, to respond to them. They are the lonely ones who need a little bit of my time; they are the vulnerable ones who need me to treat them gently; they are the ones who have hurt me and need my forgiveness. They are the many people in my life who need me to take advantage of the next opportunity I have to be compassionate, even though it would be so much easier to turn away. My *lectio* that day helped me look at almsgiving from a different perspective and to admit that sometimes it is easier for me to donate food, clothing, and money to charitable causes, worthy as they may be, than it is to respond to the people in my life who need something from me that's far less tangible but every bit as important.

Having been introduced to the richness that Scripture contains, it is with regret that I confess my lack of discipline in keeping to a regular schedule for doing *lectio* now that I'm home again. At first I tried to make it a part of my daily morning prayer routine but stopped when I found myself paying too much attention to the time it was taking. It just doesn't work to hurry through *lectio* while thoughts of the day's to-do list keep intruding. Instead, my *lectio* happens at irregular intervals, usually in the evenings when I have started to unwind and let whatever did not get accomplished wait until the next day. I need to make the journey to wherever *lectio* happens to lead without thinking about other places I have to go when I'm finished.

One of the benefits of reading Scripture has been the discovery that certain verses and phrases have found their way into my memory and pop up spontaneously from time to time like little commentaries on whatever is going on at the moment. Political ads, for example, almost always bring to mind: "See how they gabble open-mouthed; their lips are filled with insults" (Ps 58:8). If I glance out the window on a snowy day I'm reminded that "He showers down snow white as wool, he scatters hoarfrost like ashes" (Ps 147:16). On my hands and knees in my flower beds, all of a sudden I find myself remembering: "And the LORD God planted a garden in Eden" (Gen 2:8).

Short wisps and strands of Scripture are likely to come drifting unbidden into my mind at a moment's notice, and whenever it happens I feel like I have just been given a little spurt of insight about the importance of paying attention to things. It helps me remember that there is more to my life than whatever is happening on its surface and it reminds me that prayer can arise naturally and spontaneously, even in the most ordinary and mundane moments of the day.

The Book of Nature

Several weeks before leaving Mississippi Abbey for home, I made an appointment with Gail to ask her for a "word," a tradition that goes back to the fourth-century Desert Fathers and Mothers. It was the custom for monks who lived solitary lives in remote and isolated areas to ask their spiritual masters for a "word" of advice, some little bit of insight into living a spiritual life.

I liked the idea and so I decided to ask Gail for a word to take with me. We met in her office, a sunny room with two comfortable rocking chairs next to a window that overlooked the big yard behind the abbey. That morning the trees had started to leaf out and the orchards were full of pink and white blossoms. It was a glorious day.

With only a few remaining weeks to spend with the sisters I wanted to use the time well but I also missed Denny and was looking forward to being home with him again. I had started to wonder if I would forget everything I had learned from the sisters once I returned to the familiar routines and patterns of life outside the abbey, and I was anxious to ask Gail for her thoughts about how to make sure that didn't happen. The advice she gave me was not at all what I had been expecting. She simply told me to make sure to spend a little time outdoors each day. She said I should try to make it a priority and be serious about sticking to it.

I had assumed she'd tell me something a bit more esoteric, something more *monastic*, something that had a little bite to it. Gail's recommendation sounded so simple and it should not have come as such a surprise since simplicity is a hallmark of Cistercian monastic life. But that was not the main reason Gail suggested I get outside each day. It was because she knew how important it is to study the Book of Nature. "For this whole sensible world is like a kind of book written by the finger of God that is created by divine strength, and each creature is like a kind of letter, not established by human convention, but instituted through divine judgment to demonstrate and in a kind of way to signify the unseen wisdom of God."[18]

Referring to the world of nature in this way is an ancient concept. It is rooted in scriptural references that speak of what God has revealed of himself through the created universe: "For what can be known about God is plain to them, because God has shown it to them. Ever since the creation of the world his eternal power and divine nature, invisible though they are, have been understood and seen through the things he has made" (Rom 1:19-20).

Passages like this inspired early Christian writers to suggest that the natural world can be read like a book because of what it reveals about God. Origen of Alexandria, writing in the third century, put it this way: "I think that He who made all things in wisdom so created all the species of visible things upon the earth, that He placed in some of them some teaching and knowledge of things invisible and heavenly, whereby the human mind might mount to spiritual understanding and seek the grounds of things in heaven."[19]

---

18. Hugh of St. Victor, *De tribus diebus*, quoted by Constant J. Mews, "The World as Text: The Bible and the Book of Nature in Twelfth-Century Theology," in *Scripture and Pluralism*, Thomas J. Heffernan, ed. (Boston: Brill, 2005) 99.

19. Origen, *The Song of Songs, Commentary and Homilies*, trans. R.P. Lawson (London: Paulist Press, 1957) 220.

Nearly seventeen centuries later, at a time when most people had yet to hear the term "ecology" and environmentalists were few and far between, Jesuit priest and scientist Teilhard de Chardin began to passionately write about the spirituality that pervades the earth, and indeed the entire universe. "All around us, to right and left, in front and behind, above and below, we have only to go a little beyond the frontier of sensible appearances in order to see the divine welling up and showing through."[20]

Teilhard's vision of the created world as a setting for divine revelation provides a helpful context for reading the Book of Nature. Like any other book that has been well written and lavishly illustrated, it has the potential to provoke wonder and inspiration. I think that's the main reason Gail suggested I get in the habit of spending some time outside each day just as the sisters do.

It took some pretty miserable weather to keep them inside. Even on the coldest and most blustery of days they'd be bundled up in parkas and boots out tramping through the snow or gliding along on cross-country skis down past the stone house and out across the wintry fields. On stormy days they'd be out walking in the wind and sometimes even in the rain, their short veils fluttering behind them like little black sails.

Cistercians are known as lovers of the place, and it would be hard not to feel that way about Mississippi Abbey. Their property includes several hundred acres of woodland as well as a small pond, so the monastery has become home to deer and a variety of other wildlife, including many species of birds. It is hard to imagine how anyone could walk through the fields or along the wooded paths behind the abbey and fail to notice how beautiful it is.

I remember the morning I headed over to the candy house for one of my first work assignments. It was one of those pale winter days; a light snow had fallen during the night and there was no trace of the sun. The sky was the same color as the snowy

20. Pierre Teilhard de Chardin, *The Divine Milieu* (New York: Harper and Row, 1960) 89.

ground and the trees and shrubs and fence wires were lined with hoarfrost. As I started up the path, I saw Emma standing perfectly still ahead of me with her index finger pressed to her lips, signaling me to be very careful. I inched my way to where she stood and followed the direction of her eyes until I saw what had stopped her in her tracks. Sitting high up on a branch a short distance in front of her was a hawk, its brown and white feathers blending in perfectly with the dark tree in which it perched. Having determined that I had seen it too, Emma smiled and mouthed the words "so beautiful," nodding her head to confirm the loveliness of this moment the two of us were sharing. I probably would have missed it entirely. Emma, on the other hand, was so accustomed to paying attention to the winter woods that she spotted the hawk as soon as she headed off in the direction of the candy house.

I once read a book titled *How to Be a Bad Birdwatcher*, which pointed out that a person doesn't have to know a lot about birdwatching to enjoy watching birds. The author believes that because birds are so beautiful, the least we can do is get into the habit of looking at them. His advice is simply to go to those places where birds are to be found and then look around, not just because bird-watching is fun but, more important, because birds make our planet a richer place.

> Birds indicate life in its richness and its diversity, and without places where birds are, we would have a deeply impoverished planet. Without such places we are cut off from what makes us part of nature, and therefore we are cut off from what makes us truly alive. Yes, places matter, and we should visit them as pilgrims and savor the richness they bring to our lives.[21]

During the spring and fall there is an even greater abundance of birds around the abbey because the Mississippi River flyway is one of four major bird migration routes in North America. I discovered that for myself one afternoon in early

---

21. Simon Barnes, *How to Be a Bad Birdwatcher* (New York: Pantheon Books, 2004) 166.

spring when I went for a walk with Sherry. She's a genuine out-
doorswoman and can often be seen driving a tractor through the
fields, or digging up potatoes, or pruning apple trees. She has a
deep and genuine concern for the earth and is committed to
doing whatever she can to care for the land. She is also an artist—
a potter—and that seems especially fitting. How appropriate that
someone who loves caring for the earth should end up working
with clay!

That particular day felt more like April than March and we
had stopped to sit and talk in a sunny spot overlooking the valley.
Suddenly we heard the faintly audible sound of birds in flight
far above us. Sherry spotted them first but they were too far away
to identify. All we could see was the way they were flying, spiral-
ing upwards, circling higher and higher in widening arcs, their
white wings gleaming and shining in the bright sunlight. It was
a spectacular sight and we kept looking up into the sky, shading
our eyes against the sun, watching until the birds had disappeared. We stood there amazed and astonished, and asked each
other whether either of us had ever seen anything like it before.
Neither of us had.

After Vespers that evening Sherry tracked me down to say
she had done a little checking and guessed that we had seen a
flock of migrating great white pelicans riding the thermals. Evidently some people have seen as many as seventy-five of them
at one time along the shores of the Mississippi River or in the sky
overhead during the spring migration.

At Compline that night I was still thinking about them. I
remembered hearing that the pelican was commonly used in the
Middle Ages as a symbol of the self-sacrificing death of Christ.
According to legend the mother pelican gives up her own life by
piercing her breast with her beak in order to feed her young with
her blood. The words kept coming back to me: "I have become
like a pelican in the wilderness, like an owl in desolate places"
(Ps 101:7), a reminder that frequently the Book of Scripture and
the Book of Nature are filled with the same images.

One of the tasks of a good nature writer is to tune in to the
symbols found in nature. As Rachel Carson reminds us, there is
"symbolic as well as actual beauty in the migration of the birds,

the ebb and flow of the tides, the folded bud ready for the spring. There is something infinitely healing in the repeated refrains of nature—the assurance that dawn comes after night, and spring after winter."[22]

I am fortunate to live in a part of the world where there are four distinct seasons. It gives me a chance to pay closer attention to what happens in the natural world as the months come and go. I love being able to watch the changes that take place with such predictability from season to season, and I had plenty of opportunity for doing that during the three months I spent at Mississippi Abbey.

I was there from January through mid-April, and since I have lived in the Midwest all my life I know what it is like to wait for the bone-chilling cold of an Iowa winter to start melting into the warmth and exuberance of spring. I have always found wintertime to be a naturally contemplative season, a time for focusing on the interior life. And as I watched what was happening outside in the woods and fields and meadows surrounding the abbey I was even more acutely aware of the spiritual dimension of winter.

That year there was lots of snow and even a few blizzards—those blinding winter snowstorms driven by ferocious winds that make it truly hazardous to be out and about. There were bright, frosty mornings when every tree and bush and fencerow was covered with freshly fallen snow that sparkled and shone in the sunlight, and subzero days when the bright morning air shimmered with hundreds of tiny ice crystals.

Inside, one of the sisters had carefully planted a variety of vegetable seeds in large trays and placed them on a table in front of a sunny window in the common room. It didn't take long before the seedlings emerged, and from then on we were able to check on their progress whenever we went to get our mail or glance at the message board. On frigid days when snowy winds rattled the windows, I'd glance at those delicate green seedlings

22. Rachel Carson, *Lost Woods: The Discovered Writing of Rachel Carson*, Linda Lear, ed. (Boston: Beacon Press, 1998) 163.

and be reminded of a poem by Dylan Thomas about the marvel-ous energy driving all of life.[23] It is a lyrical reminder that every-thing about the natural world has been energized by the same generative spirit that bursts forth in roots and seeds pushing up fragile shoots strong enough to break through the hardened earth. It is the same force that enlivens and energizes us all. I think it's worth noting that one of the titles for the Holy Spirit is *Vivifi-cantem* from the Latin words *vivus* (alive) and *facio* (to make or do). Thus the Holy Spirit is the "giver of life," the source of that mysterious energy that surges through the created universe and animates all living things.

I can still remember the first time it dawned on me that the world really is a sacred place. It was during a family camping vacation in the Black Hills. As the oldest of six children, I was expected to pitch in and help my beleaguered parents (who must have been exhausted for most of our vacation) as much as pos-sible. Like many oldest children in large families I often envied my younger brothers and sisters their freedom from the chores and responsibilities that were mine, and truth be told I suspect my memories of those camping trips aren't quite as idyllic as my siblings'. With one notable exception.

On that particular morning I was awakened early by my father, who was already up and dressed. He had managed to clamber over the other six sleeping bags in our crowded canvas tent without disturbing anyone and had quietly slipped outside to enjoy a few moments of peace and quiet before all the hubbub of the day began. Motioning me to be very quiet, he reached out to help me climb over all the other lumpy sleeping bags without stepping on any of my siblings and setting off the usual commo-tion that went along with waking up in a crowded tent.

Outside, Dad tossed me somebody's sweatshirt and helped me tie my tennis shoes, before motioning for me to follow him. Groggy with sleep, I stumbled along after him as he headed up a short trail and stopped at an overlook with a panoramic view

---

23. Dylan Thomas, "The force that through the green fuse drives the flower," *The Collected Poems of Dylan Thomas* (New York: New Directions Books, 1939) 10.

of the mountains. The sun was about ready to rise. It was the first time I'd ever been outside early enough to notice how fresh and sweet-smelling the world is at that time of day. Until then I'd never witnessed what goes on in the sky during those moments that surround sunrise.

I think that's when I first began to realize there was more to God than what the Baltimore Catechism had told me. Good little cradle Catholic that I was, it had never occurred to me that there could be more to it than what I had been taught to believe. Standing there with my dad watching the sun come up behind the mountains was a moment of revelation for me. It was the most spectacular sight I had ever witnessed and the most intimate moment I had ever shared with anyone. It was probably my very first moment of genuine "God Awareness" and my first inkling that there is a strong connection between the glorious beauty of the earth and the sacred life of the Spirit. It was my first experience reading the Book of Nature.

It was a book I became very familiar with all those years later during the three months I lived with the sisters. As March lurched on toward April, winter began to lose its bite, even though the days were often cold and filled with ice and snow. There was a feeling of restlessness in the air, as if we could sense that the whole world was on the verge of something about to happen. By then, we were well on our way through Lent and for several weeks the liturgy had been full of watery images like this one: "For as the rain and the snow come down from heaven, and do not return there until they have watered the earth, making it bring forth and sprout, giving seed to the sower and bread to the eater, so shall my word be that goes out from my mouth; it shall not return to me empty, but it shall accomplish that which I purpose, and succeed in the thing for which I sent it" (Isa 55:10-11).

During the last week of March the first spring rains began washing away the remains of winter, sweetening the air with the earthy fragrance of springtime. The first reading at that Saturday's Mass contained these short lines from Hosea: "He will come to us like the showers, like the spring rains that water the earth" (Hos 6:3). The homilist that day reminded us that the rains of early spring have three distinct functions: to cleanse, to nourish, and to warm the earth by drawing out the frost and softening the soil to make it ready for planting, all lovely metaphors for what happens within us when our hearts are touched by the nurturing spirit of the creator. As a matter of fact, *Digitus Dei*, or "finger of God," is yet another term for the Holy Spirit. I think it is a particularly appropriate image for envisioning the work of the Spirit in our lives—touching and probing us, prodding and nudging us, pointing us in the direction we are meant to go.

Scripture is full of poetic language that invites us to marvel at the artistry of such an enormously creative God whose fingerprints are found all throughout the Book of Nature, and to ponder the astonishing fact that we have a place in it. "When I see the heavens, the work of your hands, the moon and the stars which you arranged, what is man that you should keep him in mind, mortal man that you care for him?" (Ps 8:4-5).

The psalmist was a keen observer of nature who took great delight in finding evidence that the finger of God had been at work. "How many, O Lord my God, are the wonders and designs that you have worked for us; you have no equal. Should I proclaim and speak of them, they are more than I can tell!" (Ps 39:6). That didn't stop the psalmist from trying. Well over half of the 150 psalms mention some aspect of the natural world, using the language of metaphor and poetry to evoke a sense of wonder and awe.

> You keep your pledge with wonders,
> O God our savior,
> the hope of all the earth
> and of far distant isles.
> You uphold the mountains with your strength,
> you are girded with power.
> You still the roaring of the seas,
> (the roaring of their waves)
> and the tumult of the peoples.
> The ends of the earth stand in awe
> at the sight of your wonders.
> The lands of sunrise and sunset
> you fill with your joy.

You care for the earth, give it water,
you fill it with riches.
Your river in heaven brims over
to provide its grain.
And thus you provide for the earth;
you drench its furrows,
you level it, soften it with showers,
you bless its growth.
You crown the year with your goodness.
Abundance flows in your steps,
in the pastures of the wilderness it flows.
The hills are girded with joy,
the meadows covered with flocks,
the valleys are decked with wheat.
They shout for joy, yes, they sing. (Ps 64:6-14)

Those beautiful words capture the essence of what it means to live in a world that has been so lavishly provided for by its creator, but it is the last line that speaks most eloquently. It's an exuberant reminder that the response to such an extravagant outpouring of generosity is a sense of awe and gratitude. Sedate and reserved creatures that many of us are, we may not go around shouting and singing for joy but we most assuredly know what it's like to feel as if we wanted to. Fortunately the author of the Psalms has found a way to speak for all of us. "I will praise you, Lord, with all my heart; I will recount all your wonders. I will rejoice in you and be glad, and sing psalms to your name, O Most High" (Ps 9:2-3).

This is why I have tried to be faithful about following Gail's advice the day she gave me her monastic "word." I have tried to make it a point to spend some time outdoors each day. The beauty I find there has a gentling effect on me. It soothes and restores me when I'm feeling agitated and out of sorts, and helps me regain my equilibrium when I get thrown off balance by events and circumstances that leave me shaken and distressed. Most important, it's a chance to read the Book of Nature and marvel at the artistry of its author because I've come to believe that to be moved by the beauty of the natural world is simply another way to pray.

The Book of Experience

The sisters do not make a distinction between what is going on in their lives and their search for God. They know many of the most important lessons about life can only be learned by living it with faith and conviction, trusting in God's good grace. It's one of the fruits of contemplative living. It means recognizing that the events and circumstances of life can be opportunities to learn what cannot be learned any other way, even when it involves anguish and pain.

One cold and stormy afternoon following my weekly singing lesson with Chris, I told her about a letter I had received from a friend who had just been diagnosed with breast cancer. Chris said she could understand how my friend must be feeling because a few years ago she had been given the same diagnosis. She described what an anguishing time it had been for her and how hard it was knowing that her own suffering was taking a toll on the rest of the community as well because living in a monastery is like living in a very large family. What happens to one sister has an impact on everyone else. Chris knew the anxiety and turmoil she felt was having a draining effect on everyone. Just because they were all nuns didn't make them immune to the emotional upheaval that goes along with cancer.

Until faced with a life-threatening situation no one can truly know what it is like to be so utterly vulnerable. In the midst of all that uncertainty and helplessness Chris had to let go of everything except faith in order to discover what it really means to trust in God. That was what she hung on to during those long months following her surgery while she went through all the pain and discomfort of chemotherapy, the hair loss, the nausea, and the fatigue.

But looking back on it all, she said the experience taught her some of the most powerful lessons she has ever learned about herself, her faith in God, and her relationship with her sisters. She learned what suffering is truly all about, and that she was able to endure it. She said it drew her closer to Christ, and I understood that to mean that through her own experience with cancer she gained some important insights into the suffering Christ himself endured.

Chris said she also learned things about prayer that she might not have recognized otherwise, specifically the solace that comes from being surrounded by a praying community in a time of crisis. She knew she was being carried along by so many people who cherished her—her family, her friends, and most of all her own sisters in the community. It opened her eyes to how much she mattered to other people and how much they depended on her presence in their lives. This in itself was a blessing because there is perhaps nothing quite as life-affirming as the sure knowledge that we are genuinely loved.

It was interesting to hear her story, not just because of what she had to say, but also because of the way she talked about it. Cancer is a pretty grim topic of conversation. But Chris is very expressive and she has a sparkling grin that kept breaking out while she talked. I had the impression she enjoyed the opportunity to share her cancer experience with me, which makes a lot of sense when you consider *joy* is a word that often shows up in the Book of Experience.

It is also a word that's used consistently by early Cistercian writers like Bernard of Clairvaux, Gilbert of Hoyland, and William of St. Thierry. Saint Bernard is said to have regarded the life of a monk as a vocation of joy, and the sermons of Gilbert of Hoyland are full of words and expressions that describe the joyfulness of his vocation. William of St. Thierry has this to say about monastic joy: "For when the joy of the Lord is established in a good conscience, it is not interrupted by the incursion of any earthly sadness or obscured by any vain joyousness, but continues faithfully and firmly in its steady course, always and everywhere tranquil, nor does it undergo change even though it lends itself to many things."[24]

This seems to suggest that joy doesn't necessarily mean the absence of what is painful and difficult but rather the ability to maintain a joyful attitude regardless of the circumstances in which one finds oneself.

---

24. William of St. Thierry, quoted by Jean Holman, "Monastic Joyfulness in Gilbert of Hoyland," *Cistercian Studies Quarterly* 19.4 (1984) 320.

It brings to mind a conversation I had with Kathleen a few days before I left for home. I had told her that one of the things I was going to miss was the spirit of joyfulness I'd felt during the three months I lived at Mississippi Abbey. She laughed and rolled her eyes the way many of the sisters did whenever I made one of my "it's so peaceful around here" remarks. Then she turned serious and suggested it might be helpful to learn how to practice the discipline of joy—another one of those relatively obscure monastic customs that make an awful lot of sense. Kathleen explained that it has to do with remaining alert to God's presence in all the circumstances of life—even those times when life is difficult, burdensome, and painful. Like any other discipline it takes a fair amount of effort because *joyful* isn't exactly the word I'd normally use to describe my frame of mind when things aren't going my way. I have always associated joy with exuberance, gaiety, elation, delight, words like that. But it is worth noting that while joy is one of the fruits of the Spirit,[25] exuberance, gaiety, elation, and delight aren't even mentioned. Instead, the rest of the list includes patience, faithfulness, and self-control, which can make a big difference when attempting to put the first few lines of the letter of James into practice: "My brothers and sisters, whenever you face trials of any kind, consider it nothing but joy" (Jas 1:2).

This must be what the discipline of joy is all about and, as Gail told the community in one of her chapter talks, it's our responsibility as Christians. It has less to do with feelings and more to do with attitudes, specifically an attitude of hope and trust born of the ability to recognize the hand of God in the events and circumstances of life—even those that test our strength and endurance. We can't rid the world of sorrow, pain, and injustice but we can choose to "Rejoice in hope, be patient in suffering, persevere in prayer" (Rom 12:12). "The presence of struggle and heartache in our lives does not bar us from true joy," Gail says in her book, *Seasons of Grace*. "On the contrary, it can prepare our hearts for fuller and deeper joy. The only real enemy of joy is a

---

25. See Gal 5:22-23.

melancholy that turns us inward on ourselves and makes us lose hope."[26]

The discipline of joy sounded like a great idea the day Kathleen told me about it, and I left Mississippi Abbey determined to keep it in mind. Naturally, I forgot all about it until one day the following spring when I woke up and knew something was terribly wrong with my left eye. It turned out the retina had begun to detach, making it necessary to have surgery immediately.

Surgery for a partially detached retina is pretty minor on the scale of "bad things that can happen." It was scary and painful and unpleasant. But it wasn't life-threatening, nor did it result in any permanent change in lifestyle. The worst part was that for several weeks I had to give up reading, writing, and everything else that involved using my eyes for close work. Nor could I bend and reach, which meant that during those glorious spring days I was not able to do any gardening. It wasn't all that bad and yet it was harder than I had thought it would be.

The discipline of joy probably would never have occurred to me had it not been for a phone call with Kathleen, who reminded me of the conversation we'd had shortly before I left the abbey. So for the next few weeks and during the months that followed as I went back for repeated examinations and treatment, I tried to keep that conversation in mind.

I definitely did not *feel* happy or jubilant about what was going on, and I surely would not choose to go through it again. But I learned that it is possible to face difficult and painful experiences without being overwhelmed by them. By experiencing how hard it was not being able to do the things I wanted to do, I was learning about patience. By having to get used to not being in control of what was happening to me, I was learning about trust. It was a good reminder that what's sacred about life is not limited to what leaves us feeling uplifted. Sometimes the spiritual journey takes us into uncomfortable places where all we can do is wait . . . and hope . . . and trust that in the long run all will be well.

26. Fitzpatrick, 157.

Nevertheless, I still have a lot to learn about practicing the discipline of joy, and I suspect I will find ample opportunity the longer I study the Book of Experience. The little I've already picked up has taught me the value of paying prayerful attention to the difficult and challenging things that happen to me. Life breaks us all, Ernest Hemingway is purported to have said, and if we're lucky we'll be stronger in the broken places. I believe that while we have very little control over many of the major life-altering events and circumstances of our lives, we have a great deal of control over how we choose to react to them. I know far too many people who have spent their lives being miserable because they have chosen to react negatively to the inevitable problems and sorrows they have encountered. In doing so, they have hardened their hearts beneath layers of bitterness and resentment, refusing to be open to the healing power of grace. It need not be that way. Learning what it means to practice the discipline of joy can help us be prepared to choose the path of hope and trust no matter what may be in store for us.

There is an old proverb that says the veil that hides the future has been woven by the angel of mercy. True enough. But perhaps the same angel is also busy unraveling whatever prevents us from seeing the significance of the past and the present. Both have much to teach us about the spiritual life, provided we pay attention.

Paying attention means looking—really looking—at what's happening to us in order to discover why it matters so much. Unfortunately, it's easy to get distracted. When things aren't working out right or when I run into a tricky situation with another person that leaves me feeling discouraged, angry, or upset, my tendency is to react rather than reflect. But I am learning there is value in waiting for the intensity of those feelings to pass so that I can get a better perspective on what is to be learned from them. Since the Book of Experience is full of some pretty emotional stuff I think it is important to figure out how to read the passages that deal with it.

But so much of life can be hard to understand no matter how ardently I struggle to find words to explain it. That's why metaphors and symbols can be so helpful. Scripture is full of metaphor and Jesus himself was fond of stories and similes ("The kingdom

of heaven is like . . ." "Once there was a father who had two sons
. . ." "Unless you are born again . . .") Willigis Jäger says these
scriptural parables and symbols are like glass windows that let in
the light, since it's difficult to look directly into the brightness of
light itself. "We can recognize it only in reflections. . . . The light,
that has no structure itself and can never be grasped, gets its color
and structure from the glass window."[27] Like looking through the
windows in our homes, we must learn to look for our own personal
stories and metaphors and discover what they can reveal to us.

One of the most accessible places for me to find metaphors
and symbols is the landscape I inhabit when I'm dreaming. While
not everyone agrees with me, I seriously doubt that my dreams
have much to do with what I had for dinner. More likely they
relate to what's in my heart and my soul, which probably explains why I did a fair amount of heavy-duty dreaming during
the time I was living with the sisters.

One night I dreamt my two adult sons were still little boys.
It was a particularly vivid dream and I awoke missing them terribly because even though I dearly love the young men Casey
and Brendan have become, the dream gave me a chance to meet
them once again as the children they used to be. Later in the day
I mentioned it to Emma, who listened intently because as it
turned out she had just finished reading a book by Anselm Grün
about the spiritual significance of dreams. According to Grün,
dreams help us uncover the truth of who we are because the
language of dreams is the language of our soul.

> We should listen to what God wants to communicate to us
> in this language, because we often do not hear what God
> tells us during the day. We often distort the words which we
> hear in prayer and in silence, or place our desires into them,
> or disregard what is unpleasant. In dreams, God uncovers
> the truth about us without doing anything to stop it.[28]

27. Willigis Jäger, *Search for the Meaning of Life: Essays and Reflections on the Mystical Experience* (Liguori, Missouri: Triumph Books, 1995) 17–18.

28. Anselm Grün, osb, *Dreams on the Spiritual Journey* (Schuyler, Nebraska: Benedictine Mission House, 1993) 50. Also J. A. Sanford, "Gottes vergessene Sprache," *Studien aus dem CG* (Zurich: Jung Institut XVIII, 1966).

Emma felt my dream had used "the language of the soul" to remind me of an important piece of truth about myself: namely, that being a mother has always been and probably always will be one of the most intensely meaningful experiences of my life. It is an integral part of who I am, and who I am meant to continue being. How fascinating to have had a dream like that while I was living in the company of women who would never be mothers! It was a powerful reminder of the importance of my own vocation, and the fact that the love I have for my sons has been carved into the deepest part of my identity. The feelings and convictions I have about what my sons mean to me are so powerful that I very seldom even consciously think about them. The dream gave me a chance to go to that place in my heart where I was able to immediately recognize them.

But dreams aren't the only place to find metaphors and symbols. The Book of Experience is full of them, and sometimes they show up in the form of unexpected and unwelcome challenges. Shortly after my retina surgery I developed a tear in the retina of the other eye, which required laser therapy. It was a much simpler procedure except that immediately afterwards one of the tiny blood vessels in the eye burst. There was no serious damage done but my doctor warned me that it could take up to six weeks before my vision would return to normal. For several weeks I could see nothing at all with that eye. When I covered the other eye there was only darkness in front of me. I knew then and there that I had stumbled across a metaphor.

Darkness speaks to me of how vulnerable I am in the face of all that is uncertain about life. It is an apt description for the anxiety that goes along with doubt and uncertainty, and the fear that comes with not knowing what to do or where to turn. To be in a place of darkness is to know the desperation of looking for a tiny little ray of light leading the way out. These are the very times when it is important to trust that little by little, the darkness will surely disappear.

During those six weeks of temporary and partial blindness I got up each morning long before sunrise to light a candle in my little library room. And each morning I covered my "good eye" and stared straight ahead of me. For several discouraging weeks all I could see was darkness. But one morning I noticed a barely perceptible spot directly in front of me that seemed a little less dark than the space around it. Within a few days it had turned into a dim and foggy blur that gradually began to flicker like the flame it was. Little by little, the foggy blur began to clear and the flicker from the flame grew stronger and more sharply defined. Within a week I could make out the form of the candle itself. And then one morning I opened that eye and realized I could see everything clearly once again. During those six weeks I had learned an eloquent lesson about the importance of patience and hope and trust. And I'd also had a chance to do some serious thinking about the light imagery in our Christian tradition. "Your word is a lamp for my steps and a light for my path" (Ps 118:105). "I am the light of the world. Whoever follows me will never walk in darkness but will have the light of life" (John 8:12). "For once you were darkness, but now in the Lord you are light. Live as children of light—for the fruit of the light is found in all that is good and right and true" (Eph 5:8-9).

Seeing nothing but darkness in front of me gave me a deeper appreciation for what these beautiful passages have to say. And it helped me realize that it's important to pay attention to what is often being revealed through difficult and painful experiences.

Some feel it is a waste of time to be so concerned with the interior life. Lighten up, they say; don't take yourself so seriously! And they have a point. Too much of the wrong kind of introspection can be self-indulgent and result in exaggerated feelings of importance. People can end up becoming excessively concerned with themselves, as if their experiences and expectations are all that matters. To focus only on our own needs, opinions, and perspectives is to become blind to those of others. When we are entrenched in our individual sorrows and misfortunes, we fail to recognize the anguish of those whose suffering is often much harder to bear.

Not being able to see properly gave me an insight into how hard it must be to be deprived of the sense of sight. But my brother Ed has lived his entire life with severe visual impairments. The rest of us in our family have always known it has been difficult for him but we have not experienced anything that comes close to what that hardship has been like. We've always admired the way he has accepted his disability and learned to cope with the limitations it has imposed, but none of us have really understood just what has been involved in doing that.

I thought about Ed often while I waited to regain my full vision. To be temporarily unable to see normally was nothing compared to the extent of his visual impairment. It was humbling to recognize that what I was having such a hard time accepting was only a minor inconvenience compared to what Ed has had to live with since birth. Losing and recovering my vision taught me to be more aware of what it must be like to be blind. It helped me gain a deeper insight into what my brother has had to endure all his life and what he has to teach us about suffering.

Reading the Book of Experience has taught me the value of taking time to pay attention to the significance of what is happening to me, rather than racing through life oblivious to what it is really all about. I have learned it doesn't make sense to behave as if the spiritual part of life can be separated from everything else because life itself has much to reveal about what is sacred. The world is full of opportunities for recognizing the presence of God, and the Book of Experience is where many of them are to be found. The key is learning how to read it.

ASPECTS OF THE LIFE

It is precisely because Benedictinism is a commitment to facing the challenges of real life that it can serve as an inspiration and summons to many outside its immediate circle. On an existential level, the witness of Benedictine life fervently lived can be a reminder that humanity is enhanced and not diminished by renouncing self-indulgence, possessions and power. On a more interior plane, the beliefs and values incarnate in Benedict's Rule can be for us an antidote for some of the conditioning to which we are all subjected, who live in the twenty-first century. Attempting to assimilate the counter-cultural philosophy of Benedict's Rule is not an escape into an antique irrelevance, but a movement of reflection that is becoming increasingly necessary in a society that is fearful of any critical self-analysis.[1]

Michael Casey
An Unexciting Life

Enclosure

January 20

I thought I'd be moving right into the monastic enclosure as soon as I arrived at Mississippi Abbey. Instead I'm going to be spending a couple of days here in the retreat house. Louise explained that this will give me a chance to make a more comfortable transition between the world I'm coming from with all its noisy superficiality and the life I'll be living with the sisters for the next three months.

---

1. Michael Casey, ocso, *An Unexciting Life: Reflections on Benedictine Spirituality* (Petersham, Massachusetts: St. Bede's Publications, 2005) 14.

*Once I enter the monastic enclosure, I'll be leaving behind all
the distractions and diversions that keep me from concentrating
on what's most essential—the one thing needed, the better part,
the part that often tends to get ignored outside the monastic
enclosure.*

Monks and nuns are often accused of running away from
the demands of life to hide inside their cloisters, where they can
avoid the hard work of living as productive members of society.
Obviously that is not true, but unless people understand the
importance of the spiritual life, they probably will have trouble
appreciating why anyone would want to withdraw from the
world to make it a priority.

Therein lies the reason for monastic enclosure: it exists in
order to enable men and women to make the search for God their
top priority through prayer and loving service to one another.
We are all called to be faithful to our baptismal vows by living
apart from whatever interferes with the Gospel message. It's one
of the requisites of the Christian life. Jesus himself told us that
we are not of this world (John 15:18-19), and how many times
have we heard that line about not getting too attached to the
things of the world (1 John 2:15)?

Since that is supposed to be the goal of every Christian,
why do monks and nuns need to be so literal about leaving the
world in order to devote their lives to it? It's because the things
of the world and the ways of the world can so easily distract us
from what we need to be doing as followers of Christ. That's
why monks and nuns leave it all behind by choosing to spend
their lives within the physical environment of their monastic
enclosures.

In concrete terms, the enclosure comprises that part of the
monastery that is accessible only to the monastic persons who
live there. At Mississippi Abbey this extends to the grounds behind the main monastery building itself as well as everything
inside it. It covers all those areas where the sisters live and work,
including the kitchen, refectory, chapter room, scriptorium, class-
rooms, offices, work spaces, and of course the dormitory area
where the sisters' cells are located. Enclosure also encompasses
the monastic choir section of their church where the sisters gather

in choir stalls that face each other across an open aisle for Mass and the Liturgy of the Hours. (Guests are seated in a separate section to one side of the main altar.) These areas are clearly marked because normally, no one else is allowed to enter.

There has always been an intriguing aura of mystery about those signs that say "monastic enclosure, please do not enter," as though there are secrets to be discovered within the walls and behind the closed doors of the abbey. Having been a frequent visitor prior to the three months I spent there as a long-term guest, I've always felt that it would be a major breach of monastic etiquette to cross those boundaries and wander in unaccompanied. I have grown accustomed to respecting the sisters' enclosure by making sure I stayed on my side of it. So it took me a few days to get used to being on the other side and to get over feeling that I was trespassing. The sisters had been wonderfully welcoming and with the exception of their individual cells, there were no places that were off-limits to me. Louise even made a point of showing me the boiler room when she was taking me around that first day! And every time we passed a closed door, she opened it—even if there was nothing inside but a vacuum cleaner and an assortment of cleaning supplies.

Before long I felt right at home living with the sisters inside the enclosure. There was something warm and companionable about it, and so it didn't bother me at all knowing that I would not be able to leave the abbey for three months. Not only do the rules of enclosure limit non-monastic persons from entering, they also set parameters for where and when a sister may go out. And while I was living there, I was expected to abide by the same rules.

While from the outside monastic life may look like a glorified prison, monks and nuns see it differently. True, the sisters are not at liberty to go scooting in and out whenever they feel like it, but my sense was that for the most part they didn't really want to. And neither did I. On the rare occasions when I did leave for a few hours, it felt oddly disorienting to be surrounded by the familiar busyness of the world I had temporarily left behind. Once I rode along with one of the sisters who had to run into Menards to pick up some paint. Another time I had to slip into town to have a shoe repaired. Both times it felt awfully good to be back at the abbey again. I had only left it for a short time and yet I'd gotten so used to not being inundated with all the noise and confusion on the outside, that it was a big relief to be able to leave it all behind me once again.

The monastic enclosure is not a barrier preventing the sisters from living full and meaningful lives. On the contrary, everything necessary and essential for the life they have chosen is provided and there is no reason to look elsewhere for it. I was actually a little surprised at how quickly I got used to living that way—and how much I hated to leave it when the time came.

Possibly, the fact that I moved into the monastic enclosure during a very cold and snowy winter made it easier to be inside both literally and figuratively. I think it is in our nature to want to slow down during this time of year. Perhaps there is something inside us that is in sync with what happens in the natural world during the wintertime, sending millions of creatures scurrying underground to take shelter from the harsh wind and bitter cold by curling up in snug caves and hidden burrows. "Now the woods are like a great bedroom, with various life forms snoozing away the cold days and the long nights," writes naturalist Bill Stokes. "Those of us who must stay awake through it all know spasms of envy that we do not recognize. We are related to the sleepers, but we cannot use their ways to weather the annual storm of darkness. Something deep within us regrets that."[2] Perhaps that is the reason I've always felt winter is such a contemplative season. But instead of sleeping until spring, I have to be content with staying awake during those long, cold nights and dreary, gray days with nowhere deep to go but inside my own heart. Where better to do it than in a monastic enclosure?

Winter in Iowa is often brutally cold but it is also breathtakingly beautiful, especially along the bluffs high above the Mississippi River. It's worth bundling up tightly to trudge through the snow looking for hawks and other birds, or to sit

2. Bill Stokes, *The River Is Us* (Minocqua, Wisconsin: Northword Press, 1993) 186–87.

inside feeling safe and warm on a stormy night, listening to the wind howling outside. There's something about winter that tugs at the contemplative heart. It's what nature writer Hal Borland was describing when he wrote about a walk he took one cold winter night:

> Somehow I knew that I was one with the wind and the stars and the earth itself. Winter was all around me, simple as the glittering breath from my lungs. I was a part of the mystery, the wonder and the awe, part of the holiness and the whole-ness of life and the reason beyond all my reasoning.[3]

In the middle of those long winter nights at Mississippi Abbey I would get up for Vigils and, not yet fully awake, edge my way carefully between the choir stalls, trying not to disturb any of the sisters who were already there. After a few more moments of perfect stillness, Ciaran would lean down and tap the little gong at her feet and we would all rise for the first Office of the day.

There's a sense of intimacy about the night Office of Vigils that strikes me as a good image for monastic enclosure. "In my little bed by night, I sought him whom my soul loves," wrote Gilbert of Hoyland in one of his sermons on the Song of Songs. He continues:

> What better place than one's little bed, what time more fit-ting than by night, for the exercise of love? . . . The more the spirit is freed from harness, the more it will hasten to-wards what it loves . . . Contrariwise, frequent preoccupa-tion with the world almost blunts the affections and makes the spirit callous. Preoccupation entangles, repose unravels the spirit.[4]

Gilbert's "little bed" speaks to me of the intimate quality of mo-nastic enclosure and of the richness that is found in a genuinely prayerful environment where care is taken to avoid whatever

---

3. Hal Borland, *Seasons* (Philadelphia: J.B. Lippincott Company, 1973) 107.

4. Gilbert of Hoyland, *Sermons on the Song of Songs*, Cistercian Fathers Series 14 (Kalamazoo, Michigan: Cistercian Publications, 1978) 45, 46.

"blunts the affections and makes the spirit callous." But the image of the little bed also suggests that there's something about monastic enclosure that is more important than its physical parameters. It has to do with that private space that is buried within each one of us where we are truly ourselves. This is why what matters the most about monastic enclosure is found hidden away in each sister's heart.

Gail has written about enclosure from this perspective by pointing out that while the physical aspects of enclosure are important because they define boundaries and provide space for structuring a prayerful and contemplative environment, what is most important about monastic enclosure is its spiritual dimension. Monks and nuns choose to live apart from the rest of the world in order to enter an environment where they can seek God, praying alone and with one another not only for their own sake but also for the good of the entire world. The monastic enclosure, she writes, "creates a 'safe zone,' safe from the distractions of persons and things that draw one away from the spiritual journey, and safe for the opening of one's heart to the good and the stripping away of the false self."[5]

Enclosure at Home

Each of us is called to the spiritual journey, but the majority of us are stumbling along trying to follow it through a world where the prevailing values, norms, and priorities of our culture keep getting in the way. Because we do not live within the safety zone of a monastery, we must create our own interior enclosures in order to nurture our spirits and stay focused on our search for God. For me, it's been helpful to look at it from the perspective of the ancient monastic practice of guarding the heart. In Gail's words, this means "continually discerning God's call to love so one can choose the good and exclude from one's innermost heart

5. Gail Fitzpatrick, "Enclosure: The Heart of the Matter," in *A Monastic Vision for the 21st Century* (Kalamazoo, Michigan: Cistercian Publications, 2006) 153.

the trivial, mere curiosities, and those animosities that destroy tranquility and the reign of God's peace within."[6]

The image of guarding our hearts is rich with meaning because we all use language that proves we're familiar with the inner landscape of the heart: we can usually tell in our hearts when something is right (or wrong). We know what it feels like to yearn for our heart's desire, and what it means to love another person from the bottom of our hearts. When we're willing to drop all defenses and be frank and honest with someone, we say we want to have a heart-to-heart talk. As children we used to cross our hearts when promising to keep a secret and as adults we know what it is to lose heart when someone hurts or disappoints us. We know what it is to have a heart that burns with passion or bursts with pride or sings with joy. And we also know all about heartache and what it feels like to weep as if our hearts were breaking. We know kindhearted people who are all heart, people with hearts of gold whose hearts are in the right places. And we know others who have hardened their hearts, those whose hearts are cold as ice, those who behave heartlessly.

Because the heart is such a potent symbol, Scripture often uses it to speak about that mysterious part of us that is the very core of our being: "O search me, God, and know my heart. O test me and know my thoughts. See that I follow not the wrong path and lead me in the path of life eternal" (Ps 138:23-24). "Keep your heart with all vigilance, for from it flow the springs of life" (Prov 4:23).

In fact there are over a thousand references to the heart in Scripture and most of them describe what in contemporary parlance might be called the inner person. "I pray that, according to the riches of his glory, he may grant that you may be strengthened in your inner being with power through his Spirit, and that Christ may dwell in your hearts through faith, as you are being rooted and grounded in love" (Eph 3:16-17). "Do not worry about anything, but in everything by prayer and supplication with thanksgiving let your requests be made known to God. And the peace

6. Ibid., 150.

of God, which surpasses all understanding, will guard your hearts and your minds in Christ Jesus" (Phil 4:6-7). "Do not store up for yourselves treasures on earth, where moth and rust consume and where thieves break in and steal; but store up for yourselves treasures in heaven, where neither moth nor rust consumes and where thieves do not break in and steal. For where your treasure is, there your heart will be also" (Matt 6:19-21). "A new heart I will give you, and a new spirit I will put within you; and I will remove from your body the heart of stone and give you a heart of flesh" (Ezek 36:26).

Monastic writers have used the term "heart" in this same way to connote that deep center of being that is the source of our thoughts, feelings, desires, and behaviors. Saint Benedict begins his rule by telling his monks to listen to his instructions with the "ear of your heart." "Rid your heart of all deceit," he says (RB 4.24), and "speak the truth with heart and tongue" (4.28). A monk is not to grumble in his heart (5.17) but rather "manifests humility in his bearing no less than in his heart" (7.62). Monks are to pray with "compunction of heart" (49.4) and "heartfelt devotion" (52.4).

Cistercian spirituality emphasizes the importance of coming to the truth about oneself by looking into the depths of one's heart. It is here that one goes to find God and it is from here that one's deepest prayer emerges, or in the words of Baldwin of Forde:

> It is only right and proper and just that we should give our heart to him if he himself thinks fit to ask for it. And he has thought it fit! "Give me your heart," he says to us! He who asks you to give him your heart wants to be loved from the heart. God wants our whole heart for himself, that in him, before all else, it may take its pleasure.[7]

And Isaac of Stella writes, "The heart that covets the sight of God as in a mirror must keep itself free from cares, from harmful, unnecessary and even necessary ones. It must keep itself ever

7. Edith Scholl, ocso, ed., *In the School of Love: An Anthology of Early Cistercian Texts* (Kalamazoo, Michigan: Cistercian Publications, 2000) 39.

alert through reading, meditation and prayer. Blessed are the pure of heart; they shall see God. May he grant that we do so."[8]

Early monastic writers believed that since God is our heart's desire, it is within the depths of our hearts that we will find our way to him. "If, as St. Paul says, Christ dwells in our hearts through faith (cf. Eph. 3:17), and all the treasures of wisdom and spiritual knowledge are hidden in Him (cf. Col. 2:3), then all the treasure of wisdom and spiritual knowledge are hidden in our hearts. . . . This is the treasure hidden in the field of your heart (cf. Matt. 13:44), which you have not yet found because of your laziness."[9]

John Cassian, who lived in the fifth century, traveling across Egypt and founding monasteries throughout southern France, believed that in order to guard the treasure that is hidden in the heart one must keep careful watch over thoughts. "It is, indeed, impossible for the mind not to be troubled by thoughts," he wrote, "but accepting them or rejecting them is possible for everyone who makes an effort. It is true that their origin does not in every respect depend on us, but it is equally true that their refusal or acceptance does depend on us."[10]

Thoughts are seductive. They have the potential to lead us where we don't want to go, which is why we can so easily end up giving in to impulses and temptations—whether they have to do with food, or sex, or the inclination to harbor the resentments, grudges, and frustrations that go along with anger and jealousy. Cassian taught that in order to guard our hearts we must learn to be disciplined about what we allow ourselves to think about. Simply put, it means putting a speedy end to thoughts and impulses that are destined to end in trouble if we indulge in them. In her book *Thoughts Matter*, Benedictine Sister Mary Margaret Funk explains how relevant this ancient practice

8. Ibid., 150.

9. G. E. H. Palmer, ed., *The Philokalia, Volume II* (London: Faber and Faber, 1981) 109.

10. Boniface Ramsey, OP, trans., *John Cassian: The Conferences* (New York: Paulist Press, 1997) 56.

is for us today, noting that the thought process is a powerful tool for determining the outcome of our actions and behaviors. Because we have a great deal of control over our thoughts, we can determine whether or not to be motivated by them. The key is to become aware of a thought in time to do something about it. "First thoughts beget second thoughts, which become intentions. Intentions constitute motivation and indicate where the heart resides. Motivation moves the will to decide and act on the thought. Decisions give voice to the choices we intend to act upon. Attention to our thoughts reveals our intentions."[11]

It is risky to indulge in negative thinking because it can easily lead us into more trouble. Guarding our hearts means having enough self-control to say "don't go there!" Not only is it a great way to squelch temptations at their source but it also helps us avoid nursing grudges, fanning the flames of regret, or allowing ourselves to be overwhelmed by our anxieties and fears. Ultimately, it can lead us to greater compassion for others and a deepening realization of the truth of who we are and how we are to live as followers of Christ. That is why I think the parable of the Sower is one of the most powerful of all Jesus' stories.

> And as he sowed, some seeds fell on the path, and the birds came and ate them up. Other seeds fell on rocky ground, where they did not have much soil, and they sprang up quickly, since they had no depth of soil. But when the sun rose, they were scorched; and since they had no root, they withered away. Other seeds fell among thorns, and the thorns grew up and choked them. Other seeds fell on good soil and brought forth grain, some a hundredfold, some sixty, some thirty. (Matt 13:4-8)

Whenever I read that parable I spot different aspects of myself. Sometimes I see myself in the seed that fell on the path, because I recognize all too well the times I've failed to take advantage of the opportunities I have to deepen my knowledge of what it means to grow in faith. At other times I recognize, in the seed

11. Mary Margaret Funk, osb, *Thoughts Matter* (New York: Continuum, 1998) 20.

that fell on rocky ground, how easy it is for me to lose heart during times of spiritual dryness and doubt. Most troublesome of all is what I see of myself in the seed that fell among thorns because I know how easily I am distracted by the worries and anxieties, as well as the trivial pleasures and superficialities, of life.

And yet I believe that buried deep within all of us, at the very core of our hearts, are seeds of goodness that must be protected and nurtured in order to bear fruit in our lives. It is the work of a lifetime to keep them growing because there is much that can stunt, if not totally destroy, their growth. That's why it is so important to create our own interior enclosures in order to separate ourselves from the things of the world that choke our spirits and stifle the growth of goodness within us. We must have the wisdom to cultivate what we find in our hearts and the courage to prevent entry to whatever threatens its development.

A very concrete example of what it means to guard the interior enclosure of our hearts has to do with the media, including television, movies, newspapers and magazines, e-mail and the internet. I would never go so far as to say that they are all blatantly dangerous and should be completely avoided, and I am certainly not about to stop using e-mail, abandon the internet, get rid of my TV, and never darken the door of another movie theater for the rest of my life. But on the other hand, I do believe that the media—in all its forms—can affect us more powerfully than we care to admit, and that's why we need to be selective about the way we use it. We need to be careful about the degree to which we are willing to let it into our interior enclosures. It is no secret that much of what's broadcast on television, printed in newspapers and magazines, and easily accessible via the internet is simply not good for people—people of any age. While we are justifiably concerned about the effect it has on children, I think we should be just as troubled about what it's doing to the rest of us as well. I think we are all threatened by the way violence has become a major part of the entertainment industry's standard fare. We are all being exploited by the way sex has been trivialized. We are all cheapened by the way what is vulgar, crude, and offensive has become the standard for the way people dress, behave, or speak to one another. Worst of all, it colors the way we look at our world and one another. And that is why we need to guard our hearts against it.

Denny has taped a little slip of paper to our television set with the following words from Psalm 100: "I will walk with blameless heart within my house; I will not set before my eyes whatever is base" (vv. 2-3). It's just a little reminder to think twice before plopping down in front of the TV. It's not that I'm worried I'll start itching to dress up like a hooker and hang around bars looking for someone to go home and have sex with, or that I will suddenly develop a violent streak and go out and buy a gun so I can start shooting people. And I doubt very seriously whether watching a steady diet of ridiculous reality TV episodes might change my view of reality in any way whatsoever. It's more a matter of not liking to get so upset and angry about the extent to which the kind of messages people get from the media pervade our popular culture. Nor do I like having to face up to the obviously judgmental streak that surfaces when I find myself wondering how on earth people can sit there watching such mindless drivel.

While I've tried not to be openly critical of people for spending so much time in front of their television sets, I have become much more discerning about what I allow to filter into my own environment. And the bonus for doing this has been that I have a lot more time to devote to things I truly enjoy.

But the problem goes further than the media. Outside the physical boundaries of a monastic enclosure we are bombarded with messages from other sources as well, messages that are filled with not-so-subtle pronouncements about what we should think and how we ought to behave in order to fit in with the norms and mores of our society. Unfortunately, most of it is based on values and attitudes that are in direct opposition to what enriches our hearts, minds, and souls. To find examples we need look no further than the clever slogans and catchphrases that marketing departments pay their creativity gurus big bucks to invent. "There are some things money can't buy," reads the tagline next to an image of a woman stretched out on a sandy beach; "for everything else there's MasterCard."

Ads and commercials tell us a lot about contemporary values and priorities. So do bumper stickers ("My C-average student can beat up your honor roll student"), not to mention T-shirts ("I'm not ignoring you, you're just not worth paying attention to"), coffee mugs ("The one who dies with the most stuff wins"), and for that matter, greeting cards ("Congratulations on your divorce, you should have dumped the jerk long ago"). In the midst of all this it makes sense to go back and reread Romans 12:2: "Do not be conformed to this world."

Those words challenge us to consider what monastic enclosure means from our perspective, living as we do in a world that does little to nurture the seeds of goodness within us. I think we need to create our own inner enclosures—enclosures of the heart. Guarding our hearts means protecting and cultivating our inner goodness by trying to avoid whatever threatens to destroy it. And for Christians, guarding the heart also means doing what we can to ensure that our actions and behaviors are consistent with the message of compassion, forgiveness, and loving service that we find in the Gospels. It has to do with the choices we make about how to live and how to relate to those with whom we are sharing our lives. In my view much of this comes down to the importance of enoughness, the primacy of prayer, and the connectedness to people.

The Importance of Enoughness

Simplicity is a central feature of monasticism. It is apparent in the way the sisters maintain moderation in all aspects of their lives. It is visible in the natural and uncluttered beauty of their abbey's physical environment as well as in the way their abbey buildings have been designed and furnished. And it is reflected in the demeanor of the sisters as they move through the ordinary tasks and routines of each day with such grace and ease. Having observed them for three months, I think I have found out at least one of their secrets: they have discovered there is a lot more to life than acquiring and accumulating things. They know the value of moderation—enough food, enough clothing, enough work, enough time.

I, on the other hand, am constantly battling the tendency to keep filling up my life with more of what I've already got. The irony of acquisition is that the more I have, the greater my drive for accumulating even more. This seems to apply to everything from books to socks to garden tools. And the more I accumulate, the less likely I am to pay attention to what I already have: the books I haven't gotten around to reading yet, the socks I can't find mates for, the garden tools that have disappeared into the clutter that is piling up in the garage. I would be a lot better off if I could learn to recognize when to say "enough is enough."

But acquiring too many books and garden tools is only a symptom of the problem, and so what I have to work on is a way to stop assuming I ought to have whatever looks appealing at the moment. The trick is learning to tell the difference between what I actually need versus what might be nice to have even though I don't need it at all. That's easier said than done in a culture fueled by a vast system of clever marketing techniques intended to make just about anything seem like it is absolutely essential for our happiness and well-being.

The concept of enoughness applies to other areas as well. We can develop a consumer approach to life based on the "more is better" habit of doing things that keep us constantly on the go, cramming as much as we possibly can into our already over-scheduled agendas. I call it the shopping cart approach to accumulating experiences. It is the difference between being a tourist who rushes around accumulating souvenirs and snapshots as opposed to being a traveler who sets out to savor the journey and enjoy the amazing things that happen along the way. It is a mistake to rush through life trying to get more and more out of it if it means I'm going to end up being too busy to appreciate the significance of whatever I'm in such a hurry to do. I think it was Georgia O'Keefe who said it's impossible to pay attention in a hurry. It makes sense, and that is why I need to do a better job of telling myself enough is enough in terms of what I want to do with my time. Part of what it means to create my heart's own enclosure has to do with slowing down the pace of my life so I can pay attention to what really matters.

As important as it's become for me to be guided by the principle of enoughness in order to avoid overspending, overindulging, and over*doing* things, I have also had to remind myself that there are some instances where the reverse can be true. I can end up not devoting enough time to prayer, or not doing enough to nurture the relationships I have with the people I love, or not paying enough attention to the significance of whatever happens to be going on at the moment. That is why the monastic practice of ending each day with a short *examen*, or review, can be a sort of spiritual heads-up alerting me to those areas of my life where more would definitely be better.

The Primacy of Prayer

A major reason interior enclosure is so important for the life of the spirit is because it creates an environment that's more conducive to prayer. But anyone who has ever learned anything at all about prayer knows you can pray anywhere and in absolutely any circumstance or situation in which you find yourself. So it is not simply the physical environment of an enclosure that matters so much; it's also the fact that enclosure makes prayerfulness a priority. When my attention is focused on other things, when I'm distracted and conflicted because of my busy, fragmented lifestyle, when my leisure time is squandered on meaningless diversions, chances are my prayer life is going to be pretty shallow. I can easily get so caught up in the minutia of my life that prayer gets left out of it, even though I don't intend it to be that way. That is not likely to happen within a monastic enclosure where time and space are regularly set aside for no other reason but to pray.

But at home it's different. My house doesn't have a chapel attached or bells that call me when it's time to pray. Of course I shouldn't have to be reminded, and I don't need to go to a chapel or church because prayer can happen anywhere. But outside the monastic enclosure I'm far too likely to forget.

For that matter, why bother in the first place? As a child I remember being taught that I had to pray because God needs me to. But like so many things I learned about God as a child, I simply don't believe it anymore. I cannot go along with the image of a megalomaniac deity with a relentless thirst for human adulation and affirmation. Such a creature doesn't bear much resemblance to the Old Testament Lord of the Universe who, according to Psalm 39 does not ask for burnt offerings or holocaust but rather an open ear, or the New Testament God of mercy, compassion, and forgiveness. In my view, God doesn't need me to pray. But I do.

I need to pray because something inside me longs to reach out for whatever it is that God is. There is so much more to life than what we can possibly discover by collecting information or attempting to analyze it or measure it or explain it. That "moreness" is what I think God is all about. God is more than we can ever hope to explain through our doctrines, creeds, or religions. God is a "moreness" that cannot be comprehended and yet is somehow present to me—although try as I might I'll never be able to explain how. All I know is that I need to reach out to whatever it is that God is. For me, that is what prayer is all about and by trying to create my own interior enclosure, I have tried to make it a more integral part of my life.

Just as the sisters have set aside certain times and places for prayer, it's been helpful for me to do the same thing. I may not have a chapel, but I do have that room with its comfortable chair and the shelf for all my books, and the little table that's the right size for a few candles and seasonal arrangements of flowers, gourds, or evergreens. That's where I like to go to pray. It's an important part of my enclosure.

The Connection to Good People

Those of us who live outside the physical boundaries of a monastic enclosure have made important commitments to other people in our lives. Some of us are parents and spouses; many of us are members of extended families; most of us have friends, neighbors, employers, or others in our communities who depend on us in one way or another. To neglect the people with whom our lives are connected is a gross misunderstanding of what it means to guard the enclosure of our hearts. It also runs counter to what the Gospel tells us about responding to the needs of our brothers and sisters even though it is not always convenient to do so. This suggests that instead of excluding other people from my interior enclosure, I need to find appropriate ways of inviting them in. The monastic tradition of hospitality has much to teach us in this regard. "All guests who present themselves are to be welcomed as Christ," says St. Benedict in his Rule (RB 53.1).

Although limited by space constraints, the sisters nevertheless have made their abbey a welcoming place for guests. Unless they are at prayer someone is usually on hand to greet visitors, and guests are always free to stop by the church for Mass or the Liturgy of the Hours, or simply to make use of a quiet place for prayer. Even though Mississippi Abbey doesn't have the space or the resources to operate a full-scale retreat house, the sisters have several different options available for men and women looking for a tranquil place to go for a personal retreat, including an old stone farmhouse, a comfy two-bedroom duplex, and a semisecluded one-bedroom cabin. Having had opportunities to stay in all three of them over the years, I have been on the receiving end of the sisters' hospitality countless times. The refrigerators and pantries are always well stocked (retreatants are on their own when it comes to mealtimes), umbrellas are handy in case it's raining when it's time to make the short walk to the guest chapel, and there are always little notes from the guest mistress attached to the door just to make sure everything is going OK. One of the ways the sisters extend hospitality to those who are on retreat is by making sure they have plenty of peace and quiet. Nevertheless, I have always had the feeling that should I need anything at all, someone would be there to help.

Once while making a personal retreat I was surprised to run into a friend of mine who had come over to the abbey that evening for Vespers. Afterwards I invited him to join me in the retreat house for a light supper. We had just sat down at the kitchen table when there was a rap at the door. "Is that man bothering you?" asked the always spirited and vivacious Sister Rebecca, who had seen a strange man follow me back to the retreat house and just wanted to check to make sure I was all right. She looked like she was prepared to toss him out on his ear if I wasn't and knowing Rebecca, she could have done it too! It struck me as a great example of how ready the sisters are to help protect the solitude of their retreatants.

There's an important lesson to be learned from the monastic tradition of hospitality—especially for those of us who are introverts and tend to value our solitude. It is tempting to use that as an excuse for keeping people at a distance. But hospitality requires that I make an effort to be gracious and welcoming, even when I'd rather be left alone. It goes a lot further than simply being willing to answer the doorbell when it rings. Hospitality means I must never allow my interior enclosure to isolate me from others or prevent me from treating them with the compassionate and forgiving love that Christ himself has modeled. At the same time I must learn to balance my responsibilities toward others with the care I must take to conserve my own physical, emotional, and spiritual energies. It reminds me of the instructions parents are given about using oxygen masks in case of an emergency while flying. Before they can help their children, they need to put on their own face masks; otherwise they won't be able to function. It is the same with the spiritual life—if we starve our spirits and allow our hearts to be consumed by the needs and concerns of those who depend upon us, eventually there will be nothing left to give them.

> Never, never, never
> Said Fr. Alberic in his homily about the ten virgins with
>   their lamps,
> Never give away your oil.
>
> Do not ever surrender to another
> The fuel that enflames your spirit.
> Hold fast
> To whatever it is that sets your soul on fire
> And causes your heart to burn within you.
> Use it to ignite the lamp that lights your steps
> And leads the way
> To places only you can go.

This is why I have had to think long and hard about the kinds of boundaries that need to be established in order to balance the responsibilities I have to others with what I must do to feed my own spirit. Gail says that discernment is needed in order to tell the difference between an interruption that may be "Christ in disguise" versus something that we would be better off ignoring. She offers the following advice:

> Discernment can be described as a filtering process that
> takes place as one asks of every stimulus, activity, or rela-
> tionship: "How does this help me achieve my goal of living
> a spiritual life, of seeking God in everyone and everything?"
> Filtering thus helps cope with sensory overload and our
> culture's fascination with what is "different."[12]

This can be tricky because it means recognizing that, blunt as it
sounds, certain people and situations simply are not good for
my spirit. I know that I am susceptible to the depressing impact
some people can have on me. I feel threatened around those who
are bitterly angry, sarcastic, and cynical, or those whose negative
and pessimistic attitudes affect everyone around them. There is
nothing to be gained by hanging around with people like that,
or for that matter with people who are scornfully critical of my
lifestyle and value system. As Eleanor Roosevelt said, "No one
can make me feel inferior without my consent." Nor can they
leave me feeling threatened, put down, insulted, or demeaned
unless I have given them access to the enclosure of my heart.

But boundaries are not there just to keep people away. They
also help define who may come in. And here again it's helpful
to follow Sister Gail's advice in order to grant entrance to those
whose presence in my life is a nurturing source of growth and
enrichment. I need to depend on the encouragement, support,
and example of good people. I need people in my life whom I
can look up to and whose insights and wisdom inspire me. That
is why I choose my friends carefully. That is why I go to monasteries. That is why I belong to the Associates of the Iowa Cistercians. It's because I need to have good people in my life so that
I can learn to be a good person too.

My experience living with the sisters gave me a chance to
discover just how important it is to be surrounded by people
who have made the serious business of searching for God a priority. That is what the sisters are doing inside their monastic enclosure and that is the reason they have left the things of the
world behind in order to do it. As the authors of *Walled About*

12. Fitzpatrick, "Enclosure," 161.

With God, a study of monastic enclosure, have written, "material enclosure stands as an unshakable reminder that what is of supreme importance is found within us, and that all we have to do is look for it untiringly."[13]

It is what each of us must do as well and that is why we need to build interior enclosures to guard and nurture what is sacred within us. At the same time we must be careful not to intrude upon what is sacred in others. This is something we must remember about the enduring relationships that bond us to the people we love. Genuine love requires us to be open, honest, and available to another person. And yet even here there must be boundaries if we are to avoid making unreasonable and inappropriate demands, or desire more than what the other one is able to give. Even in our most intimate and enduring relationships we must remember that there are sacred places within the hearts of the people we love and we have no right to intrude upon them.

Those of us who live outside the physical boundaries of a monastery can learn to build our own interior enclosures by refusing to be seduced by the things of the world and the ways of the world that interfere with our responsibilities as Christians. It means nurturing the seeds of goodness within us so that we may live the way we have been called to live.

Work

January 14

My first work assignment (helping to paint the refectory) left me completely exhausted and feeling like a real wimp. I guess it just goes to show how unaccustomed I am to manual labor. The morning work period starts at 8:30 and by 9:00 I was longing for it to be over. My back was sore, and my knees were killing me, and the muscles in my shoulders felt like they were on fire. It was embarrassing to be so slow and awkward, having to interrupt Louise

13. Dom Jean Prou, OSB, and the Benedictine nuns of the Solesmes Congregation, *Walled About With God*, trans. Br. David Hayes, OSB (Herefordshire: Gracewing, 2005) 158.

all the time to ask such stupid questions. (Should I be painting
underneath the window ledges too? What do I do about the paint
spatters that I just noticed are drying on the floor? Is there a trick
to getting the lid off the paint can? Should I go back and give
everything a second coat?) Louise and Emma were zipping along
like pros. You'd think they've spent their entire lives scrambling
up and down stepladders, slapping paint on walls and meticu-
lously trimming around window frames and baseboards as if it
were the easiest thing on earth. At one point I think Louise noticed
how miserably slow and inefficient I was because she smiled en-
couragingly and whispered that it was perfectly okay to take my
time since we were in no hurry.

The sisters divide the day into two work periods. The first
is in the morning from 8:30 to 11:30, and the second begins at 2:00
in the afternoon and is over at 4:00. Amazingly enough, they're
able to walk away from what they are doing when it's time to
quit instead of staying behind to keep working. It's completely
different from the way the rest of the world approaches work,
often spending our most productive hours and creative energies
consumed by jobs that leave little time for anything else. The
sisters have a more sensible approach. They limit the amount of
time they spend attending to the various tasks and jobs that need
to be done in order to balance work with other aspects of their
lives that are more important. Only on rare occasions will a sister
go back to finish up something that didn't get completed by the
end of that day's work period. They don't skip meals or ignore
the responsibilities they have to one another just so they can get
more work done. Nor do they work late into the night or on
Sundays. And work is never allowed to take precedence over
time spent in prayer. For the sisters, prayer comes first; it's the
dominant theme that is woven through each and every day of
their lives. Everything else is secondary. After all, they haven't
entered the monastery because they see it as a career option.
Monastic life is a vocation, not a professional opportunity. And
that probably explains why monks and nuns have such a radical
approach to work.

It's an approach that is deeply countercultural. There are no
"employees of the month" in monasteries. There is no way to

compete for coveted positions, or jockey for the best position on the career ladder because there are no career ladders in monasteries. The sisters do not expect to be rewarded or even praised for what they do; instead their work is done out of a sincere love for God and a genuine desire to be of service to one another.

Watching the sisters balance their various responsibilities and tasks with their commitment to prayer gave me a glimpse into what it's like when work is not allowed to dominate life. Nevertheless, the sisters still need to support themselves. Their main source of income is their candy industry, which requires working together to cook, wrap, package, market, and ship their Trappistine Creamy Caramels. In addition to candy production, the sisters also cultivate their own organically certified farmlands. They rent some of the land to neighboring farmers for pasture, but raise their own soybeans, corn, and oats, as well as many of their own vegetables.

But that is only the beginning. They also have to take care of all the housekeeping and maintenance details that are part of running and maintaining a large household. There are outside chores that need to be done in order to keep the monastery's buildings and grounds in good repair. Inside, there's laundry, cooking, shopping, and kitchen work to do, the accounts must be kept and the bills paid, the liturgy needs to be planned, the sick and infirm require care, and guests must be welcomed. The sisters' life is not an easy one by any means and they are every bit as busy working at their various tasks as anyone else. But there are some important differences.

For one thing I noticed a strong spirit of mutual service in the way the sisters share the workload at the monastery. A perfect example of this happens each day when it is time to clean up after the main meal. Each week a few sisters take turns being on the "wash-up team" responsible for the plates, glasses, and flatware. But everybody else helps with the other cleanup chores. At the end of the meal, everyone takes their place settings (plate, glass, cup, and flatware) to the wash-up station at the back of the room, where one of the members of the "wash-up team" is standing by to rinse and stack dishes in the dishwasher. Then each sister pulls on an apron and heads for the kitchen to lend a hand with whatever needs to be done. I was amazed at how quickly and efficiently a community of over twenty women could clear off the dining room tables; dispatch the leftovers to the refrigerator; wash, dry, and put away the dishes; scrub the pots and dispose of the garbage; sweep the floors and wipe up all the counters—all in a little over ten minutes. And in silence!

No doubt the sisters would be amazed to hear me say this, but the truth is I always enjoyed being part of mealtime cleanup because it was such a great example of what it means to work together as a community. Regardless of who is assigned to the kitchen and wash-up crews, the rest of the community always jumps in and helps with what needs to be done at the end of the meal. No one at Mississippi Abbey is exempt unless she is ill. Even the senior members of the community pitch in and do what they can. And there was nothing at all unusual about noticing that the abbess had rolled up her sleeves and was up to her elbows in soapy dishwater.

The other chores and tasks are handled just as efficiently and in the same spirit of mutual service. A chart is posted with weekly assignments: candy crews, kitchen crews, housekeeping crews, laundry crews, grounds and maintenance crews, and from spring through fall there are gardening and fieldwork as well. Tasks are rotated so that all the sisters pitch in and help. No one is excluded, from the abbess right on down to the newest members of the community, and even the older sisters have jobs to do. In addition, individual sisters have specific responsibilities: librarian, infirmarian, liturgy coordinator, bookkeeper, guest mistress, etc. Interestingly enough, a sister's educational level or training does not necessarily determine what her work assignment will be. A woman with a PhD in computer science may find herself doing the spring planting and fall harvesting. Likewise, a sister with an advanced degree in theology but no culinary training can end up preparing the meals, while someone else who left behind a career as a nutritionist to enter the monastery might end up in charge of the abbey's library. To an outsider this may seem like a rather inefficient way of using people's skills and abilities. But there's value in that approach. For one thing, it's an equitable way of sharing the workload. More important, it serves to remind everyone that being of service to the community is more important than being invested in one's job title.

Even though the sisters take turns sharing the work in the candy house and elsewhere throughout the abbey, some of them are especially well suited to particular jobs. Everyone knew, for example, that there was a treat in store when certain sisters were assigned to the kitchen. I was fortunate to be there at the same time as Sister Hanne Maria from Norway and she was well known for her spectacular breads, pastries, and cookies. She also had a knack for whipping up the most amazing dishes using whatever happened to be available.

Because cooking is definitely not my forte (happily for both of us, my husband is an excellent cook), I kept hoping I would never be assigned to the kitchen during my three-month stay in the abbey. But since tasks are rotated, I knew that sooner or later I would have to take my turn. The first time it happened I got off easily enough. I spent the morning peeling potatoes and carrots and doing dishes for Hanne Maria (which was a little like being in the movie *Babbette's Feast*). But the second time I was assigned to help out on the day the main cook was called away. Chris, the choir mistress, was pressed into service and with no one to help her but me, she was at a distinct disadvantage. There were some major problems with timing and the frozen vegetables never did come to a boil. On the other hand, the noodles were ready almost half an hour too soon, most of the veggie burgers were burned, and when I nuked the buns in the microwave I miscalculated— with disastrous results. It probably goes without saying that that was the last time I was assigned to the kitchen.

But I was impressed with the way Chris managed to pull things together that day so the sisters didn't go away hungry. Like everyone else in the community, she can be counted on to help out with what needs to be done to keep things running smoothly and efficiently. But while Chris is a fine cook, it's her beautiful voice that is her real gift and I was able to benefit from it as much as anyone.

Because I've never really felt I could sing, I had been afraid that the sisters would ask me not to join in during the times we were in choir. Instead, Chris offered to meet with me for what turned out to be a series of private half-hour voice lessons. Each week she patiently helped me work up the confidence I needed to hold the pitch and stay in tune as we practiced all the antiphons, psalm tones, and hymns scheduled to be sung that week. I know it meant extra work for her, but her willingness to share her particular gift with me meant I was able to participate with the rest of the sisters whenever we were singing in choir.

So even though I have a great deal of admiration for the way Chris was able to pull together a decent meal that day in the kitchen, her role as choir mistress made a far greater impression on me. It is an example of the special gift she brings to the community and I can't help wondering if the other sisters feel the same way as I do about it. Or if, as often happens in large families, they end up taking for granted the special talents and abilities each of them has been blessed with. In addition to Chris, there are a number of other fine musicians in the community who add a special richness to the liturgy. There are also several artists and a potter whose work can occasionally be seen in the abbey's gift shop. Some of the sisters teach classes in the novitiate, and others have written articles that have been published in monastic journals. Sister Gail herself is the author of *Seasons of Grace*, a book based on chapter talks she has given to the community over the years.

Humility prompts monastic people to regard their particular talents and abilities as gifts from their creator, intended to be used for the good of others. Whether or not they are noticed or complimented isn't supposed to matter. On the other hand, I suspect the sisters have the same needs we all do to be valued and appreciated. And yet, one of the fruits of humility is the grace to recognize and use the gifts we have been given without expecting to be praised for doing it.

One thing that struck me about the sisters' approach to work was how attentively they did it, regardless of whatever it happened to be. There didn't appear to be much multitasking going on in the monastery. The sisters' way is to do one thing at a time, carefully and deliberately, without rushing or hurrying—be it scrubbing carrots in the kitchen, cataloging books for the library, or stirring up a big batch of caramel in the candy house. It took awhile for me to catch on to doing things that way. In fact, I constantly needed to be reminded that it was okay to take my time at whatever I had been assigned to do during that day's work period. "There's no need to hurry" was a refrain I heard again and again by the sisters who explained my various jobs to me. Whatever didn't get accomplished that day could wait till tomorrow when either I or someone else could get back to it.

What struck me about the carefully deliberate approach the sisters take to their work was how much they tend to accomplish because of it. One week I was assigned to a work crew that set out like a tiny army ready to do battle against the forces of dust, dirt, and grime that had taken over the liturgy room. Armed with buckets, mops, vacuums, dust rags, and an arsenal of environmentally friendly cleaning products, we set out under the benevolent leadership of the always-smiling Hanne Maria, who calmly and sweetly took command of the situation. Within minutes we'd been given our orders and the room began to buzz with the silent hum (monastic work is always done in silence) of our combined efforts to spruce up that sorry-looking room. I was set to work oiling the wood paneling behind Emma, who was two steps ahead of me scrubbing it, while Kathleen wiped off the dusty window frames. Next to her was Julie perched precariously on a stepladder, doing a magnificent job of washing the ceiling (it had never even occurred to me to wash my own ceilings!). Meanwhile Chris swept around the room with the vacuum cleaner ahead of Hanne Maria, who followed behind with the rug shampoo machine. In the space of only a few hours we managed to get most of the room finished. Then the bell rang for Midday Prayer and everything came to an abrupt halt, even though there was still work to be done. Within the space of a few minutes I was back in choir surrounded by the sisters with whom I'd been working all morning. It was time for a different kind of work—the *Opus Dei*, or Work of God. Prayer.

But the sisters don't wait until the bell rings to pray during their working day. They also pray *while* they work—to the extent their various jobs allow for it. Some jobs, especially those that are tedious, repetitive, or based on familiar routines, lend themselves especially well to prayer, and the fact that the sisters work in silence means they don't have to put up with the blare of radios or the chatter of gossipy coworkers. I was especially aware of what a difference a prayerful work environment makes during the times I was assigned to be a "squiggler" on the chocolate coating crew. We squigglers have the extremely important but horribly boring job of standing at our posts waiting for the caramels to glide by in neat little rows on the conveyor belt. They have just emerged from being decadently covered with glossy coats of melted chocolate and it is up to us to lightly tap each of them with our neatly sanitized and gloved index fingers. This forms the characteristic diagonal line that is the traditional confectioner's mark indicating "caramel inside." I dreaded being assigned to "squiggle." It was bad enough constantly having to fight off the temptation to pop my chocolate-coated index finger into my mouth every couple of seconds. But what made the job even worse was that it was so excruciatingly monotonous. That's when I caught on to the value of using that time prayerfully the way the sisters do. Some of them see it as an opportunity to pray the ancient Jesus Prayer over and over again, or to recite other formulaic prayers, psalms, or Scripture verses silently to themselves.

Obviously, that kind of prayer is not feasible for every kind of job. Many tasks require mental concentration. Handling mail orders, balancing the account books, preparing reports and presentations, planning the liturgy, practicing music, writing articles, and attending to the numerous administrative tasks are hardly the kinds of jobs that can be done without putting a great deal of thought into the process. The sisters believe that this kind of work can be a type of prayer in itself when it is done mindfully and is not allowed to lead to feelings of pride and aggrandizement.

During the three months I lived with the sisters I was given a variety of jobs. I started out working in the laundry room under the capable direction of Colum, who was extremely patient with me since I wasn't used to operating the big, institutional-sized washing machine and dryer. During the winter months the dryer is used for bedsheets, towels, and work clothes. The sisters mark these items with their laundry numbers so the person in charge of sorting and folding them can put them away in their proper places on shelves in the wardrobe room. That's also where the sewing machine, irons, and ironing boards are located and I used to love going there on bright winter mornings with the sun streaming in the windows as I ironed the sisters' long white choir robes and cowls. It took a while because of the yards and yards of heavy fabric used for each one of them. I marveled at the rich, creamy color and texture of those lovely white robes—especially the older ones that had been washed, ironed, and mended so many times that they had taken on a shimmery patina all their own.

One of the benefits of working silently is that it leads to a heightened sense of attentiveness. I usually have a hard time paying attention when I am surrounded by a lot of noise, or when I am rushing around trying to get a lot of things accomplished in a hurry. But I have noticed that when it is quiet and I can move at a slower pace, things often come into sharper focus. That was the way it was at the abbey and nowhere was it more evident than when I was working in the candy house.

Having never been a part of an assembly line or worked at a job that was highly repetitive and monotonous, working on the candy crews was a new experience for me. For one thing, it gave me a glimpse into what it is like for millions of people who work hard to make a living that way day after day all throughout their lives. But working in the sisters' candy factory isn't the same as working elsewhere. One big reason is because work isn't the only thing that goes on there. Instead, when the bell rings, work is temporarily halted and everyone gathers in the little candy house chapel to pray Terce. Not only does it provide them with a break in their routine but it also helps the sisters keep work itself in perspective. Gathering together in their candy house chapel is a tangible reminder for the sisters that their main work is prayer, rather than candy production.

Work at Home

Like most of the good intentions I brought home with me from my three months in the monastery, changing my attitudes

and behaviors with regard to work has been difficult to imple-
ment. Even though I have been retired for several years now, it
has become obvious that during the course of my professional
life I acquired a set of habits and patterns with respect to work
that has not been easy to change.

I spent most of my professional life working for a large land-
grant university's cooperative extension service. Basically our
aim was to translate research-based information into knowledge
and skills that could be used by people throughout the state. It
was a worthy goal but I always felt it was ironic to work for an
organization whose objective was to improve the quality of other
people's lives while neglecting the things that were important in
my own. My job required me to put in long hours, frequently at
night and over the weekends, and often I had to be away from
home during the week. Looking back, I think I poured too much
time and energy into tasks and projects that didn't always warrant it; and no matter how hard I worked or how many extra
hours I put in, there always seemed to be more to do. It was crazy,
but I did it, and so did most of the other people in the organization. Some were genuine workaholics—people who did not seem
to have any other priorities in life or were so addicted to their
jobs that it was impossible for them to be involved in anything
else but work. Even sadder were those colleagues of mine whose
sole sense of identity appeared to be tied to their professions or
careers. But the vast majority of people I knew were just as frustrated as I was. No matter how many time-management and
priority-setting seminars we attended, nothing seemed to change
the fact that we were hopelessly entrenched in an approach to
work that seriously interfered with our ability to live balanced
and healthy lives.

Part of the imbalance had to do with our tendency to take on
heavier and heavier workloads, confident that we could handle
them by becoming more efficient, better organized, and more
adept at multitasking. While I was still working, it often seemed
that my life consisted of staying on top of my calendar in order
to keep track of everything that needed to be done from one hour
to the next. I used to hurl myself through each week frenetically
trying to keep up with a schedule that was just too full of lengthy

to-do lists. The fact that I was able to get a lot accomplished was a pretty good indication that it is possible to become efficient, well organized, and adept at doing several things at the same time. But it is also true that I resented living that way. Just about every busy working person I know feels the same. Talk to most people about the pace of their lives and chances are they will tell you they wish they could find a way to slow down. I have come to believe the only way to do that is by learning the difference between what is important and what is urgent.

Anyone who has ever taken a time-management course has probably come across the urgent/important quadrant: some tasks and responsibilities are important but not urgent because they need not be done immediately (writing a letter to a friend). Then there are those urgent tasks that simply must be taken care of in a timely fashion even though there are more important things we would much rather be doing (tracking down a plumber who'll be willing to come out on the Fourth of July to unplug the kitchen drain). Other things are both urgent and important, requiring immediate attention (calling 911 because an elderly neighbor has fallen and appears to have had a stroke). Finally, there's an endless array of activities that are not at all urgent and aren't particularly important (playing solitaire on the computer).

One reason the sisters have developed such a healthy attitude about work is because they maintain a sensible balance between what is important and what is urgent. It probably all goes back to St. Benedict, who set up specific times throughout the day for labor and prayer, thereby ensuring that work would not dominate a monk's life, leaving little time or energy for spiritual growth. So there is a natural rhythm to the way the sisters live because work is just one aspect of it. The same should be true for everyone, but many of us have yet to figure out how to keep work from interfering with other things that matter to us.

"Too busy" has turned into the standard response to the greeting "how have you been?" And it is not just because of what goes on in the workplace. We are also up to our ears managing homes, fulfilling family responsibilities, and following through on civic and volunteer commitments. But I have noticed there is a big difference between being busy and being frenzied. The difference has to do with choices we make about where to direct our energies, and the degree to which we are able to be attentive and mindful of what we are doing. To be busy is to be fully engaged and purposeful about doing the work at hand. To be frenzied is to be engulfed in the struggle to do more and have more and accomplish more. When the boundaries between what is truly important and what really doesn't matter that much get blurred, our priorities get mixed up and it becomes harder and harder to slow down and concentrate on paying attention to any of them.

The sisters aren't immune to busyness; and it would be inaccurate to give the impression that their life is free from the tensions and stresses of having too much work to do. Despite the prayerful rhythm and balance of the monastic schedule, I discovered it's not always as easy to stick to it as it might seem. Occasionally one of the sisters—still wearing her work clothes rather than having changed back into her habit, as is the custom for Midday Prayer—would dash into the church while the opening hymn was being sung. I knew the abbess frowned on this kind of tardiness ("Gail doesn't like us to be late for the Office," one of the sisters had told me) and from time to time it would come up in her chapter talks. I also noticed that every once in a while some sisters hurried back to their desks to squeeze in a little extra work during the *meridian* (nap time) that came between the noon meal and the afternoon work period. Now and then a sister stayed on after the afternoon work period had ended. So, yes, sometimes the sisters are guilty of working too hard just as the rest of us are. The difference is that they have a better system for catching themselves doing it.

For one thing, living in community means they have agreed to be accountable to one another. They depend on each other to help stay focused and, if necessary, to be reminded because it is the responsibility of each sister to support the others in their vocation of prayer. And so they can count on one another to call it to their attention if they are working too hard or too long, or if they are neglecting other responsibilities because their energies are being sapped by their work. It makes sense. Wouldn't we all be a lot better off if we could depend on someone to tap us on the shoulder now and then and remind us to slow down? That doesn't usually happen outside monastic enclosures—especially if we work in jobs and professions that keep demanding more and more of us. What a difference it would make if we all worked in environments where we were supported in our attempts to balance work with other things that are of vital importance to us! Because the truth is, once we have crossed the line that separates being busy from being frenzied, we are usually too caught up in what we're doing even to notice that it's time to stop.

Unfortunately, the rest of us can't rely on someone else to help us maintain a balanced perspective about the work we do each day. We've got to handle this one on our own. And for me that's been tricky. Like most retired people, I quickly discovered it is every bit as easy for my days to fill up with busyness as it was when I was employed. So when I came home from the monastery, I very carefully assigned myself specific times to work on the various tasks and projects that require my attention and energy from one day to the next. Nice try! After only a few days it became obvious that it wasn't working because life kept interfering with my schedule: meetings and appointments, unexpected family responsibilities, phone calls and e-mails; so much of what went on in my life from one day to the next couldn't be scheduled in advance. I need to maintain a degree of flexibility in order to keep up with it all, and so I have had to reevaluate what it means to create a more balanced approach to the work I do.

Since I'm a list-maker, I decided to try balancing each work-related task on my to-do list with something equally important. There would be one column for things that *needed* to be done (get groceries, pay bills, write up and distribute a committee report, plan a presentation for a conference that's coming up). Next to that column there would be a corresponding number of equally important, non-work-related things I wanted to do (try out some new music, catch up on some spiritual reading, take a walk with Denny, write a long letter to a friend instead of dashing off another hurried e-mail).

Even though it was a pretty hokey idea, I have to admit I fall back on it every once in a while. If nothing else, it's a bit of a reality check—much like keeping track of food choices when trying to develop healthy eating habits. When I notice the only things I have crossed off my to-do list have been work-related, it tells me it's time to put more effort into maintaining a healthier balance.

Another way to take stock of how I have been using my time is the practice of making an *examen*, a monastic habit I acquired while I was living with the sisters. Twice daily—after Midday Prayer and again at Compline—the sisters spend a few moments silently reflecting on what they have done (or not done) that day. It's something I've been trying to do at home as well. In fact it's a great way to take a short break from all the flurry and flutter of a busy day and gain a little perspective on it in order to identify those areas of my life that are clearly out of balance. Perhaps I'm feeling tense and conflicted about a problem I need to look into. Maybe I've done or said something I really shouldn't have and I need to make amends. Going back over what's happened while it is still fresh in my mind prompts me to figure out what I need to do about it. It's a little like checking my heart rate while exercising just to see if I'm on target, or monitoring my blood pressure to make sure I'm in the right range. Doing an *examen* encourages me to be accountable for the things I have done (or not done) and the degree to which I have been able to use my time in a focused and prayerful way.

People who live in monasteries take to heart St. Paul's admonition that we must "pray without ceasing" (1 Thess 5:17). Both *ora* (prayer) and *labora* (work) are expressions of love, writes Cistercian monk Charles Cummings, who says they each involve giving of oneself to another.

> Self-forgetful service of the community is, like prayer, a movement out of myself toward the other, a movement of giving, of love. . . .When work and prayer are put in the context of love and of adhering to the will of God, then conscious, rational thought processes become secondary. It is enough to be working out of love for God and for my brothers and sisters.[14]

14. Charles Cummings, ocso, *Monastic Practices* (Kalamazoo, Michigan: Cistercian Publications, 1986) 57–58.

The monastic attitude toward work, with its emphasis on being of service to others, has helped me recognize that I have a responsibility to pitch in and help out when I notice that someone could use a hand. It means not waiting to be asked to do something or assuming that it is up to someone else to take care of whatever it is that needs to be done. This applies to everything from emptying the trash when the trash can is full to volunteering to take the minutes at the next committee meeting. And it means doing these kinds of things without waiting to be noticed and affirmed, or as is often the case, expecting someone to return the favor.

But just as important is the connection between work and prayer. "First of all, every time you begin a good work, you must pray to him most earnestly to bring it to perfection," says St. Benedict (RB Prol. 4). It's a good idea but I need to be reminded to do it. Since much of my work involves sitting in front of a computer screen, I've tried taping short prayers and poems all around my work space. They're just simple little lines that someone else has written, but glancing at them helps me quiet my mind for just a moment in order to be mindful of God's presence in the work I am doing.

I have discovered that the internet is a great resource for integrating prayer into the work I need to do at my computer. I've found and bookmarked a number of sites that I go to regularly as a way of helping me try to keep a prayerful focus while working. In addition to universalis.com, a couple of my other favorites include gratefulness.org, which Benedictine monk Br. David Stendahl-Rast has helped to develop, and sacredspace.ie produced by the Irish Jesuits.

Praying online is a far cry from the monastic ideal of balancing work and prayer. For me it's simply another attempt to include prayer in my daily life. Even though it is not feasible for me to schedule my workday around prayer the way the sisters do, I have been trying to create routines of my own in order to develop a more prayerful focus to the way I live. Slowly I have been learning that even though I don't have a bell to remind me, I can still keep the work I do each day in balanced and prayerful perspective.

Formation

The scriptorium is located right down the hall from my room and it's always open! What a treat! It means if I want, I can get up in the middle of the night, roll out of bed, and be only a few steps away from a library! I have only been here a few weeks and have already checked out over twenty books and I'm running out of room here in my little cell. I've got to do something about this book lust of mine since I probably won't be able to read half of what I end up checking out. And every time I set foot in the scriptorium, I find something else that looks intriguing. If ever there was a case of "so many books, so little time!" this is it.

Mississippi Abbey's scriptorium is a large, sunny room completely lined with shelf after shelf of books. In the middle of the room are sturdy tables with plenty of space for spreading out notebooks, pens, and stacks of reading materials. Down the center, separating the room into two sections, stands a row of book carts containing reference volumes, concordances, journals and periodicals, seasonal reading, and recently acquired additions to the library collection. At the far end of the room there's a little sunporch overlooking one of the numerous flower gardens to be found at various places around the abbey.

It is up to the librarian to order new books and catalog them when they arrive, as well as to serve as a one-woman circulation department. I don't know how the sisters feel about it but if I lived in the monastery, that would be the job I would hope to be given. As it turned out my favorite work assignment was assisting Carol, who was the librarian at the time. Maybe whoever was in charge of work assignments was being deliberately kind—or it could be that after my disastrous stint in the kitchen she knew it was to everyone's benefit to put me somewhere else. Whatever the reason, I ended up spending a fair amount of time assisting Carol and that was just fine with me.

The library checkout system is pretty lenient. You write your name and the name of the book on a card and leave it behind in the box located on a shelf in the library office. There is no maximum number of books you can check out and you don't run the risk of fines for bringing them back late. Once a year the librarian does an inventory of what has not been returned for a while and sends out gently worded overdue notices. In the meantime, if someone needs a book and you've had it for a while, you will get a polite note kindly requesting that it be returned.

I loved having access to so many really good books. There were all the great spiritual classics of course—books I have known about but never got around to reading, like St. Augustine's *Confessions*, the works of St. John of the Cross and St. Teresa of Avila, *Imitation of Christ* by Thomas à Kempis, and so many others. Naturally there were shelves and shelves of books by and about the great Cistercian writers, including helpful commentaries and scholarly reviews of their work. There were whole sections of the library devoted entirely to Scripture study, theology, Christology, and church history. There was another section on prayer, another on the sacraments, and another on spirituality. And that was just the beginning.

There is not enough room upstairs in the scriptorium for all the books the community owns. Like just about everything else at the abbey, books are communal property, which means anytime someone gives a sister a book as a gift it's a safe bet it will end up downstairs in the library annex, where it is possible to find everything from aerobic exercise to container gardening to origami to Zen Buddhist poetry. There is a biography section, a history section, books about science, books about the arts, and books about nature. I spent a fair amount of time browsing through the literature and poetry section, which also included some popular fiction and even a few mysteries.

One reason there are so many books at Mississippi Abbey is because learning is such an important part of the sisters' life. There is much for them to discover about the life to which they have been called—a life that is rooted in a heritage of wisdom that has been evolving for centuries. I suspect that the sisters need to be lifelong learners in order to discover what it really means to be Cistercians, because with the vow of *conversatio morum* Cistercian men and women commit themselves to making serious changes in their lives so they can be faithful to monastic values and practices. They try to leave old patterns and behaviors behind in order to embrace a countercultural way of life. In one of his letters St. Bernard described Cistercian life in the following words:

> It is humility, voluntary poverty, obedience, peace, joy in the Holy Spirit. Our way of life is subjection to a teacher, to an abbot, to a rule, to discipline. Our way of life is to apply oneself to silence, to practice fasting, vigils, prayer, manual work, and above all to hold on to the more excellent way which is charity, advancing in all these observances from day to day, persevering in them until the last day.[15]

It's not an easy life and learning to live it becomes the task of a lifetime for each sister as she discovers more and more about what monastic life entails. That's why formation is such an important aspect of the life. It is an ongoing process of tapping into the wisdom and traditions of monasticism in order for the sisters to deepen their understanding of their vocation and the changes they need to make in order to be faithful to it.

Formation begins when a woman first enters Mississippi Abbey. It continues during her novitiate as she explores the historical, philosophical, emotional, and theological foundations of her vocation and gains a deeper—and more realistic— perspective about what's involved in living in a Cistercian community. Formation has to do with all aspects of a sister's life—the temporal as well as the spiritual—and it does not end with a sister's solemn profession but continues throughout her life as she perseveres in fidelity to her vows. Formation helps her integrate her life of prayer with the demands and responsibilities of living a communal life in charity and love. Formation helps her remain true to her own dignity as a child of God, someone whose life is unfolding with its own special challenges and particular graces.

Mississippi Abbey is a true learning community, committed to the concept of continuing education, and the sisters are skilled

---

15. St. Bernard of Clairvaux, Letter 142, in "Conversion of Life," Monk? Blog, posted July 21, 2005, http://monasticism.org/monk/2005/07/21/conversion-of-life.

at sharing their knowledge and insights with one another. They are bright and competent women, several of whom have advanced degrees in various fields. In addition to calling upon each other to teach the various classes that comprise the community's novitiate and juniorate programs, they also work together to plan and present a variety of other classes, seminars, and workshops on an ongoing basis.

Some years there is a specific theme chosen for the community to study together. While I was there the focus was on First Corinthians, and so each month everyone gathered in the scriptorium, notebooks and pens in hand, to listen to a presentation by one of the sisters on some aspect of Paul's first letter to the fledgling Christian community at Corinth. I was fascinated by the topics the sisters had volunteered to teach, and impressed by the amount of time and research they put into preparing in-depth presentations from a variety of interesting perspectives. I listened to presentations that included St. Bernard's use of 1 Cor 13, a literal approach to 1 Cor, the liturgical uses of 1 Cor, music and poetry in 1 Cor, and a discussion of spiritual gifts as presented in 1 Cor. For each presentation the scriptorium was transformed into a classroom complete with overhead projector, blackboards or flip charts, and the presenters came prepared with supplemental reading materials and handouts. (One of my favorites was a cartoon captioned "Paul hears from his mother." It depicted a sheepish looking Paul unrolling a scroll that read: "You have time to write to the Corinthians and the Galatians, but never to me?")

In addition, there were other opportunities for the sisters to get together in small groups to explore specific subjects that interested them. These classes were optional and did not always deal with such obviously spiritual themes as the First Corinthians class. I remember barging into the chapter room one day and stumbling across a gathering of sisters, all dressed in sweatpants and sweatshirts. They looked completely out of context and it took me a moment to register that the reason they were all sprawled out across the floor in what looked like extremely uncomfortable positions was because they were there for their yoga class.

I passed up the yoga class and opted instead for the Cistercian forum that took place on an informal basis and functioned in much the same way as a book discussion group. The sisters took turns selecting an excerpt from the writings of various Cistercian fathers and mothers on which to focus. We had a chance to read the passage in advance and think about the discussion questions that had also been prepared. Then on the appointed day we met for a short talk and discussion led by the sister whose turn it was to facilitate. I was grateful to be invited to participate because it was a good opportunity to be introduced to the work of writers I might have missed otherwise. In addition to reading excerpts from the work of Bernard of Clairvaux, I dipped into the writings of Gilbert of Hoyland, Beatrice of Nazareth, Aelred of Rievaulx, William of St. Thierry, and Isaac of Stella—names that aren't likely to show up on the New York Times' list of influential writers.

Because of the Cistercian forum, I discovered that I had been greatly mistaken in assuming that such writings, which emerged so many centuries ago from medieval minds, are completely inaccessible to modern readers. It was fascinating to hear the sisters talk about them with as much enthusiasm as other people talk about Oprah Winfrey's latest book recommendations. I was especially intrigued at how easily the sisters were able to find ideas from early Cistercian writers that are relevant to life in a twenty-first-century Cistercian monastery. What was even more fascinating was how often I was able to make connections between what had been written in the Middle Ages for monks and the kinds of experiences and challenges nonmonastic people encounter all these centuries later.

An example is Bernard of Clairvaux's Second Sermon for Easter Sunday, which is full of practical advice about how to talk to another person about problem issues that need to be addressed. The monastic term for it is "fraternal correction" and since medieval writers were big on metaphor and analogy, Bernard uses a Gospel passage as a point of reference for what he has to say about it. He says the women who bring spices to anoint the body of Jesus for burial illustrate the importance of handling a difficult situation with charity and love. The three women, who represent the role of the mind, the tongue, and the hands, exemplify the need for using the "spices" of discretion, moderation, patience, and compassion.[16]

Bernard's point is that there are three things to keep in mind about dealing constructively with the kinds of problems that crop up between people. First, he tells his monks to think about the nature of the problem and how they can best respond with compassion and discretion. Second, he says they must choose their words carefully and avoid speaking out in anger or resentment, pointing out that "the spoken word we can't unsay; beyond recall, it wings away."[17] He recommends focusing on specific behaviors and why they are problematic, rather than blaming, criticizing, or berating the other person for what he or she has done. Finally, he reminds his monks that since their actions and behaviors speak volumes, what is really important is to be a good role model because the most powerful and efficacious lessons are taught not by words but by consistently behaving in a way worthy of emulation.

As I read Bernard's sermon, I was amazed at the similarity between what he was suggesting to his monastery of medieval monks and what today's communication specialists say about resolving conflicts at home and in the workplace. Even though terms like "interpersonal communication" and "relationship issues" don't show up in Bernard's writings, he seems to have instinctively understood what they were all about. Twenty-first-century psychologists, therapists, counselors, and communication specialists advise their clients to focus on the behavior rather than criticize the person. They point out that it is best to choose words prudently, careful to avoid taking a harsh or judgmental tone. They say the best way to teach a person how to behave is by being a good role model. Bernard said the same thing back in the twelfth century.

16. Bernard of Clairvaux, "Second Sermon for Easter Sunday," *St. Bernard's Sermons for Seasons and Principal Festivals of the Year* (Westminster, Maryland: The Carroll Press, 1950) II.

17. Ibid., 194.

It was interesting to hear the sisters' perspective on this because it was so similar to my own. We all agreed that we hate conflict—especially when it involves people with whom we live and/or work! But while we would much prefer not ever having to deal with these kinds of problems we know from experience we can't get off that easily. Life is complicated and there are times we must approach another person about something unpleasant that has happened between us. To avoid the issue or wait for it to disappear on its own isn't going to do anyone any favors.

We talked about how much we liked Bernard's compassionate approach and his advice about addressing problems thoughtfully instead of lashing out at another person in anger. Then the sisters shared things they personally try to do when they're having trouble with someone in the community. Before approaching another person, one sister makes a prayerful effort to think about what the other one might be feeling. Everyone felt Bernard's point about needing to be good role models is crucial to living together in community, and especially when dealing with newcomers to monastic life. Instead of simply telling a novice her behavior is inappropriate, it is wiser to provide a good example. One sister added that it's important for her to be honest with herself whenever she feels inclined to point out another person's mistakes. If it is because she relishes the sense of superiority and likes the satisfaction of pointing out another person's shortcomings, then that's clearly the wrong reason for approaching her in the first place. But if what she wants to tell the other person will truly help her in some way, then it becomes an act of charity.

As the sisters talked about their experiences I kept thinking of my own, because it was obvious that Bernard's sermon applied to me as well, especially as a wife with a tendency to be pretty judgmental about things my husband says and does. Even though I try to avoid being outwardly critical, inwardly I often end up judging him rather harshly when he doesn't live up to my standards and expectations (which admittedly can be rather unrealistic). I would be better off if I paid more attention to my own faults and failings instead of being so concerned about his. Then there's the tricky issue of being honest with myself about my motivation for wanting to confront him about something he has done or not done that I find problematic. Just whose problem is it anyway? Do I genuinely believe he will be grateful for having me point out that in my estimation he's made an error (you're wearing THAT shirt with THOSE pants after all the times I've already told you they look terrible together)? Or is it because telling him will make *me* feel better?

I find it easy to focus on what bothers me about other people while conveniently overlooking the things about myself that I should not ignore. From what they tell me, the sisters struggle with this same problem. It's not as if we don't know better. It's just that it is so easy to excuse ourselves and avoid going to the trouble of changing. In the monastery, however, it's a little harder to do that because the sisters are continually being formed in what it means to live the way they know in their hearts they are meant to live.

Formation at Home

The commitments I have made to marriage and family life are just as binding as the vows a sister makes to monastic life, and I know that in order to search for God I must follow the path that leads through the life to which I have been called. But I cannot help thinking it might be easier to find my way if, like the sisters, I could learn from the wisdom of others who have traveled the same route and are able to provide guidance and support as well as practical information about what to expect along the way. It's no secret that living happily ever after in the married state is a lot harder than the storybooks make it sound. It means letting go of unrealistic expectations and accepting the challenges that go along with loving someone during those difficult times when love involves self-surrender and sacrifice.

But there's no opportunity to go through a novitiate program before making marriage vows. Instead, those vows come right at the very beginning of a marriage with scant preparation beforehand. I suspect most newlyweds haven't the slightest idea what they are committing themselves to. It's unfortunate that they have to figure out everything on their own, especially since the divorce statistics are a pretty grim indication that well over half of them never do.

It's no different with parenthood. True, a healthy approach to pregnancy encourages many women to make sure their babies get off to a good start before they arrive, and today's mothers are often well prepared for the actual birth itself. But once the baby is born, parents are pretty much left to muddle through on their own. There is no training expected of them prior to taking on the most awesome responsibility in the world, nor are there any continuing education requirements. The world is full of evidence that we would probably all be a lot better off if men and women were given some guidance about how to be parents.

Instead we keep stumbling along, making mistakes we should not have to make, and when that happens it's all too easy to assume the sacred dimension of life has nothing to do with what happens on a day-to-day basis. I need to be reminded of the connection between what it means to be a spouse and a parent and what it means to look for God. I need to be supported in my attempts to be faithful to the commitments I've made so that my fidelity will be a source of growth not only for myself but for my husband and sons as well.

My spiritual path is located right smack in the middle of my life, but unfortunately I do not always have a very good understanding of what it means to follow it. I need a formation program, but I have had to be in charge of coordinating it myself. I'm not so sure I am the right person for the job, because while everyday circumstances and relationships are where I am most likely to encounter the sacred, they are often the source of what prevents me from recognizing it. How much have I missed of God's presence in my life simply because I was too preoccupied or distracted even to notice? How often have I failed to see Christ in the people I live and associate with because I am too busy focusing on the things that irritate me about them? Have I stumbled right over opportunities to apply forgiveness, compassion, and all the other Gospel values because it has been so much easier not to? I know that what is most routine and commonplace about life, including what is most difficult and burdensome, has the potential for teaching us how we ought to be living it, but I can't help thinking it's easier for monastic people. They can count on carefully developed and ongoing formation programs to help them make sense of their vocations and what it means to live them. The rest of us are left to fend for ourselves, and we could use some guidance. We need resources to help us deepen our understanding of the content of religious faith—its foundation in Scripture, its theological depth, the grace of its sacraments, and the richness of its liturgy. We need practical information and guidance about what it truly means to shape our lives around the beliefs we profess. We need the support of dedicated men and women we can look to for encouragement and advice, people whose lived experiences can serve as sources of inspiration.

This kind of spiritual formation is not so easy to find outside the monastery. It might seem logical to look for it in churches, but in all honesty I can't say I have had a great deal of luck finding it there. Catholic parishes have directors of religious education who work hard to coordinate programs for children and teenagers, an understandably important priority. But most adults move past the spirituality of childhood and adolescence, and while some parishes are fortunate in being able to employ full-time adult faith formation directors, others lack the financial resources needed to provide substantive programs that move beyond entry-level spiritual development. True, many parishes offer "adult faith enrichment" opportunities in the form of Bible study, book and movie discussions, small faith-sharing groups, and occasional presentations during Lent and Advent, as well as periodic talks by guest speakers wedged in between Sunday Masses or on nights nothing else has been scheduled in the parish center. Usually coordinated by dedicated and hardworking volunteers, these programs are a step in the right direction but I have found they are not designed to provide the depth of insight and level of support many adults are looking for. It is probably not even fair to ask for that kind of help at the parish level. Not when you consider all the many demands today's parishes are facing in an era of dwindling resources.

So I have had to put together my own jerry-rigged formation program, bumbling along in fits and starts, hoping that somehow I will be able to keep myself on track. Being an ex-English major has helped to a certain extent because I can't imagine getting through life without books that mine the depths of human experience and uncover insights I can use to make sense of life. They have helped to shape my most cherished values and convictions, and have given me some important clues about how to live accordingly. Reading these kinds of books is like pitching a tent near the place where wisdom dwells in order to peer through her windows and listen at her doors.[18]

Books have introduced me to a wide range of ideas about God and the many and varied attempts at understanding him through the ages. Sometimes what others have tried to articulate about the world of the spirit has a ring of truth that speaks directly to the part of me that most needs to hear it.

Books can provide insights into questions I grapple with, challenging my assumptions and priorities, inviting me to explore them from different perspectives, sometimes even providing fresh perspectives I have not thought about before. And the same thing can happen when I listen to a particularly articulate speaker or participate in a workshop.

I have attended several weeklong seminars at Saint John's University in Collegeville, Minnesota, and returned determined to sign up for more. In fact, I told myself that henceforth I would follow the example of a good friend of mine who has carefully adjusted her budget to include the expense of participating each summer in continuing education workshops offered by theology departments throughout the country. I'm still convinced it is something I ought to be doing, but I keep putting it off. I suspect that one reason monastic formation works is because of the built-in accountability factor that goes along with living in a monastic community. It is probably more likely that you will stick with the program when you know your sisters are there to help keep you from slacking off.

That is one of the benefits of having a good spiritual director—someone upon whom I can depend to help me stay on track. It is not a matter of being told what to do but rather a chance to be listened to by someone who can really hear what I am saying— as opposed to what he or she thinks I should be saying—in order

18. See Sir 14:20-27.

to help me clarify what I really mean. My experience with spiritual direction has been generally quite positive, although it doesn't always work out that way. Sometimes well-meaning people can be more concerned with pushing their own particular beliefs and agendas than with helping a person explore his or her own. My spiritual director is someone with whom I can be open and vulnerable, someone I can trust enough to confide my most troubling doubts and concerns, someone with whom I can be honest about my struggles to be a person of faith, someone I am willing to let challenge me and comfortable enough to question when I can't see the point.

Lacking the support of a monastic community, it has become increasingly important for me to find other people with whom I can be comfortable talking about God. In a society where religion has become highly politicized, introducing religious beliefs and values into a discussion can lead to an argument, or at best to an embarrassed lull in the conversation. Isn't it strange that the very mention of the G-word is often considered rude and offensive and yet the f-word has become more and more socially acceptable? And I find it ironic that people who would most likely be offended were I to mention my religious beliefs might not mind at all were I to start discussing my sex life.

On the other hand, I am strengthened and inspired by fellow-seekers who are asking many of the same questions that I am. What a difference it makes to hear their stories and trust them enough to share my own!

Most of all I am grateful for the incredible gift of being married to someone who is traveling the same path and whose unfailing support and loving presence has been the single most important influence in my life. By being my husband, he has helped me understand what it means to be his wife. Over the years we have had to help each other learn how to be faithful to our marriage and family commitments, because like all married couples we made our final vows without having completed a novitiate program beforehand. Yet by some great gift of God's grace, we have been able to learn from our experiences and grow together in the same direction. Just as the sisters help each other with their formation, Denny and I have done the same thing with ours, and nothing in my life has had a greater impact on me than what I have discovered in the process.

Humility

March 20

The sisters read aloud from the Rule of St. Benedict each time they get together to listen to one of Gail's chapter talks. Lately they have been reading from chapter 7—that's the one about humility and some of it is pretty grim. In fact, parts of it sound downright unhealthy to my twenty-first-century ears. But then I keep re-minding myself that people who lived in the ninth century prob-ably had other things on their minds that kept them from worrying about whether their self-esteem was being threatened. Especially since psychology hadn't been invented yet!

It was impossible to live for three months in a Cistercian mon-astery and avoid hearing about humility. It came up in the readings we listened to at Vigils, in the homilies that were preached at Mass, in some of the excerpts from monastic writers as they were being read and discussed by the sisters, in several of Gail's chapter talks, and even in casual conversation. More important, it was evident that humility wasn't something the sisters merely studied and talked about; it was part of the way they lived. In fact, I got the distinct impression that one of the reasons they are able to live together as harmoniously as they do is precisely because they are well versed in what it takes to put humility into practice.

Once I got over my initial hang-up about the way St. Benedict wrote about it, I was able to take a closer look at what humility really means and to discover that it has nothing to do with de-meaning oneself or sacrificing one's dignity. It is not the same thing as humiliation—something most of us have experienced in one way or another and have no desire to willingly inflict upon ourselves. Choosing deliberately to belittle, embarrass, or de-mean oneself, or intentionally to disgrace or bring shame upon oneself, is psychologically unhealthy. It is a grievous violation of our dignity as persons who have been created in the image and likeness of God. Psalm 8 reminds us that we are "little less than [gods]," crowned with glory and honor. Humility helps us realize that we share this birthright with others who have also been crowned with glory and honor. In other words, I am not the only star in the universe. I share that brilliant mark of distinction with everyone else. Humility shows me how to behave accordingly and if I were pressed to come up with a good reason for making it a goal, it would be because humility makes living harmoniously with others come naturally.

But there's more to it than striving to live amiably with others. Humility also teaches me to be more honest about the way I see myself—particularly those things about myself that I would just as soon ignore. It takes a fair amount of energy to keep up appearances, especially when it means pretending I am not who I really am. I may be skilled at justifying and excusing myself from what I'd rather not have to admit about myself, but deep down I usually know the truth. Humility takes me to the heart of the matter and forces me to stop trying to fool myself.

Benedictine and Cistercian monks and nuns have made it their business to take all this very seriously. It is a full-time priority and they have discovered that it can help them learn to be content with who they are, while at the same time appreciating the value and dignity of others. Their model for doing this is Jesus himself "who, though he was in the form of God, did not regard equality with God as something to be exploited, but emptied himself, taking the form of a slave, being born in human likeness. And being found in human form, he humbled himself and became obedient to the point of death" (Phil 2:6-8).

No wonder St. Benedict devotes so much attention to the topic of humility in his Rule. It's one of the cornerstones of a monastic person's life, as it should also be for the rest of us. That could be why when I asked Gail to recommend a monastic value to study a little more closely during the time I lived at Mississippi Abbey, she recommended humility. I couldn't help wondering if maybe she thought I was sorely in need of a little more of it! But regardless of her reasons, it turned out to be a good choice. Over the next three months I met regularly with Sister Martha to dig a little deeper into what humility is really all about.

Naturally we started with chapter 7 of St. Benedict's Rule because that's where he outlines his famous twelve steps of humility, likening each of them to the rungs of a ladder. It was a tough climb. It wasn't so much because of what he was saying but rather because of how he was saying it. By the time I got to steps six and seven (about being "content with the lowest and most menial treatment," considering oneself a "poor and worthless" worker, being convinced that one is "inferior to all," etc., etc.), that ladder was feeling pretty unsteady. Fortunately Martha was around to help me see the wisdom of what Benedict was saying instead of getting sidetracked by his sixth-century worldview.

Before accusing Benedict of sounding archaic or even psychologically unhealthy, I think it is worth noting that we belong to a society where a great deal of attention is paid to making sure we come out looking better than others. We are furiously competitive and dreadfully narcissistic, constantly trying to demonstrate our merit and call attention to our superiority. Sometimes even that isn't enough to satisfy the insatiable drive to be number one. I am reminded that not too many years ago a national youth organization came out with the catchy slogan "To make the best better." It was intended to inspire youth to work hard and push themselves to achieve higher and higher levels of accomplishment. But I cannot help wondering at what price. I know too many adults who are living unhappy and miserable lives because being the best has never been enough to satisfy their relentless hunger for more recognition, more money, and more status. Instead of socializing our kids to fall into the same trap, we would be better off teaching them how to use their own talents and skills, while also recognizing the merits and achievements of others. Instead of pushing our kids to become better than everyone else, St. Benedict would teach them how to identify and appreciate what is best about *others*, not just themselves.

Perhaps we have gone overboard when it comes to helping our children feel good about themselves. We run the risk of turning them into approval junkies, desperate for that intoxicating emotional fix that comes from being honored, complimented, affirmed, and fawned over. Certainly it is important for children to grow up knowing they are loved. But in our haste to avoid damaging their self-esteem, we may applaud them too strenuously for behaviors and accomplishments that don't really merit that kind of response. There is a big difference between praising a child for working hard to break a bad habit or acquire a new skill, versus heaping adulation on a child for finishing his or her homework before turning on the TV. Sooner or later children have to learn to do the right thing—whatever it happens to be—simply because it is the right thing to do, regardless of whether or not anyone is there to notice and compliment them for doing it. I think that is why humility is such an important virtue for all of us to acquire. It teaches us to do what is right and just even when there's nothing for us to gain by doing it.

Humility has nothing to do with lack of self-esteem, as I was to discover during the course of my "independent study project" with Martha. In addition to the Rule, we also used a more contemporary text by Michael Casey,[19] who explores Benedict's twelve steps of humility in practical terms, pointing out that it is actually the opposite of artificiality and pretense.

> The Pharisee, we remember was condemned for being an *hupocrites,* a word that means play-actor, pretender, dissembler. Humility means setting aside the mask. . . . We present ourselves to others transparently, in all our imperfection and vulnerability. We depend on their good will for acceptance and love, not on the success of our efforts at self-promotion.[20]

According to Casey, true humility is an attitude that enhances rather than diminishes human life and leaves a person feeling content and "at home" being who he or she is. It involves looking at ourselves honestly, and that means being just as willing to recognize our strengths and abilities as we are prone to worry about our shortcomings. It's true we have limitations that prevent us from reaching our potential. But we also have gifts that must not be wasted. In the long run, humility enables us to develop a realistic attitude about ourselves and the relationships we have

---

19. Michael Casey, ocso, *A Guide to Living in the Truth: St. Benedict's Teaching on Humility* (Liguori, Missouri: Liguori, 2001).

20. Ibid., 25.

with others. Michael Casey's book about humility, *A Guide to Living in the Truth*, couldn't have been more aptly titled. Humility helps us come to the truth about ourselves and how to recognize and respect it in others.

With that in mind, and my weekly meetings with Martha to guide me, I set about to explore the seventh chapter of the Rule of St. Benedict. For starters, she suggested that I identify the exact opposite of what Benedict was describing in each of his twelve steps. It turned out to be an excellent strategy for recognizing that if humility sounds unappealing, its opposite is even more unpleasant.

Benedict begins by noting that the first step of humility teaches the monk to keep "the fear of God always before his eyes" (RB 7.10). As I understand it, the "fear of God" has to do with responding to the wonder and incomprehensible mystery of what is sacred about life. It means keeping myself open to evidence of God's presence and alert to what it means to live mindfully. The opposite of this first step of humility is to allow myself to be seduced by trivialities that prevent me from discovering what lies deeper. I suspect it can be a terribly empty and meaningless way to live.

The second step on Benedict's ladder of humility is that a monk "loves not his own will nor takes pleasure in the satisfaction of his desires" (RB 7.31). The opposite is to become selfishly and willfully focused on myself. Once I start letting myself be driven by my passions and desires, what began as a lack of self-control can turn into the kind of self-indulgence that puts pleasure and fulfillment ahead of everything.

The third step is that a monk "submits to his superior in all obedience" (RB 7.34). On the other hand, I know how much trouble I can cause myself and others by assuming that I should always be the one in control. My tendency to expect everyone else to go along with my way of doing things, based on a firm conviction that it's the best way, can make me a very difficult person to get along with. Expecting everyone to conform to my standards makes it hard on everyone—including myself.

The fourth step of humility is that the monk's mind "quietly embraces" patience (RB 7.35). Impatience probably causes me more trouble than I care to admit. It's responsible for poor choices and impulsive decisions, not to mention all sorts of careless and sometimes hurtful remarks I end up wishing I'd never made. It also makes it extremely difficult to be supportive and compassionate—qualities I would like very much to cultivate in myself.

The fifth step of humility is that the monk does not conceal evil thoughts but "confesses them humbly" (RB 7.44). Conversely, when I know I'm responsible for something I'd rather not have to admit, there's a strong temptation to deny what happened or at least to try wheedling my way out of any blame. If that doesn't work, it's easy to get defensive rather than risk the vulnerability that goes along with admitting that I was indeed at fault. None of this is very helpful when trying to resolve the kinds of conflicts and problems that arise in relationships—especially in a marriage.

The sixth step of humility is that the monk is "content with the lowest and most menial treatment" (RB 7.49). Sadly, I have gotten used to wanting to be treated exactly the opposite. I've grown accustomed to a whole range of privileges that are denied to others simply because of their socioeconomic level, ethnic background, education, or other factors that have deprived them of resources and opportunities I take for granted. This aspect of humility reminds me that there is danger in becoming so content with my life that I become indifferent to the plight of others.

The seventh step is that a monk believes "he is inferior to all" (RB 7.51). Michael Casey points out that the texts that elicit negative reactions are often the ones we need to pay the most attention to. Most likely the reason I tend to bristle at what Benedict is suggesting here is because, as much as I'd rather not admit it, I know I have a tendency to be quite judgmental. Instead of believing that I am inferior to others, all too often I end up congratulating myself for being just the opposite, noting that their way of doing things isn't nearly as admirable as mine.

The eighth step "is that a monk does only what is endorsed by the common rule of the monastery and the example set by his superiors" (RB 7.55). Benedict was writing his Rule for a group of men who, in order to live together, needed to come to an understanding about how to go about doing it. The same thing is true for the rest of us, particularly those of us who live in families. Without some structure and consistency in my life, "togetherness" can become chaotic and counterproductive.

The ninth step "is that a monk controls his tongue and remains silent" unless asked to speak (RB 7.56). Like many people, I'm often guilty of doing just the reverse of that by jumping in with my two cents' worth because I'm so convinced that whatever I have to say is more important than what is already being said by someone else. But St. Benedict's point is that I'd be better off keeping my mouth shut in order to put my energy into listening to what the other person is trying to say—something that is almost impossible to do if my main objective is having the last word.

The tenth step is that the monk "is not given to ready laughter" (RB 7.59). Sometimes I try to hide my insecurity and discomfort by forcing myself to act amused. Sometimes I try to say things that I hope will come across as being witty and clever because I am at a loss for anything else to say. Sometimes I pretend to laugh even though I have no reason to. It's because I'm not humble enough simply to be who I really am. I feel compelled to hide behind a mask of laughter that isn't even real.

The eleventh step "is that a monk speaks gently . . . seriously and with becoming modesty, briefly and reasonably, but without raising his voice" (RB 7.60). As a wife and a mother I know how important it is to remember that spoken words are powerful—they can bond us to the people we love, but they can also tear us apart. So it's worth paying attention to how I choose to use them. And it's just as important to be equally attentive to the importance of keeping still in order to hear what others are trying to say to me.

Benedict's twelfth and final step of humility "is that a monk always manifests humility in his bearing no less than in his heart" (RB 7.62). Perhaps the opposite of this would be the inability to recognize the truth of who we are. It's hard acknowledging those things that keep me from being the person I would like to be, because it means facing who I really am—as opposed to who I would like to fool myself and others into thinking that I am. It doesn't mean I should stop trying to change what I would rather ignore. Nevertheless, avoiding the truth of who I am can make it difficult for me to live in a way that is consistent with my values and beliefs. I would like to be able to arrive at a point in my life where doing the right thing comes naturally to me and goodness becomes a way of life. It's a lofty goal and most likely I'll never get there, but I'm pretty certain that unless I can be more humble, I haven't got much of a chance.

Humility at Home

Meeting with Martha each week to talk about humility helped me recognize that of all the monastic virtues this is probably the one I need to take to heart the most. It is also the hardest to apply. So why bother trying to cultivate a virtue that can be so tough to put into practice? Michael Casey says it is because true humility actually enhances our lives because it enables us to become comfortable being who we truly are.

> The fruit of humility is . . . naturalness. Being at home with ourselves. Being ourselves. Grace extroverts itself. It begins subtly in the depths of our spirits, but in the course of a lifetime evangelizes all levels of our being until it becomes outward, visible, communicable. It can never reach that point if we are in the habit of hiding behind a façade so that our true self is always concealed.[21]

Recognizing the truth about ourselves also opens our eyes to the humanity of others and tends to make it more likely that we will respond with compassion, empathy, and support to those around us. It often calls for self-sacrifice on our part and no matter how noble a ring that has to it, putting it into practice is something else entirely.

Like so many other virtues, it's the little day-to-day details that make self-sacrifice so tiresome. Most of us have no trouble

21. Ibid.

being generous and unselfish during times of crisis. It is one of our most admirable traits as a human race that when tragedy and disaster strike, we tend to respond with compassion and assistance, even though the persons involved may well be perfect strangers. Consider the tremendous outburst of sympathy, concern, and financial aid that poured out for the victims of the 9/11 tragedy, or the devastation wreaked by Hurricane Katrina, or the suffering caused by the Asian tsunami. Our hearts are touched with sorrow when something truly horrible happens to others and our response is to want to reach out in some way, even if all we can do is make a donation or offer up a silent prayer.

Unfortunately I've discovered it is not that easy to respond in the same spirit of generosity to the more mundane needs and concerns of those who are closest to me here at home. Why do I have to give up my plans so you can be home in time to watch the Green Bay Packers game? How come you always leave it to me to remember all the birthdays and anniversaries? Why should I have to spend part of my vacation traipsing through cemeteries looking for genealogical information when I couldn't care less? If I were a more humble person, I'd respond with a little more generosity when these kinds of opportunities arise, especially since they all involve the person closest to me, with whom I have chosen to share my life.

Humility reminds me that my life is not mine alone. I believe we are all meant to help shoulder one another's burdens, share one another's joys, and affirm the goodness in one another. This is impossible if my choices and priorities are always made on the basis of what's in it for me. But the more I see of life, the more convinced I am that it's a mistake to take such a self-indulgent stance. "What are we here for," asked George Eliot in her novel *Middlemarch*, "if not to make life less difficult for each other?" And several centuries earlier St. Benedict said something very similar when he urged his monks to bear "one another's weaknesses of body or behavior" with patience (RB 72.5). It is what self-sacrifice is all about.

More often than not, the business of making life less difficult for people involves doing things that impinge upon my time, energy, and emotions. It means being willing to suspend my tendency to act out of my own self-interest and to give someone else the option of having it his or her way. It means yielding to them. Being willing to go along with their ideas, decisions, or plans. Putting my own opinions on hold for a while. Lowering my expectations.

Self-sacrifice requires that I get used to the fact that people won't always be inclined to treat me the way I think they ought to. Some of them may very well take my generosity for granted and others may even take advantage of it. Things won't always work out the way they should and most likely I will end up getting hurt now and then. When St. Benedict says we need to be content with this kind of treatment, I don't think he was suggesting that we should let ourselves be abused or diminished by what others do or don't do to us. Rather, we need to remember that the way others treat us does not interfere with who we are as persons who have been created to live lives of goodness and love.

Ultimately humility forces us to accept the fact that life does not always unfold conveniently, comfortably, and painlessly. Often it just doesn't make sense. Hardest of all to understand or accept is the fact that sometimes it is painfully unfair. Cruel and terrible things happen to innocent people and we cannot escape the fact that each one of us must come face-to-face with the reality of what it means to suffer.

For the Christian, the cross is the only possible way to approach the problem of suffering. That doesn't make the question any easier to grapple with because the appalling image of the suffering Christ on his cross is a disturbing one. In response, St. Paul has this to say: "For the message about the cross is foolishness to those who are perishing, but to us who are being saved it is the power of God" (1 Cor 1:18). This forces me to come face-to-face with something I simply cannot comprehend. It is a deep mystery that lies at the very heart of everything I have been taught about my faith, and I have spent long hours trying to get comfortable admitting that I simply do not understand it and cannot possibly begin to explain it.

I remember once having a conversation with a good friend of mine who asked me in all seriousness how I could possibly believe such an utterly absurd story. After bumbling around attempting to mouth all the pat answers my Catholic tradition has handed to me throughout the years, it suddenly occurred to me that not a single one of them made any *sense* because there really aren't any logical explanations for something that is impossible to comprehend in the first place. That conversation was a crucial one for me because even though I was unable to come up with the kind of answer I wanted to give my friend, it forced me to take a closer look at what I am doing each time I say I believe in the mystery of the cross. It is a conscious decision, an act of the will rather than of the intellect. It is a choice to put aside what my mind cannot fathom in favor of what I sense in my heart, even though I lack the vocabulary needed to speak of it. And so for years I've struggled with the question Jesus posed to his disciples when he asked, "who do you say that I am?" (Mark 8:29). My only response is that whoever Christ is, he is completely beyond my ability to comprehend. Yet I cannot deny that he is real. Furthermore, in some inexplicable way the cross and resurrection are key elements in a reality that is far more significant than anything I could possibly imagine, because somehow, as strange as it sounds, suffering is part of the whole picture.

I am drawn to what Jesuit priest and writer William O'Malley says about the suffering of Christ. For O'Malley many of the traditional theories (including the idea that the ghastly death of Jesus was necessary in order to appease God and atone for our sins) seem to suggest that God is a vengeful and dangerous force to be placated and paid off rather than a merciful and forgiving source of love and compassion. O'Malley suggests that what we really need to understand about the suffering and death of Jesus is that they are profound examples of how we are to deal with the big and the little sufferings we encounter in our own lives.

> He endured his passion simply to show us *that's the way things are.* Suffering is inevitable in human life—a self-evident truth even no atheist could deny. What Calvary is saying is that there is no way to enrichment of the human soul other than through surmounting unwelcome challenges. That is

the glory: the aliveness of the human soul inspirited by God
just as Jesus was, because Jesus was.[22]

For Christians the problem of suffering is an invitation to
ponder the mystery of the cross and as Michael Casey says, it is
a way to "enter a level of human truth not accessible by any other
means. When we identify with Christ crucified, our spiritual life
takes on reality and solidity. . . . Through suffering, one comes
to depend less on external things for satisfaction, and to confront
inward reality more squarely. From here it is a small step to
God."[23]

Suffering is something others cannot do for us no matter
how deeply they may sympathize with what we are going
through. Ultimately no one else can bear the pain of it or endure
the agony of what it means to be defenseless and vulnerable in
the presence of what is often unspeakably anguishing. Here is
where suffering can take on a more numinous meaning for Christians who are mindful that in the torment of the cross Jesus himself reached this same place of desolation. We know that in the
throes of gruesome torture he summoned enough breath to cry
out, "My God, my God, why have you forsaken me?" (Mark
15:34). The fact that Jesus experienced the torment of having to
suffer a hideous death, feeling utterly alone and abandoned by
God, is worth noting because the story doesn't end there. We are
told that moments before taking his final breath, Jesus cried,
"Father, into your hands I commend my spirit" (Luke 23:46).
Somewhere between those two statements Jesus took that small
step toward God that Michael Casey has written about. In order
to understand anything at all about the problem of suffering, we
need to keep that small step in mind because of where it can lead
us. Our Christian heritage tells us that ultimately suffering does

---

22. William O'Malley, *God: The Oldest Question* (Chicago: Loyola Press, 2000)
167.

23. Michael Casey, ocso, *Toward God: The Ancient Wisdom of Western Prayer*
(Liguori, Missouri: Liguori, 1996) 155, 156.

not end with the cross but with the promise born of Christ's resurrection.

I doubt if I would have given much thought to any of this had I not had the chance to learn a little more about humility during the time I lived with the sisters. I see it as a way to keep things in perspective in order to arrive at a point where I am better prepared to accept the reality of my life, including what's unjust and painful, with patience, courage, and trust. In a world filled with suffering and sorrow, humility teaches me that it is possible to rise above it and be at peace.

There's no doubt that of all the monastic virtues humility is among the most challenging. It means confronting our weaknesses and faults and recognizing what our words and actions say about us. But it also means recognizing that we have been given certain strengths, talents, and abilities to be used appropriately, while valuing the strengths, talents, and abilities of others. Perhaps this is one reason genuine humility takes us to a place of tranquility within ourselves where we are able to recognize the truth of who we are, free of any need to compete with or envy others. It makes it easier for us to do the right thing regardless of how inconvenient or irksome it may be at the time, and helps us realize that love is not love unless we are willing to respond to the needs and concerns of others instead of insisting that it be the other way around. The book of Sirach says that three things are beautiful in the sight of God: "agreement among brothers and sisters, friendship among neighbors, and a wife and a husband who live in harmony" (Sir 25:1). We'd probably see a lot more of all three of them were we able to live a little more humbly with one another.

THE VOWED LIFE

In the misery and disorder of our lives, true love thus demands—like monasticism, but in a more humble and apparently more prosaic way—asceticism and sanctification. Moreover, it implies, with man as with woman, an "interiorized monasticism" . . . the healthy solitude that each must respect in the other in order to keep alive the sense of one's otherness. At times, only distance allows one to perceive the unity; only an awareness that the more the other is known the more he is unknown creates the deepening and the renewal of love.[1]

Olivier Clement, from the foreword to
The Sacrament of Love

From This Day Forward

April 25

I'm back home again and it doesn't seem possible that the three months I spent with the sisters went by so quickly. That last morning we all gathered together in the community room and as I made my way from sister to sister, stopping to embrace each one of them and exchange a few final words, it was so hard to say good-bye. But I knew Denny had driven around to the back door of the kitchen and was expecting me, so I didn't want to make him wait much longer. Kathleen, Louise, Kate, and Carol helped carry my things out to the car and then it was time to drive away. I didn't want it to be over, even though at the same time it felt so

---

1. Olivier Clement in the foreword to *The Sacrament of Love*, Paul Evdokimov (Crestwood, New York: St. Vladimir's Seminary Press, 2001) 11.

good to feel Denny's arms around me once again and know that
we were headed for home. And now here I am ready to take up
where I left off but anxious to make sure I won't forget what has
happened in the meantime.

The morning I left Mississippi Abbey, Denny and I drove
down the narrow asphalt road to the edge of the abbey, past the
stone entryway, and along the gravel road that led to the high-
way, where we turned and headed back in the direction of my
ordinary life. It was a beautiful spring day and I had the distinct
impression that everything around me was happening for the
first time. It was exactly the same feeling I remember having had
over forty years ago on our wedding day as Denny and I left the
reception and took off on our honeymoon.

Those were the days when brides still changed into carefully
coordinated "going away ensembles" before departing on their
honeymoons, and on that hot and muggy June day I was attired
in a three-piece suit, with matching shoes, handbag, and—amazingly enough—gloves! There was no air-conditioning in Denny's
beat-up, old '58 Chevy and we had rolled down all the windows
in a desperate attempt to cool off during the sweltering eight-
hour drive across Iowa. But in spite of the heat and the ridiculously uncomfortable clothing (including all sorts of underwear
that women have finally had the good sense to realize they can
do without), I was happier than I had ever been before. I remember thinking over and over again that my real life was just beginning and everything that truly mattered was happening to me
for the very first time. It had suddenly hit me that the entire
course and direction of my life had been set into motion by what
had taken place earlier that day. I was *married* now. I had pledged
to spend the rest of my life with this person sitting next to me in
the car. He was my husband. I was his wife. What had I gotten
myself into when earlier that day I had taken him for my lawful
husband and promised to have and to hold him from this day
forward, for better for worse, for richer for poorer, in sickness
and in health, until death?

It has been over four decades since that day and I am still
discovering what those marriage vows entail. Ironically, it was

something I spent a fair amount of time thinking about during the time I spent in the monastery because the fact is, I missed Denny a lot more than I had thought I would. Over the years I had grown so accustomed to being with him that I had almost forgotten what it was like not to be. It didn't take long to remember. It was an unsettling kind of feeling, a yearning for his presence, a longing and desire I had not felt for a while. Missing him the way I did became an important part of my monastic experience. It was a chance to step back from the familiarity of being married long enough to do some serious thinking about my marriage vows.

I remember being taught that a vow is a binding promise made to *God*. In the exchange of marriage vows, that binding promise also establishes a covenant between a man and a woman, and the *Catechism of the Catholic Church* tells us it is so sacred that Christ has raised it to the level of a sacrament.

> The sacrament of Matrimony signifies the union of Christ and the Church. It gives spouses the grace to love each other with the love with which Christ has loved his Church; the grace of the sacrament thus perfects the human love of the spouses, strengthens their indissoluble unity, and sanctifies them on the way to eternal life.[2]

This is grandiose language and in all honesty it has always puzzled me. I know the Church sees marriage as a symbol of the love between Christ and his Church. But in fact marriage can be fraught with hostility, anger, and resentment. In some marriages, it results in psychological as well as physical damage being done to one or both spouses, and it can end in bitterness and divorce. These realities are totally incompatible with the love of Christ.

With due respect, sometimes I feel the Church does not have a very realistic perspective on what is actually involved in building the kind of relationship that can function and endure in the manner described in the *Catechism*. True, the Church tries to help

---

2. *Catechism of the Catholic Church* (Washington, DC: United States Catholic Conference, 1994) 1661.

people prepare for marriage and invests an awful lot of time and energy into making it clear that divorce is not a viable option. But once the wedding is over, most couples are left to muddle through on their own. When it comes to supporting husbands and wives in their efforts to understand what it means to build a truly sacramental and grace-filled relationship, it has been my experience that the Church has not been very helpful. It has been up to those of us who are married to find reliable resources for learning what we need to know about following through on the vows we have made. Ironically, some of the best insights I have gained have come from taking a look at the vows monks and nuns make.

Living a vowed life—either as a married person or a professed monastic—means making sure that the choices we make about the life to which we have been called are consistent with the binding promises we have made to God and to one another. I think the monastic vows of stability, obedience, and conversion contain a great deal of wisdom about what is involved in building a strong and lasting marriage.

The connection between monastic vows and marriage vows actually begins with the liturgical celebrations in which they take place. Having had the opportunity to witness several solemn monastic professions and numerous nuptial Masses, I've been struck by the similarities between the two.

The rite of marriage begins with the priest asking the couple if they are entering into marriage freely and without reservation, resolved to give themselves totally to one another for life—to which both bride and groom respond in the affirmative. Similarly, during a monastic solemn profession the abbess begins by asking, "What do you seek?"—to which the nun responds, "the mercy of God and of the Order." While the bride and groom are questioned about their readiness to undertake what is expected of them in the vocation of marriage, similarly the nun is asked a series of questions that illustrate her willingness to give herself to God alone, in solitude and silence, in persevering prayer and willing penance, in humble labor and good works.

In a wedding ceremony the bride and groom take each other by the hand as they declare their love and commitment to one another. At a monastic profession, the newly vowed nun moves throughout her community embracing each member in turn and asking for her prayers. All dressed up in bridal gown and tuxedo, the bride and groom exchange rings as symbols of their love and fidelity, as well as their intention to do God's will by living together in faith and peace. The newly professed nun is clothed with the monastic cowl, a beautiful long-sleeved garment in the shape of a cross, which is a symbol of dedication and self-sacrifice.

Both ceremonies include a solemn blessing invoking God's special grace for the person or persons who have just vowed to be faithful to their calling in life. Again, the similarities are striking. At a wedding the priest prays that God will bless and sustain the newly married couple through whatever trials and tribulations lie ahead for them. Similarly, the solemn prayer of monastic consecration invokes Father, Son, and Spirit, asking for special graces to enable the newly professed nun to persevere in her resolve to remain faithful to monastic life through whatever trials and difficulties there may be.

It is no wonder that these special prayers are an integral part of a solemn monastic profession and a nuptial Mass. In both instances the parties involved are entering, in good faith and with the best of intentions, into a way of life that could well turn out to be dramatically different from what they hope it will be.

It would be hard to say which life contains the greater risk. Both involve learning to recognize our strengths and weaknesses, what we are capable of as well as what we are limited by, and the qualities that cause us to grow as well as those that diminish us. In marriage, as in monasticism, we are promising to persevere in fidelity to a way of life that will require us to move beyond our own self-interest. The monastic vows of stability, obedience, and conversion of life have much to teach us in that regard.

Stability

By the vow of stability within her community a sister obliges herself to make constant use of the means of the spiritual craft there, trusting in the providence of God who has called her to this place and to this group of sisters.[3]

Constitutions and Statutes of the Monks
and Nuns of the Cistercian Order
of the Strict Observance

With the vow of stability the sisters promise to live the rest of their lives at Mississippi Abbey. They do not have the option of moving to a different community should they decide they would like a change of scenery or a wider range of options for advancement. After all, a monastic vocation is not the same thing as a career. Monastic people do not simply pack up and move on to a new community if they run into problems trying to get along with the people with whom they are currently living, or if the current style of leadership or the customs of the house are not to their liking.

In making the vow of stability a sister freely chooses to remove herself from the familiar world of family and friends, and the many pleasures that come with being able to come and go as she pleases. There are no vacations, no Thanksgiving and Christmas holidays at home surrounded by parents, sisters and brothers, aunts, uncles, and cousins. For that matter, there's no chance of being on hand to welcome a new baby into a relative's family or to be there for the baptism, First Communion, high school graduation, or wedding.

That does not mean, however, that the sisters cut themselves off completely from their families. At Mississippi Abbey relatives are constantly coming and going in and out of the guesthouse on frequent visits, during which they are affectionately welcomed by the rest of the community as well as the sister they have come to see. From what I observed, the families of the sisters at Mississippi Abbey tend to get adopted by everyone in the community. In a sense they become one big family of people who know each other well and share each other's joys and sorrows.

---

3. Constitutions and Statutes of the Monks and Nuns of the Cistercian Order of the Strict Observance (Rome, 1990) 9.

While the sisters are not at liberty to jump on a plane and scoot home for birthdays, anniversaries, high school graduations, and the like, their vow of stability does not keep them from the side of a parent who has died or is seriously ill. In addition, it is sometimes necessary for a sister to leave the monastery on a temporary basis in order to assist another community in some way, or possibly even to help form a separate community under the sponsorship and with the support of her own. In fact, that is exactly what happened in 1999 when five sisters from Mississippi Abbey were sent to the island of Tautra in central Norway to found a new monastic community there, close to the ruins of a medieval Cistercian monastery.

But for the most part the vow of stability means that a sister is committing herself to live her life in the monastery she has entered, and where she has already spent her formative years as a novice. And just as marriage vows would be meaningless were it not for the love that bonds a husband and a wife, I wonder if maybe the same isn't true of the vow of stability a sister makes on the day of her solemn profession. Henceforth, bonds of love will unite her to this community of women who will be her family and this sacred place that will be her home until she dies.

Stability at Home

In thinking about the similarities between the monastic vow of stability and the marriage vows I exchanged with Denny on our wedding day, the first thing that comes to mind is a picture my younger son drew when he was a little boy. It's a drawing of four lopsided figures, each with a big heart colored on its chest, standing hand in hand inside an outline of a house. Next to it, carefully printed in lopsided letters, are the words: "Home is the space that fills up the walls of the place where our family lives."

That is what stability means to me. It is not so much *where* we live but rather *how* we live inside that place that matters. Stability means creating a warm and nurturing environment of support and acceptance so the people who matter most to me in the entire world are safe to come and go, secure in the knowledge that I will love and cherish them for as long as I live. It is something I pledged on the day I was married even though the word "stability" was never mentioned.

Without stability in our marriages it's difficult to make homes out of the places we live—something that is especially critical for those of us who are trying to remain faithful to our marriage vows in the midst of what has been called a culture of impermanence.

We're surrounded by evidence of how easy it is to throw away, update, replace, move out, and leave behind just about every aspect of life, from the clothes we wear and the computer software we use to the towns in which we live, the groups we join, and the job titles we're given. Words like *new, improved, revised*, and *latest version* constantly show up in ads designed to capture our attention, and we are accustomed to hearing terms like *restructuring, downsizing, cutback*, and *eliminate* to describe decisions that impact us in our workplaces, schools, and even our churches. We have grown accustomed to saying good-bye to people we love because they—or we—move on to something new. And for thousands and thousands of children, that "something new" involves a divorce.

All this has made it necessary for us to learn to adapt, to be flexible, to deal with the present rather than try to return to the way things were in the past or expect them to stay that way into the future. One of my favorite expressions is "Our happiness depends on how well we adjust to Plan B!" It's so true. In a culture of impermanence we have got to know how to handle the changes that are sure to come our way. We have got to figure out how to cope with ambiguity and uncertainty. The alternative is to become helplessly entrenched in anger and frustration over events that are beyond our control.

What does it mean, then, to cultivate a sense of stability in the midst of so much that is unstable about our lives? I suspect it is easier in a monastery, where constancy and centuries upon centuries of tradition come with the package, so to speak. For those on the outside it's a different matter. Stability is something we have to create for ourselves by the choices we make and the lifestyle we create. But having been introduced to a tiny dose of monastic stability, I have picked up some insights that apply to my own life as well. Cistercian Abbot André Louf has given me some clues. In pointing out that older members of monastic communities have usually been there for half a century or more, Louf reminds us that they have become part of a way of life that has deep roots.

> It treasures its own past and tradition, which it recalls and safeguards with love, for they are its support. A community passes on its heritage from one generation to another with every day of its life, and in this way its spirit lives forever.[4]

It is the same with our families. When Denny and I married, not only did we join each other's family of origin, but in promising to accept children as a gift from God we were looking ahead to what we hoped would be a family of our own as well. Over the years we have established our own tiny community shaped by a heritage of values and history we have inherited from past generations. No matter how unstable life may be, we can preserve an enduring sense of permanence for our children and ourselves by making it a point to recognize and treasure our family's history and heritage.

I am fortunate that both my husband and my mother are avid genealogists who have spent hours in dusty historical society libraries poring over microfiche records of census reports, immigrant ship passenger lists, and assorted other documents that have given us links to people who are part of our family, even though we have never met. I think it is important to know about them because as part of our family's past, they have contributed to who we are today. Without them our family would not have any roots. Their choices and decisions, often made at great cost, set in motion a whole trajectory of events and circumstances that have had an impact on all of us who followed them.

4. André Louf, ocso, *The Cistercian Way* (Kalamazoo, Michigan: Cistercian Publications, 1989) 121.

For me, stability means recognizing my connection to those people who have come before me. I can see myself in some of the old photographs I have been given of my grandmother when she was my age—we have much the same build and even our facial features are similar. I even have a tendency to tilt my head slightly to the side when having my picture taken, just as she did.

And there are other similarities as well. I have the diary she kept the year my mother turned sixteen. In fact she was the one who gave it to me the year my oldest son turned that same age. Reading Grandma's diary entries that year felt like we were sharing some of the same frustrations and joys that are part of raising teenage children. The fact that her challenges had to do with my mother and mine with her grandson just made it all the more significant.

A strong sense of our heritage also teaches us that our family's roots have been watered by the often painful sacrifices of those who came before us. My husband's natural father was killed during the Battle of the Bulge in Normandy. In 1985 we took our two sons to the tiny village of Comblain la Tour in Belgium, where we stayed with a woman whose family had housed some of the American GI's who were stationed there, including Denny's father in the months before he was killed. We slept in the same home where he had slept and ate his meals, went to Mass in the church he had attended, walked the narrow streets he had walked. We talked to people who remembered him and visited the cemetery where he had been buried.

It was a powerful experience for all of us, a reminder that there probably is not a family among us whose identity has not been shaped in some way by that war. Not only was Denny's father killed somewhere in the Ardennes forest in 1944 but in addition, the man who later became his stepfather had been captured in North Africa and marched all the way to Germany to be held there as a prisoner of war. Among our family's most cherished possessions is the rosary he made during those long and harrowing months of imprisonment. Along with it came the amazing story of how he had made it using foil from cigarette packages, plastic from a toothbrush handle, and the windshield of a German plane that had been shot down and smuggled into the camp by Russian prisoners.

Most of us will be spared having to endure imprisonment or death for the sake of our families, but with our marriage vows we are making a commitment to look after and care for one another come what may. "To have and to hold" means we belong to each other and must not forget that there is something greater than our own self-interest at stake. As long as we live together, our lives will not be ours alone. We will be called upon to respond over and over again to one another, our children, and all the other people in our families who need us to give of ourselves, even when it would be so much more convenient not to. Even when we know we have already done more than our fair share. Even when it feels like once again the bulk of the work has fallen upon our shoulders. Stability doesn't happen without a fair amount of effort. And sometimes it doesn't feel particularly good, especially when, in putting other people first, it seems like we're coming out last.

Stability is also connected to the physical as well as the emotional environments in which we live. Both have a powerful effect on us. It's something I experienced while I lived with the sisters in the "sacred space" of their beautiful abbey. Since then I have discovered that my best chances for recognizing what's sacred are probably to be found in the ordinary moments that happen from one day to the next right here in the place where I live. I suspect that may explain why many elderly people find it so terribly painful to have to leave their homes and move into extended care facilities. It's because they're being taken away from a place that has become sacred to them. Recently I heard a ninety-year-old man tell his daughter that it would simply break his heart if the time ever came for him to move out of the house where he had lived for over sixty years. I think that house contained a part of his heart and soul and I wonder just how long he could survive trying to live anywhere else. I wonder what it will be like for me when that time comes. I wonder if it will break my heart to have to leave this sacred place that has become a symbol for what is permanent and enduring about my life.

Our homes are sacred to us because regardless of how modest they may be, they express so much about what we cherish, as do the things with which we surround ourselves inside our homes. Recently my parents made the decision to move into an apartment because it was getting too difficult for them to manage the upkeep that their larger home required. The process of downsizing gave them a chance to sort through items they no longer need in order to get rid of a lot of clutter they've accumulated over the years. But just as important, it was an opportunity to recognize why the things they weren't willing to part with had become so significant to them and why they needed to take them along to their new apartment. And so along with the furniture, the clothing, the pots, pans, and dishes, we helped my parents carefully pack and unpack several big boxes containing other items that were much more valuable. Things like the big crucifix that hung on the living room wall all those years, my dad's battered briefcase with his slide rule and a few old blueprints still inside, the crystal cake platter that was used each time there was a birthday to celebrate (and since there were six children it got a fair amount of use). Without these treasured reminders of what has mattered to my parents over the years, their new apartment would lack a sense of stability. It would be difficult for them to feel genuinely at home there.

Watching my parents go through the process of moving was a good reminder that what is sacred about our homes has more to do with how we live in them than with the length of time we reside there. What we do with our homes and the way we care for them express a lot about us. So do the things with which we surround ourselves inside our homes. Denny and I have discovered that even the simplest and most commonplace of objects can take on a special significance if it holds a memory, or reminds us of something (or someone) that's meant a lot to us. That is why we use my grandma's dishes and Denny's mother's silverware for our special family dinners. It's why he keeps three ragged and weatherworn rocks piled on top of his dresser as a reminder of the day he spent on the remote and windswept island of Skellig Michael just off the rugged coast of western Ireland. It's why I can't bear to part with the beat-up, old ironing board in the basement, even though it rarely gets used. It's because it was one of the very first purchases the two of us made after we were married.

Perhaps we hang on to these things for some of the same reasons toddlers cling to their security blankets. In their own small way I think they're powerful symbols of stability because they remind us of what's lasting and permanent in our lives.

But stability must be nurtured and protected because there is much about our culture that can pollute it. I'm reminded of a folk song Pete Seeger used to sing in the seventies about the way we're slowly filling up our minds with garbage by living shallow and superficial lives. Denny and I have tried to eliminate much of this kind of garbage from our environment, and one of the best methods we've found has been to keep the television set turned off as much as possible. Just as we keep our trash cans out of sight, we've also wanted to prevent our TV set from interfering with the ambiance of a room by becoming the central focus for what goes on there. So it has been relegated to the basement, where it is much less likely to get flipped on indiscriminately. Without the noise and distraction of television our home becomes a much more tranquil and relaxed place to be, and it has given us an opportunity to pay more attention to what's beautiful about living here.

I think beauty is an important part of the spiritual life because to be deprived of it is to run the risk of losing sight of what makes our lives so marvelous and awe-inspiring. Beauty, in all its many and varied forms, is surely what the psalmist had in mind when he wrote, "How many, O Lord my God, are the wonders and designs that you have worked for us" (Ps 39:6). How sad, then, to litter our lives with whatever prevents us from seeing it.

To be a lover of the place we call home begins with an appreciation of the beauty that can be found in simple things. It's there in the patterns on the wall made by the morning sunlight streaming through our bedroom window, a patch of alyssum outside our front door that reseeds itself year after year, the sound of the wind blowing through the trees in our backyard. We are surrounded by so much that is beautiful and all of it speaks of God's presence. *Vocatus Atque Non Vocatus Deus Aderit* reads the inscription over the front door of psychologist Carl Jung's house. "Bidden or not bidden, God is present." It's up to us to notice.

In one of her books, Joan Chittister says, "We believe in work. We commit ourselves to people. We give ourselves up to schedules. We even play. What we spend far too little time on is beauty."[5] She feels that because God gave us beauty in order to enrich our lives, we have a moral responsibility to prepare our hearts to receive it, not only by appreciating the beauty that exists in simple things, but also by taking advantage of whatever resources we have available for surrounding ourselves with what's beautiful. I've found that I need music in my home; I need books full of poetry and books full of wisdom and insight and books that speak of what has happened in the past and is possible in the future; I need to look at and use beautiful things that have been fashioned by the hands of artists and other creative people. "Look around the room you're in," Chittister advises. "Is there anything in it simply because it is beautiful? . . . Places that are barren, sterile, or unharmonious are like acid on the soul. They look harmless but they agitate us to the core."[6]

In other words, beauty is not a luxury. We need it because of the effect it has on us and the way it helps us experience God. It enhances the sacred space of the home we have created and teaches us a little more about what it means to be blessed. It helps us maintain a sense of stability in an ambiguous and impermanent world.

Obedience

> By the vow of obedience a sister desiring to live under a rule and an abbess promises to fulfill all that lawful superiors command in accordance with these Constitutions. In thus renouncing her own will she follows the example of Christ who was obedient until death and commits herself to the school of the Lord's service.[7]
>
> Constitutions and Statutes of the Monks
> and Nuns of the Cistercian Order
> of the Strict Observance

---

5. Joan Chittister, osb, *The Psalms: Meditations for Every Day of the Year* (New York: Crossroad Publishing Company, 1996) 57.

6. Ibid., 60.

7. *Constitutions*, 10.

Of all the monastic vows this is the one I would probably have the hardest time with, were I a sister. I suspect that it might be the case for many of the sisters, although I can't say for sure because I never felt gutsy enough to come right out and ask. That is not to say I wouldn't have liked to, because I couldn't help but wonder what it was like having to go along with what someone else told them to do or not to do. Sure, now and then we all have to do that. But what if it was that way all the time?

A case in point: Shortly after I arrived, the new job assignments were posted on the bulletin board outside the refectory. These included everything from major responsibilities (head cook, infirmarian, guest mistress, librarian, etc.) right on down to the more ordinary tasks and chores that have to be done in order to keep things moving smoothly (someone to feed the fish and keep the aquarium clean, someone to make sure the garbage and trash gets emptied, someone to keep the driveways and sidewalks cleared of snow in the winter).

Jobs are rotated throughout the community and the abbess consults with each sister involved before posting the list. While individual talents and skills are taken into consideration, the lack of previous experience doesn't necessarily excuse a sister from a job assignment she was hoping she wouldn't get. Someone who may never have operated a sewing machine before in her life may very well end up being in charge of all the mending and sewing. Conversely, a sister may have considerable experience doing a particular job very well. But that is no guarantee she won't be assigned a different job when there is a need.

I had the impression that some of the sisters were less enthusiastic than others about their new assignments. For some of them it meant they had been assigned to a job they had hoped would be given to someone else. For others it meant giving up a job they thoroughly enjoyed in order for someone else—possibly someone not nearly as qualified—to take over. And for some it may even have meant having to shoulder more responsibility than they were prepared to handle. Regardless of how they may have felt about what they had been assigned to do, their vow of obedience meant it was highly unlikely that anyone would try to be excused from the assignment unless she had a compelling reason. And even though a sister might want to, it was highly unlikely that she would out-and-out refuse to abide by the decision the abbess had made.

That was only one example of what it was like to be bound by a vow of obedience. There were others as well and I couldn't understand how the sisters could possibly be so compliant about living that way. Occasionally one of them would casually mention that Gail had (or hadn't) given the go-ahead to a request. For example, one day I met a sister as she was preparing to run into town for an appointment. She was wearing street clothes because that's what most of the sisters do when they have errands to run in the secular world. When I mentioned how nice she looked, she told me it was a hand-me-down from a relative back home who didn't want it anymore. "I had to check with Gail first to see if I could keep it and she said it was okay," she added. I couldn't help wondering whether she resented having to ask. I surely would have.

During the three months I lived with the sisters I heard that same line—"I'll have to check with Gail first"—over and over again. I never really got used to it. When I tried to put myself in their place, all I could do was bristle at what seemed to me to be an unnecessarily restrictive way to live. There was something vaguely disturbing about all those bright, intelligent women agreeing to whatever they were told to do or not do regardless of how they felt about it.

But then it's no wonder I found it so hard to get used to the idea. Like just about everything else about monastic life, obedience is about as countercultural as it gets. It's likely to be considered a liability rather than a virtue. The notion of being obedient to anyone raises all kinds of red flags because we equate it with weakness, powerlessness, and the loss of freedom rather than looking at it the way the sisters do. For them obedience is a way of being united to Christ by responding to the needs and wishes of others just as he did by living a life of self-sacrifice: "For the Son of Man came not to be served but to serve" (Mark 10:45).

Monks and nuns see Christ as a model for being of service to others and an example of what it means to abandon oneself in trust and confidence to the will of God. "I seek to do not my own will but the will of him who sent me" (John 5:30). Obedience is at the root of it all, and that's why it's one of the vows a sister makes on the day of her solemn profession. It's worth noting, however, that she is promising to be obedient not only to her abbess but to the rest of her sisters as well. Not in the sense of mindlessly going along with what someone else orders her to do but rather choosing to be motivated by something other than her own self-interest. Cistercian Abbot André Louf calls this an attitude of the soul and a strategy of love and says that it is the "daily grind" of ordinary life that enables the monk to put obedience into practice.

> Right through the day, he discovers a thousand occasions for giving way to another's wish, for listening to or accepting his brother's advice so he may know the truth which his brother has, and try to resolve the differences between them. In the ordinary works and services of the monastery he will carry out his tasks without seeking to impose either his own methods or his own opinions.[8]

Louf's words can also be applied to those of us whose "daily grind" involves sharing the tasks, routines, and burdens of life with a spouse. Regardless of whether we have made monastic vows or marriage vows, we cannot be faithful unless we are willing to commit ourselves to a life that involves self-sacrifice.

On the day Denny and I exchanged our marriage vows, the priest read the following words to us:

> It is most fitting that you rest the security of your wedded life upon the great principle of self-sacrifice. And so you begin your married life by the voluntary and complete surrender of your individual lives in the interest of that deeper and wider life which you are to have in common. Henceforth you belong entirely to each other; you will be one in mind, one in heart, and one in affections. And whatever sacrifices you may hereafter be required to make to preserve this common life, always make them generously. Sacrifice is usually difficult and irksome. Only love can make it easy;

8. Louf, *Cistercian Way*, 66.

and perfect love can make it a joy. We are willing to give in proportion as we love. And when love is perfect, the sacrifice is complete.[9]

I've heard it said that obedience can be the form love takes. But if that's the case, why do so many of us (especially us women) react so strongly to the idea of being obedient to our spouses? We bristle at the very thought. And with good reason. We have seen too many marriages where domineering and self-centered husbands have made life an ordeal for their wives, and too many wives who have allowed themselves to be manipulated and taken advantage of by their husbands. It must also be admitted that we have seen our fair share of unhappy husbands who have spent their lives trying to satisfy the wishes of their demanding and overbearing wives. If that's what it means to be obedient, who can blame anyone for wanting to have nothing to do with it?

But I don't think that's what it's all about. I don't think mature obedience has anything to do with being subject to the whims and demands of others—especially when what they are asking is dangerous or harmful or manipulative. Nor is it an excuse for taking advantage of someone else's good intentions or for excusing ourselves from the responsibility to make wise choices about our own behaviors.

Similarly, obedience is not a ploy for avoiding tough decisions. In all honesty there are some situations I would rather not have to confront, even though I know I must. When that happens I have to admit it would be a lot easier simply to bow out and leave everything to Denny. Or if I am feeling ambivalent about a tough decision I can't seem to make, it would simplify matters immensely if Denny just out and told me what to do, saving me the trouble of having to figure it out for myself. At the very least, I wouldn't have to take the heat if it turned out to be the wrong course of action.

But I doubt if any of this has much to do with obedience as a form of love. No, obedience stems from our freedom to act

9. *The Mass on the Day of Marriage* (St. Paul: Leaflet Missal Co., 1967) 10–11.

responsibly because it's the loving thing to do. As husbands and wives we are called to that kind of obedience not because we are being forced to, or have no choice in the matter, but rather because we are committed to doing the right thing, the loving thing. Seen from this perspective, obedience is a tool that can help us do that.

Those of us who are married know that doing the loving thing doesn't always feel good. As much as I love my husband, I doubt if anyone would believe me if I said living with him day after day, year after year has been nothing but pure bliss. Every husband and wife knows there are days when the person they have promised to cherish all the days of their lives just doesn't strike them as being particularly easy to love and honor. Or to understand, accept, or forgive.

But of course I wasn't thinking about that on the day I got married. Back then I was caught up in the glow of the way it felt to love someone who made me feel so loved in return. I assumed this would be enough to carry us both through whatever lay in store for us. It's a common enough assumption to make. Just consider the number of love songs that are variations on the theme of how wonderful it feels to be in love.

So I suppose it's only natural to equate love with the way it feels to love someone. After all, it's one of the most beautiful and profound experiences we'll ever know. But there is so much more to love than the feelings it stirs up. It's not just a movement of the heart. It is also an act of the will. It has to do with choices and decisions. That's why it has been helpful for me to look at the role obedience plays in my own marriage. I have a tendency to want to focus on myself instead of Denny—or at least to want to feel good about the times I do put him first. Obedience reminds me that it's important to do the loving thing even when it would be so much easier and more convenient not to.

But like so many other women my age, I was in the early years of my marriage during the seventies—that turbulent time when women's roles were undergoing profound changes. Typically enough, I belonged to a consciousness-raising group that met each week to talk about how oppressed we were. We called each other "sister" and vowed to support one another in every effort to free ourselves from the ugly yoke of male domination. (I smile now every time I think about those meetings because at the time I didn't drive and so I had to rely on Denny to drop me off each week. When the meeting was over I'd sneak away from the "sisterhood" long enough to make a furtive phone call letting him know I was ready to be picked up and taken home.)

Every one of my friends had a bumper sticker that read "uppity women unite!" for we were intent on asserting ourselves whenever there was an occasion for demanding fair treatment and equal opportunity. Admittedly it was an exciting and liberating time to be a young woman. In addition to learning to value the experiences and opinions of other women, I learned to speak up for myself, to challenge myself, develop confidence in myself, and make goals for myself that I set out to fulfill. It was a vibrantly stimulating and energizing period in my life and I am glad I lived through it. Except for one thing. The focus was squarely aimed at—myself. I was so intent on insisting on my rights that I came dangerously close to overlooking the responsibility I had to treat others—especially my husband—as equitably as I expected to be treated.

At the time I would have been righteously indignant had the topic of obedience in marriage been raised. And yet looking back I think it would have been to my advantage had I been able to recognize early on that obedience is a way to balance the responsibilities that go along with the rights in a marriage. It would have been easier for both Denny and me had we realized a little sooner that even in the most egalitarian of relationships there are simply going to be situations and circumstances where it is impossible to be 100 percent fair and equal. These are the times when we have a chance to do the loving thing, regardless of whether or not we're going to end up feeling good about doing it.

I wish I had caught on to this a little earlier. It might have made me easier to live with had I learned how to focus more on what Denny has needed from me rather than the other way around. It might have helped me recognize when to put my own wishes on hold for a while in order to go along with what he wanted, even if it would have been tedious or irritating to do so.

I might have been more likely to do something about my need to be in control and in charge; maybe I would have been a little less insistent that things be done my way and a little more open to going along with his way instead.

Thinking about all this has been a reminder that the vows I exchanged with Denny so many years ago are still in effect! It's probably a good idea to look at them once in awhile from the perspective of what I've figured out in the meantime. In this case I've come to the conclusion that obedience isn't nearly as bad as it once sounded—provided it's mutual, adds the uppity woman left in me!

It probably goes without saying that none of this comes easily, which is probably why St. Benedict referred to "the *labor* of obedience" when he wrote about it in his Rule. It's because of all the effort that goes into it. Not surprisingly it requires a fair degree of patience.

I have always thought it was interesting that patience is the first thing to be mentioned in the oft-quoted scriptural definition of love that's such a popular choice for weddings (1 Cor 13:4-7). I see it as a sort of scriptural heads-up about what's in store for the bride and groom once they get down to the serious business of building a genuinely loving marriage. Saint Paul is pretty specific about what they're going to have to do—and not do—to make that happen, and the first point he makes is that it's going to take patience. Without it, chances are they won't get very far with the rest of what he has to say about love. Husbands and wives need quite a bit of patience in order to refrain from insisting that they have their own way. Patience is called for in order for them to treat each other with kindness instead of spitefulness. They need to be patient with each other in order to develop trust (and to restore it if ever it gets tarnished). It takes patience to avoid jealousy, boastfulness, and conceit, as well as to overcome rudeness, selfishness, and resentment. Saint Paul has spelled out in no uncertain terms what it takes to get in the habit of doing the loving thing and it's a tall order. No wonder he warns us at the outset that we need to be patient with each other if we're going to be able to bear all things, believe all things, hope all things, and endure all things.

Obedience at Home

Since it takes a lot of patience to keep plugging away at the labor of obedience, it would simplify matters greatly were I not so inclined to react impatiently when I'm frustrated, irritated, and upset. It's hard enough being patient about perfectly mundane things—like how long it takes for the light to turn green at a busy intersection, or the fact that sometimes my internet connection takes a few seconds more than what I am used to. Knowing how impatient I can be about such trivial matters, it's pretty obvious that I'm going to have a harder time being patient when I am annoyed with Denny.

If I were more patient, I would probably be a better listener. Instead of interrupting to let him know I disagree with him, I might do a better job of paying attention to what Denny has to say about whatever it is I don't want to hear. If I were more patient, I would probably be more able to go along with what he prefers when I prefer it a different way. Maybe I would be more willing to follow through on his suggestions and ideas rather than wanting it to be the other way around. If I were more patient, I might find it easier to cut him some slack instead of expecting him to live up to my standards.

Given how important patience is in a marriage, you'd think there would be more done to help us learn how to develop it. But aside from the reading in First Corinthians, my guess is that most of us don't hear that much about it. I know I certainly haven't. But it's different for monastic people. Fidelity to their vow of obedience means they have had a lot of experience learning about patience and how to put it into practice. Saint Bernard of Clairvaux outlined the following seven important points to keep in mind about obedience[10]—and all of it has to do with being patient. Although intended for medieval monks, Bernard's advice strikes me as being surprisingly up-to-date. I think it's full of

---

10. Bernard of Clairvaux, "On The Seven Degrees of Obedience and The Term to Which They Lead," *St. Bernard's Sermons for Seasons and Principal Festivals of the Year* (Westminster, Maryland: The Carroll Press, 1950) III.

insights about what it takes to make mutual obedience a cornerstone for building a more genuinely loving marriage.

Obey with a Good Heart

A good heart is a patient and accommodating heart. There is nothing very loving about going along with what Denny is asking if my whole approach to it leaves him wishing he had never brought it up in the first place. To obey with a good heart means patiently stifling the urge to make quite sure he knows just how inconvenient or burdensome it will be to follow through. It means patiently resisting the temptation to behave as if what I am doing for him is further proof of how much he owes me in return. There's no sense going along with his way of doing something if I keep reminding him that my way would be so much better (even if I'm convinced it would be).

Obey with Simplicity

Saint Bernard noted that it was not uncommon for monks to question what they were being asked to do. "Why does it matter?" "What's the point?" "Is it really all that necessary?" It's not that unusual for me to do exactly the same thing—especially when whatever I'm being asked just doesn't strike me as much of a priority. Sometimes it's all too easy to simply ignore a request Denny has made by assuming that if it's really that important, he'll go ahead and do it himself sooner or later anyway. A more loving approach would be to recognize that what he is asking of me is important to him even if it doesn't seem that necessary to me. To obey with simplicity means going ahead and patiently doing it, regardless of all the reasons I can come up with for not having to.

Obey with Cheerfulness

Saint Bernard must have been used to hearing monks grumble and complain about what they had been asked to do; otherwise he probably would not have bothered to mention this point. But it is an important one to keep in mind because too often I hear myself saying, "Oh, all right! Have it your way! It doesn't make any difference what I want!" Or I manage to get the message across nonverbally so he knows I am really ticked off about going along with what he has asked of me and he had better keep in mind that I am not doing it willingly. To obey with cheerfulness is patiently to keep in mind St. Paul's words: "Each of you must give as you have made up your mind, not reluctantly or under compulsion, for God loves a cheerful giver" (2 Cor 9:7).

Obey with Promptitude

I have a tendency to get so caught up in my own priorities that I forget all about the ones that are at the top of Denny's list. It is not that I necessarily intend to ignore them; it's just that since mine seem so much more important at the time, naturally it's okay to postpone getting around to what Denny needs me to do. But St. Bernard obviously knew that saying we'll get around to it sooner or later often means it won't get done at all. To that, Bernard has this to say: "The truly obedient person does not know what it is to delay; he abhors procrastination; he is a stranger to tardiness."[11] To obey with promptitude means making what we have been asked to do a priority in order to follow through—and the sooner the better.

Obey with Fortitude

Sometimes I don't want to do what Denny has asked me to do because frankly, I just don't want to be bothered. Instead I try to talk my way out of it on the grounds that it's too burdensome, or too time-consuming, or that I do not have the necessary information. I have even been known to use flattery to get out of something I don't particularly want to do by assuring Denny that since he would obviously do such a better job of it than I, why doesn't he just go ahead and do it himself? To obey with fortitude, however, is to face up to the fact that even though I may think I have some fairly good reasons for not following through, I'm going to go ahead and patiently try to give it my best shot.

11. Ibid., 470.

Obey with Humility

This is a tricky one because it means I need to be honest with myself and face up to the fact that it is possible to go along with what Denny needs me to do more for my sake than his. Is it because I am simply looking for opportunities to feel good about myself by demonstrating how self-sacrificing and generous, how thoughtful and supportive, how kind and helpful I am? To lend a hand so that I can feel pleased with myself for doing it is a pretty self-centered way of behaving. So lest I congratulate myself for an outstanding performance in the obedience category, St. Bernard cautions me with these words: "It avails nothing to obey if at the same time you are unhappily proud at heart."[12]

Obey with Perseverance

Saint Bernard wraps things up by reminding his monks that just as he has noted in his Rule, the labor of obedience requires a great deal of unwavering effort. It calls for determination and persistence in order to keep at it. Having vowed to love and honor my husband for the rest of our lives, I have promised to be his helpmate there at his side when he needs me. It means recognizing that I cannot ignore or minimize his needs and concerns and that I have committed myself to do the loving thing even though at times it will be challenging, difficult, inconvenient, or even tedious to follow through. It means paying attention to the way I react to the things about married life that make it difficult and burdensome. It means recognizing when I am being inflexible and insisting on having my way. And it also means being careful about the way I handle my own irritation when he is the one who's being inflexible and demanding.

Like just about everything else about monastic wisdom, all of this goes against the grain of contemporary sensibilities. And yet, as much as we may bridle at the very thought of it, there is much to be gained by considering how the monastic approach to obedience can help us be faithful to our marriage vows. Mutual and mature obedience can be the connecting point between the

12. Ibid., 474.

rights and the responsibilities of husbands and wives, as well as a means of patiently following the advice St. Paul so wisely outlines in the thirteenth chapter of First Corinthians. Obedience doesn't mean doing what we're told to do because we have no choice. It's a matter of choosing to do it because we know it's the loving thing to do. Maybe we could say that *mutual* obedience is the form *married* love can take.

Conversatio Morum

> By the vow of *conversatio morum* or fidelity to monastic life a sister who, in the simplicity of her heart, seeks God by the following of the Gospel, binds herself to the practice of Cistercian discipline. She retains nothing at all for herself, not even authority over her own body.[13]
>
> Constitutions and Statutes of the Monks
> and Nuns of the Cistercian Order
> of the Strict Observance

Loosely translated, the Latin term *conversatio morum* refers to a conversion or change of life that implies turning away from whatever interferes with the ability to focus one's mind and heart on seeking God. In making this vow a sister commits herself to changes that seem utterly incomprehensible to many people in the outside world. She is giving up the exhilarating pleasure and intimacy of a sexual relationship as well as the joys of marriage and motherhood, the happiness that comes with being able to get together with family and friends whenever she pleases, and the freedom to pursue a career path and enjoy the benefits that come with being employed. She's turning her back on the chance to own a home, a car, lovely clothes, or just about anything else money can buy. She won't be making any more appointments to have her hair styled, nor will she be doing any more shopping for lipstick, mascara, or perfume. You'll never see a Cistercian sister with her nails polished or decked out in jewelry of any

13. Constitutions, 10.

kind. She's agreeing to forgo vacations, shopping trips, movies and television, and won't even have the option of ordering out for a pizza or meeting friends on the spur of the moment at a coffee shop for casual conversation over a latte. She's giving it all up just as she's passing by opportunities for success, prestige, fame and fortune. In fact, she is readily choosing to do without just about everything our society holds dear in order to embrace a lifestyle that embodies an entirely different set of values and priorities. Why go to such extremes, we may ask. Because according to the Constitutions and Statutes of the Cistercian Order, "those who prefer nothing to the love of Christ make themselves strangers to the actions of the world."[14] Their goal is to grow in union with God through a simple life of prayer and service to one another.

It is certainly a worthy goal and yes, it is a beautiful life. But what must it be like to do without so much that the rest of us take for granted? It was one thing for me to live the way the sisters lived for three short months, but I wonder if I could do it for a lifetime. Would I ever get used to having only one small room with a bed, a few shelves, a chair and a desk to call my own? Actually it wouldn't really be my own because I wouldn't be free to spruce it up by choosing a brighter color for the walls or new curtains for the window or a different bedspread for my narrow bed. I couldn't have a CD player in the corner or even my own computer on the desk. As for a cell phone—forget it! And how on earth would I survive spending the rest of my life in a room with so little closet space?

In making her vow of *conversatio morum* a sister turns away from the comforts, pleasures, and conveniences of the secular world and commits herself to a lifetime of being content with less, not because she's trying to prove that it is possible to live that way or to pass judgment on those who cannot. Rather, she has a different goal in mind, and for her the monastic life is the way she hopes to attain it. It is a lifestyle designed to help her guard her heart and overcome the barriers that stand in the way

14. Ibid., 22.

of her search for God. As Michael Casey says, the monastic life-style is a way to rid the heart of complexity and reduce the level of inner division. He adds that "monks serve as a reminder that a life of ease and pleasure is not the best way to find ultimate fulfillment."[15]

> The monk has to confront and by grace to overcome the instincts and tendencies that complicate his life and muddy the surface of his mind. This is difficult to achieve so long as he is embroiled in the inevitable turmoil associated with family and career. So he abandons a normal existence, makes an effort to live as a monk, and after years of un-dramatic struggle comes to a point of self-transcendence where the spiritual world begins to form part of his every-day horizon.[16]

The monastic vow of *conversatio morum* is all about fidelity. It is a commitment to be faithful to changes that need to be made over the course of a lifetime. In this sense I think it's similar in many ways to the promise husbands and wives make to each other when they exchange marriage vows. In fact, the very words they say as they place the rings on each other's fingers are "take and wear this ring as a pledge of my fidelity . . ."

And so not knowing what was ahead, Denny and I plunged right into it by promising to remain faithful to each other come what may. The sisters did exactly the same thing by promising to be faithful to the monastic life even if it turned out to be different from what they expected it would be. Regardless of whether we committed ourselves by monastic vows or marriage vows, there was a great deal of uncertainty involved because we simply did not know what we were getting ourselves into. Yet we went right ahead and promised to be faithful anyway! What on earth were we thinking?!

---

15. Michael Casey, ocso, *Strangers to the City* (Brewster, Massachusetts: Para-clete Press, 2005) 14.

16. Ibid., 17.

Conversatio Morum at Home

What I was thinking on my wedding day was how much I loved Denny and how much I wanted to be with him for the rest of my life, no matter what might be ahead of us. I figured that regardless of whatever might happen, it would be okay because we would be together—in love—and that was all that would matter.

Looking back I wonder how on earth I could possibly have been so naïve. I had absolutely no idea that it would take a lot more than love and togetherness to make our marriage work. After over forty years of learning what it does take, I am sometimes tempted to think I have been just plain lucky. But I know better. It hasn't been luck. It's been grace.

And as much as I would hate to argue with Michael Casey, who is one of my favorite writers, I do have to admit to being a little put out by part of the passage I quoted earlier. One could misinterpret his comments about the difficulty of being "embroiled in the inevitable turmoil associated with family and career" and wonder whether he meant to imply that married people don't have much of a chance of arriving at "a point of self-transcendence where the spiritual world begins to form part of [their] everyday horizon." Most likely that is not at all what he meant. For one thing, marriage, unlike monastic consecration, is a sacrament, which suggests that the relationship Denny and I have is a source of God's grace and presence in our lives.

In his book *The Sacrament of Love*, a unique reflection on marriage and monasticism, Paul Evdokimov says that instead of setting one way of life against the other, there is value in recognizing how each of them functions as a channel of God's grace. We are all on the path to holiness and for all of us it is a lifelong journey.

> The two ways, contrary to human reason, are found to be inwardly united in the end, mysteriously identical. It is sufficiently clear by now that the best, and perhaps the only, method to fathom the value proper to matrimony is by comprehending the greatness of the meaning of monasticism.

One will better understand the vocation of marriage in the
light and the school of monasticism.[17]

We have all been called to holiness. But for those of us who
are married, that bumpy path leads straight into the world rather
than out of it. Trying to answer a call to holiness in the midst of
a culture that seems like it's about as unholy as they come is
challenging, to say the least. We are surrounded by much that
undermines our attempts to build an authentic spiritual life. But
it is not impossible provided we are able to turn away from whatever impedes us. It's really a matter of *conversatio morum*. We can
learn simultaneously to live in the world and to reject those
things about the world that get in the way of what Michael Casey
calls the "singleness of outlook that permits the experience of
God."[18]

For those of us who are married, *conversatio morum* is a matter of taking a close look at what it means to be faithful to the
commitments we made when we exchanged our marriage vows.
Consider the following lovely and lofty words taken from the
Pastoral Constitution on the Church in the Modern World:

> Fulfilling their conjugal and family role by virtue of this
> sacrament, spouses are penetrated with the spirit of Christ
> and their whole life is suffused by faith, hope and charity;
> thus they increasingly further their own perfection . . . Let
> married people themselves, who are created in the image
> of the living God and constituted in an authentic personal
> dignity, be united together in equal affection, agreement of
> mind and mutual holiness.[19]

Those words have a glorious ring to them. And yet, one may ask,
just how are husbands and wives to go about furthering their
perfection in the light of how difficult it can be to nurture and
sustain a marriage? If, as Michael Casey says, they are "embroiled

17. Evdokimov, *Sacrament of Love*, 73.
18. *Strangers to the City*, 17.
19. Pastoral Constitution on the Church in the Modern World 48, 52 (St. Paul:
Office for Social Justice), http://www.osjspm.org/majordoc_gaudium_et_spes
_part_2.aspx.

in the inevitable turmoil associated with family and career," just where does the part about suffusing their lives with faith, hope, and charity enter the picture? I think the answer has to do with *conversatio morum*, with the changes we need to make over the years. This means recognizing the significance of what's taking place in our lives because that's where transformation occurs.

But it's easy to overlook what's going on if we get so used to scurrying around on the surface of our lives that we miss noticing what's happening within us. And it is all too easy for that to happen because of all the activity that takes place on the surface. Weddings are a good example. According to a survey conducted in 2005, the average cost of a wedding was nearly thirty thousand dollars. "The bridal industry is now a life stage that encompasses fashion, travel, home furnishings and more," said Daniel Lagani, vice president and publisher of the Fairchild Bridal Group.[20] He was referring to the fact that weddings have turned into a multimillion-dollar industry and most of it is concerned with what's going on at the surface. I find it fascinating that so much energy (and money) is focused on wedding preparations while precious little gets done to prepare for marriage. Too bad it can't be the other way around. And if, as we are told, Christ is supposed to be the model and focus of a Christian marriage, at what point does he get included in the planning? I know for a fact that as far as many couples are concerned, the main reason for having a "church wedding" is because it provides a lovely setting in which to stage the ceremony.

And yet the Church keeps telling us Christ is central to our lives as a married couple. In a Catholic wedding, the nuptial blessing itself asks that God strengthen the newly married man and woman in order for them to be witnesses of Christ's Gospel to others. The key to living out one's marriage vows is said to be there in the words and example of Christ, and one way to learn what it means to be a source of grace to one another is by taking

---

20. Grace Wong, "Ka-ching! Wedding price tag nears $30K," *CNNMoney.com*, May 20, 2005, http://money.cnn.com/2005/05/20/pf/weddings/.

his message seriously. But often we do not. It's not that we deliberately set out to ignore it. But many of us simply do not see the Gospel as being all that relevant when it comes to setting goals and priorities that have to do with the way we want to live our lives. I once heard a pastor of a large, urban church note with sadness that while most of his congregation is faithful about coming to church regularly, he has the sense that few of them see much of a connection between the message of Christ and the reality of their lives.

Obviously, the sisters see things differently. With their vow of *conversatio morum* they are committing themselves to a way of life that takes Christ's message very seriously—so seriously that they are willing to spend the rest of their lives trying to figure out what it means to put it into practice. Those of us who make marriage vows are called to do the same thing. Both vocations are meant to be Christ-centered. Both involve a conscious decision to embrace a way of life that is based on what Christ himself has taught us about how to live. Both involve making lifelong changes that will require determination, dedication, and prayer in order to remain faithful.

But it's not as if we have to figure everything out on our own. Fortunately we have all been given some pretty clear guidelines. Here are just a few examples:

> Let love be genuine; hate what is evil, hold fast to what is good; love one another with mutual affection; outdo one another in showing honor. Do not lag in zeal, be ardent in spirit, serve the Lord. Rejoice in hope, be patient in suffering, persevere in prayer. . . . Live in harmony with one another; do not be haughty, but associate with the lowly; do not claim to be wiser than you are. (Rom 12:9-12, 16)

> As God's chosen ones, holy and beloved, clothe yourselves with compassion, kindness, humility, meekness, and patience. Bear with one another and, if anyone has a complaint against another, forgive each other; just as the Lord has forgiven you, so you also must forgive. Above all, clothe yourselves with love, which binds everything together in perfect harmony. (Col 3:12-14)

> Finally, all of you, have unity of spirit, sympathy, love for
> one another, a tender heart, and a humble mind. Do not
> repay evil for evil or abuse for abuse; but, on the contrary,
> repay with a blessing. It is for this that you were called—that
> you might inherit a blessing. (1 Pet 3:8-9)

It is probably worth mentioning that while we all have access to these passages, monastic people tend to be more familiar with them than the rest of us. One reason is because they are accustomed to steeping themselves in the words of Scripture on a daily basis through liturgical and private prayer, and the monastic custom of *lectio divina*. In addition, the sisters use the scripturally rich Rule of St. Benedict as a sort of handbook to living the monastic life.

Chapter 4 of the Rule of St. Benedict, titled "The Tools for Good Works," is a good example. Here Benedict tells his monks that there are some specific and necessary tools they'll need in the years ahead and that by using them, life will be different from the way it was before. The tools themselves—as well as the instructions for using them—are God's commandments and the teachings of Christ. They are tools of the spiritual craft, says Benedict, and they are meant to be used by anyone who is serious about following the example of Jesus Christ.

The tools of the spiritual craft are not the exclusive property of monks and nuns, because we have all been called to holiness. So those of us who are husbands and wives can paraphrase the words of St. Benedict by remembering that the workshop where we are to toil faithfully at all these tasks is in our homes and through the stability of our marriages. It is a continual process of growth and change.

It's obvious from the photos that were taken at our wedding that Denny and I have changed a lot since then. Not only do we no longer look like the same two persons but the fact is, we are not the same two persons. And thank goodness for that. We were so very young then and so naïve and clueless. I wouldn't want to live my entire lifetime being the person I was when I was twenty-two years old—inexperienced, uncertain, immature, so focused on trivial details that had to do with the surface of life.

And as much as I loved that handsome boy I married, I am awfully glad we were only together for a short time. I much prefer the man I am married to today because he is so much more genuinely loving as well as a whole lot more responsible, levelheaded, and interesting to be with.

The point is we are not the same people we used to be and I think this is one of the riskiest things about marriage. On the day people get married, they promise to love and honor each other for the rest of their lives. But when they make that promise, they have barely started becoming the persons they will end up being in five, ten, twenty, forty, sixty years. Change is at the very heart of what happens over the course of a marriage. It has the potential to transform us and help us become who we were created to be. But sadly, change can also spell disaster for people who have not learned what to do with it when it happens, and the way a person deals with it when it does has a great deal of impact on his or her spouse.

I would like to hear more about this from a strictly psychological perspective. We know all about how important parents are during the formative period of a child's life. And we've been told that adolescents need strong and supportive adult role models in order to develop into healthy and mature young people. But people don't simply stop growing and developing once they reach adulthood. As far as I'm concerned, marriage itself is a "developmental stage"—and probably the longest one for those of us who are husbands and wives. So I think there ought to be far more attention given to the effect spouses have on one another's personal development—especially since the marriage ceremony itself hints at it.

> This union then is most serious, because it will bind you
> together for life in a relationship so close and so intimate
> that it will profoundly influence your whole future. That
> future, with its hopes and disappointments, its successes
> and its failures, its pleasures and its pains, its joys and its
> sorrows, is hidden from your eyes. You know that these
> elements are mingled in every life and are to be expected
> in your own. And so, not knowing what is before you, you
> take each other for better or for worse, for richer or for

poorer, in sickness and in health, until death. (Exhortation before marriage)[21]

When Denny and I first heard these words on that June day in 1967, we were being told not only to expect changes in the years ahead but to be aware that the way we handled them would have an effect on us. In other words, it's not just what happens to us that matters in the long run. What is important is how we deal with what happens because that's what has the biggest impact on a marriage. All we have to do is look around at the marriages of other people to see proof of this. How do husbands and wives help each other cope when something they hope for ends up in disappointment? What do they do to support one another when what should have led to success turns out to be a failure? Are they able to help each other endure the pain they encounter, or bear the burden of sorrow?

If a person becomes embittered, resentful, angry, cynical, and mean-spirited, it's going to leave an imprint on that person's spouse. On the other hand, the opposite is true as well, which is why it is worth learning how to maintain a sense of equilibrium and prayerful optimism about life in order to meet adversity with courage, faith, and resilience.

"Rejoice in hope, be patient in suffering, persevere in prayer," says St. Paul in Romans 12:12, and in 1 Corinthians 13, we are reminded that love "bears all things, believes all things, hopes all things, endures all things." These words remind us of what it means to be open to the transformative nature of God's grace and how we can be a source of it for one another. That's what *conversatio morum* means as far as I'm concerned. It is all about responding to our unique call to holiness through marriage—a way of life that will involve change from one wedding anniversary to the next. Fidelity to our marriage vows means making choices and decisions that reflect our efforts to take the Gospels seriously and remain open to the way God is working in our lives.

---

21. *The Mass on the Day of Marriage*, 10.

A Few Words about Poverty and Chastity

> She renounces the capacity of acquiring and possess-
> ing goods for herself. For the sake of the Kingdom of
> heaven, she makes professions of perfect continence and
> celibacy.[22]
>
> Constitutions and Statutes of the Monks
and Nuns of the Cistercian Order
of the Strict Observance

Poverty and chastity are included in the sisters' vow to be
faithful to monastic life. It means the sisters commit themselves
to living frugally, sharing their possessions rather than owning
anything privately, and living a celibate form of chastity. This
flies in the face of contemporary attitudes about sex and
money.

Take the notion of frugality, for example. So much of our
way of life here in the United States centers on money—and the
tendency to spend it buying things we don't necessarily need.
As soon as children are old enough to watch television they are
introduced to the notion of acquisition. For proof that marketing
strategies aimed at toddlers and young children are effective, all
we need to do is watch what happens when parents who take
their youngsters grocery shopping hit the breakfast cereal aisles.
It's not by chance that the more nutritious choices are located on
the topmost shelves and the garishly illustrated boxes of crunchy,
sugarcoated stuff are to be found within easy eye level of children. It's done to make sure the kiddies will be able to spot what
they have seen advertised on TV in order to set up a fuss should
mommy or daddy choose something else. As for their older
siblings—it's estimated that one out of every ten teenagers uses
credit cards and it is a safe bet that most purchases are influenced
in one way or another by the marketing and media industries.
Unless they are among the thousands of children who are living
in real poverty, they are growing up with the attitude that it's
okay to spend money they don't necessarily have in order to

---

22. Constitutions, 10.

purchase things they don't necessarily need. Most likely frugality is something with which many of them have very little experience. The idea of people consciously choosing to live frugally is probably even more far-fetched.

But for the sisters, frugality is an important part of how they live out their fidelity to the monastic lifestyle. Unlike some monastic communities in third world countries, the sisters at Mississippi Abbey do not live in impoverished conditions. They are able to support themselves quite well with their candy business. In addition, they are able to count on the financial support of friends and generous donors when circumstances require additional funds for special projects—such as the new candy facility that was built several years ago because the old one was no longer functional.

At Mississippi Abbey, then, "poverty" does not mean doing without the essentials and necessities of life but rather making do with what's needed. The sisters' lifestyle is grounded in simplicity and based on the premise that there is no reason to acquire something unless it is really needed.

Their approach to clothing is a great illustration of how comfortable they are getting along just fine with only a little. Personally, I don't know many women whose closets contain only the barest essentials—just enough underwear to get by plus something to work in, something to wear when running errands in town, and something to sleep in. But I know it is that way at Mississippi Abbey because one of my jobs was to help out in the laundry room folding and sorting clothes. The same "outfits" (if you could call them that) kept turning up week after week. And when it came to sleeping attire, even my old flannel nightgowns looked positively luxurious in comparison to some of the sisters'. I could swear that some of them have been using the same pajamas they brought with them when they first entered the monastery. It's not that they couldn't afford to run into Wal-Mart and pick up something new. It's more likely they just didn't think they needed to because they were perfectly content with what they had.

I folded many a pair of jeans that had been neatly patched and repatched, and even a fair number of socks that had been carefully darned (something I have never learned to do). If a button was missing, it got replaced; if a blouse was torn, it got mended—and in a timely fashion. Unlike here at home where several items in my mending basket have been there for a couple of years at least. It's not that I deliberately keep ignoring them; it's just that I can afford to make mending a very low priority because I have quite a few other things I can wear in the meantime. The sisters, on the other hand, have chosen a lifestyle where there are fewer options. For them, less is preferable to more, and doing without is better than accumulating too much.

And so living with the sisters has prompted me to take a closer look at the amount of "stuff" I tend to accumulate. Not only have I attempted to divest myself of some of it, I've also been trying to prevent myself from acquiring things I don't really need. It's not as easy as I thought it would be, probably because old habits and patterns don't disappear without a struggle. But I have made a conscious effort to be intentional about the things I purchase rather than allowing myself to be persuaded by ads or tempted by what I see other people doing or having. I have been trying to ask myself if I really need whatever it is that has caught my eye. And sometimes I've even been able to talk myself out of an impulse purchase by trying to imagine what one of the sisters would say if I asked her advice about whether or not to go ahead and buy it. (It doesn't take a lot of imagination to figure out what the answer would be!)

As for my true weakness, books, I've discovered there are some nifty alternatives to Barnes & Noble, Borders, and Amazon. com. To begin with, there's always the public library. And in this age of electronic databases I can easily access a list of our library's holdings, search for what I am interested in reading, and then request that a copy be placed on hold until I'm able to pick it up at the nearest branch. I have also discovered that the internet is alive with possibilities for book lovers! I like to click on to the Amazon.com web site to "browse" because it's so easy to get information about books, including book reviews and reader reactions. Once I have found a book I'm interested in reading, I simply click on to our public library web site and search for it there.

Thanks to Emma, I've also discovered another way to simplify my approach to books. She introduced me to paperbackswap.com, a treasure trove of a web site for thrifty book lovers. Actually it is very monastic in its underlying purpose, which is to provide a means for people to share their books with one another. Once you have decided which books you are ready to give away, you simply enter them into the database so other people know they are available. When someone requests one of your books, you drop it in the mail and as soon as the other person gets it he/she notifies the web site so that you can select a book in exchange.

To be honest, though, I need to remember that merely using the internet to help locate people with whom I can swap books hardly establishes me as a paragon of frugality. Nor does the fact that I have been making an effort to avoid impulse shopping or that I'm trying to get rid of a lot of the clutter that has accumulated over the years in our basement. While there is value in learning to make do with less rather than keep accumulating more, it's equally important to remember why it even matters.

It matters because there is danger in becoming overly attached to the comfortable lifestyle to which I am accustomed. If it becomes important to acquire and experience more and more of whatever looks appealing at the moment, chances are I'll end up spending an awful lot of time, energy, and money pursuing it. I have seen this happen with friends of mine. I can see how much pleasure they derive from what their money enables them to do with their lives. And there's really nothing wrong with that except that it really can interfere with what seems to me to be more important—that part of life that has nothing to do with material possessions and enjoyable pastimes. Certainly this is what Jesus meant with his pithy little saying about the camel and the needle. I can't believe that when he made that statement about how difficult it is for people with a lot of money to enter the kingdom of heaven, he meant to suggest that wealth per se is a bad thing. More likely he was pointing out that if we let ourselves be seduced by the pleasures that come with what money can buy, we run the risk of losing sight of everything else that matters so much more.

By their conscious choice of poverty the sisters choose to separate themselves from a way of life that includes many of the material possessions and pleasurable experiences to which the rest of us are so attached. In their hearts they know they don't need all that to be happy. By turning away from it they are choosing to be faithful to a way of life where priorities are shaped by the world of the Spirit. It's a lifestyle that's closely aligned with what the Gospels have to say about material and nonmaterial realities.

> Do not store up for yourselves treasures on earth, where moth and rust consume and where thieves break in and steal; but store up for yourselves treasures in heaven, where neither moth nor rust consumes and where thieves do not break in and steal. For where your treasure is, there your heart will be also. (Matt 6:19-21)

Thinking about monastic poverty is a means of keeping things in perspective by being more mindful of the negative implications of acquisitiveness, materialism, and pleasure seeking.

But if monastic poverty is contrary to the tenor of our times, it's nowhere as out of sync with popular sensibilities as is the notion of chastity, the very thought of which probably strikes some people as being hopelessly outdated. Consider that statistics reveal the average American teenager views about 14,000 sexual scenarios each year as a result of watching TV and going to the movies.[23] The lyrics to popular hip-hop, rap, pop, and rock music are full of raunchy language having to do with sex, and all manner of hard-core internet pornography is readily available online. Then there's the fact that sexual imagery and innuendo shows up again and again in ads for everything from hand lotion and headache remedies to running shoes and soft drinks. All this is having an effect on kids, says the American Academy of Pediatrics and others who have been conducting research about teen-

---

23. American Academy of Pediatrics, Committee on Public Education, "Sexuality, Contraception, and the Media," *Pediatrics* 107, no. 1 (January 2001), http://aappolicy.aappublications.org/cgi/content/full/pediatrics;107/1/191.

age sexual activity. Given the heavy emphasis on sex in our society, it should come as no surprise that 61 percent of all high school seniors report having had sexual intercourse at least once and 21 percent have had four or more partners.[24]

In the midst of statistics like these, the very mention of the word "chastity" has a distinctly archaic ring to it for many people. "To defend chastity publicly seems like fanaticism and even its practice is regarded by many as eccentric and even unhealthy," says Michael Casey. "Priestly celibacy and monastic chastity that involve the renunciation of all direct sexual activity are scarcely believable in many cultures. This is why it becomes necessary to build up a fund of beliefs and values that support chastity."[25]

I suspect there is a great deal to be learned from monastic men and women about chastity because like so many other virtues, it is something we are all called to practice regardless of whether we are married, single, monastic, nonmonastic, gay, or straight. Chastity has to do with the choices we make about our sexuality. Monastic men and women choose to commit themselves to a celibate form of chastity that entails living without the sexual intimacy that goes along with being married, as well as the joy of having children and raising a family. Those of us who are married choose to commit ourselves to a form of chastity that includes all the responsibilities that go along with enjoying a monogamous sexual relationship.

I suppose it's natural for those of us who are sexually active women to think of celibate chastity strictly in negative terms; all we seem to think of is the "no sex" part. Being accustomed to what it *feels like* to experience all the sensual pleasure that goes along with making love, it's difficult for us to imagine what it must be like to commit oneself to a life without it. As women, we know there is a rich and voluptuous quality to our sexuality that has to do with the way our bodies respond. Celibacy means doing without those sensually exhilarating experiences that are the result of living inside a body that can do amazing things when

24. Ibid.
25. Casey, *Strangers to the City*, 52, 53.

connected to another body. As well as what can happen as a
result.

Choosing voluntarily to give it all up seems like an awful
lot to ask, especially since there's more to being a celibate woman
than doing without the passionate experience of sexual intercourse. It also implies that there will be no chance of getting
pregnant, giving birth, nursing a child, and experiencing everything it means to be a mother.

I'll admit not every woman waxes eloquent about the joys
of pregnancy and childbirth. Many women choose not to become
mothers for a variety of reasons. But as far as I'm concerned,
maternity is one of God's true gifts to those women who are
disposed to welcome it. I am definitely one of those women. For
the first half year of marriage I fretted and fussed each time my
period came because I wanted so desperately to be pregnant.
And among the most exciting words I have ever heard were those
spoken by the gynecologist as he poked and probed and finally
said with a grin, "that feels like a very pregnant uterus."

With the exception of morning sickness I loved everything
about being pregnant. I delighted in what was happening to my
body and took great pride in the way I began to fill out and take
on the distinctive look of pregnancy. If it were possible to relive
just one experience that I will never have again, I would ask to
go back and relive a few days of being pregnant. Nothing has
ever come close to what it was like to feel another life stirring
within me. At first it was just a little quiver, not much more than
a wisp of a flutter. But before much longer it had turned into a
thrumming sort of feeling, and soon I was able to clearly feel
that tiny little life kicking and squirming around inside me. As
my pregnancy advanced and I grew bulkier and bulkier, I used
to stretch out in the bathtub and watch my huge belly make
ripples in the water as the baby moved around. I can remember
actually "playing with the baby" by gently poking at what could
have been a tiny knee or maybe even a miniscule elbow, and
waiting to see if there would be an answering response. There
always was. It was all thrilling to me, even the nights when it
was hard to get to sleep because as soon as I would get comfortable, the baby would start moving around—sometimes so vigor-

ously that it would wake Denny from a sound sleep next to me.

As a wife and a mother it is difficult for me to comprehend what it must be like choosing to live with everything monastic celibacy involves. But Benedictine nun Mary Margaret Funk puts a positive spin on it in her book *Thoughts Matter*.

> The reason for monastic celibacy that makes the most compelling sense today is that the mind needs to be focused, without the complexities created by having and being responsible for a spouse. The focused mind meets God not only in heaven, but also in this life. The mind is stabilized through the sublimated sexual energies.[26]

One of the things that constantly amazed me about the sisters was how they managed to maintain their spiritual focus day after day and week after week. Maybe it has to do with celibacy. Just because they are celibate women doesn't mean they are asexual. Surely they have sexual feelings and drives and thoughts and so they must have learned how to channel all that energy in other ways. I wonder if their celibate lifestyle brings with it a keener ability to take delight in other sensory pleasures. After all, having an active sex life is not the only way to be sensual. Does celibacy lead to a heightened ability to perceive, through the senses, what is truly sacred about life? Perhaps that kind of awareness brings with it a greater clarity and depth to the contemplative, prayerful dimension of the sisters' lives.

I have also heard it said that celibate men and women have a more balanced and respectful approach to relationships because they are not so likely to be driven by the purely physical side of intimacy. Trappist Abbot General Bernardo Olivera spoke about this aspect of celibate chastity in a letter to the monks and nuns of the Trappist Order: "Chastity allows one to establish harmonious relationships with others. Basically, this harmony consists of accepting differences, respecting privacy, discerning the proper

26. Mary Margaret Funk, osb, *Thoughts Matter* (New York: Continuum, 1998) 41.

distance and gestures, communicating in a person-to-person way, being totally present in the relationship."[27]

The abbot general goes on to stress that although monastic people have chosen to live without marriage and the pleasures of conjugal sex, this does not mean they have also given up the warmth and intimacy of loving relationships. Living with the sisters gave me a close-up view of the deep bonds of love and affection that connect them to one another in strong and lasting relationships. They have created a warm and nurturing environment, a place of acceptance, affirmation, support, and friendship. It seems to echo what Dom Bernardo said in his letter to the monks and nuns of the order in emphasizing the importance of establishing harmonious relationships with others. "When the affective climate of the community is positive," he wrote, "both interior integration and harmonious relationships are more easily attained."[28]

So there is definitely a relational aspect to celibate chastity but unlike relationships that are driven by the desire for sexual gratification, there is not as great a likelihood for possessiveness, domination, or mutual exploitation to occur. It appears that intimate relationships between celibate persons are rooted in a deep respect for the dignity of each person. The same thing should be true of the relationship between husbands and wives as well.

Regardless of whether we are monastic people or married people, chastity plays an important part in helping us integrate our sexuality with our vocation in life. But the Church hasn't given us a lot of help in this regard. For too long now we have been given the impression that there is something dirty, if not downright unholy, about sexuality. (I remember how anxious I was to make my first confession so I would no longer have to worry about dying and going directly to hell as a result of my mother's insistence that I bathe with my little sister. I was con-

---

27. Bernardo Olivera, ocso, 2003 Circular Letter: On Consecrated Celibacy and Virginity (Rome: January 26, 2003), http://www.ocso.org/HTM/aglet2003 -eng.htm.

28. Olivera, 2003 Circular Letter.

vinced that all those "impure thoughts" about our naked bodies were mortal sins!)

It's not fair to blame St. Paul even though chapter 7 of 1 Corinthians does make it seem like sexual activity, even when it's between spouses, is a bit of a handicap when it comes to the spiritual life. Regardless of who's to blame, I think we have been left with the impression that truly devout men and women are not likely to have anything at all to do with sex. Just look at all those "holy virgins" who have attained sainthood over the years. Surely there were scores of sexually active yet holy wives and mothers whose lives were equally virtuous. But they haven't shown up in the lives-of-the-saints books. Why should the fact that a woman has had sex matter that much? Apparently it doesn't for the men. I can't help noticing that we seldom (if ever) hear anything about whether the male saints were virgins.

Why is it, I wonder, that the Church is so uncomfortable about sex? It certainly wasn't that much of an issue for Jesus, as the beautiful story of the woman caught in the very act of adultery attests. Nor was it a problem for him that the woman at the well was obviously quite sexually experienced, having had seven husbands!

Despite centuries of uneasiness about sex, the *Catechism of the Catholic Church* acknowledges that sexual activity is an important and "honorable" part of the marriage relationship:

> Sexuality, in which man's belonging to the bodily and biological world is expressed, becomes personal and truly human when it is integrated into the relationship of one person to another, in the complete and lifelong mutual gift of a man and a woman. . . . The acts in marriage by which the intimate and chaste union of the spouses takes place are noble and honorable; the truly human performance of these acts fosters the self-giving they signify and enriches the spouses in joy and gratitude. Sexuality is a source of joy and pleasure.[29]

29. *Catechism of the Catholic Church* 2337, 2362.

Sex, then, is not something nasty and immoral that can leave us tainted, stained, and befouled. It is something that enhances life and enables us to be united to another person in the most deeply intimate of all human relationships. Perhaps the key to using our sexuality in such a profound manner lies in the extent to which we understand what chastity means.

Even though we are called to chastity regardless of our state in life, I'm guessing that those of us who are sexually active probably don't think about it as much as our celibate brothers and sisters do. In a culture where sexual activity is so highly valued, chastity doesn't sound very relevant if we assume it's the same thing as sexual continence. I think we need to take a closer look at what chastity does mean because it has more to do with figuring out how to be sexual than with assuming we shouldn't be—as if that would even be possible.

Whether one is a priest or monk or nun, whether one is single or married, whether one is heterosexual or homosexual, it's probably a safe bet to say that learning what to do with one's sexuality is a major part of coming to know and become comfortable with oneself. Chastity is part of that process. It is a means of coming to the truth of who we are as sexual creatures and it helps us build and nurture intimate relationships with each other as men and women. "Before chastity is a moral mandate about sexual behavior, therefore, it is first of all a radical stance of the heart—a way of standing before other people," say the authors of *Tender Fires: The Spiritual Promise of Sexuality*. "Chastity is *reverence in relationships*. It is the call to integrate eros in our lives with trust, mutuality, and respect for others."[30]

For husbands and wives chastity goes far beyond the responsibility they have to be faithful to one another by refraining from engaging in sexual activity with someone else. Clearly, marital infidelity is a grievous offense against what is sacred about marriage. But I think it is a mistake to assume that for a married person chastity is simply a matter of resisting the temp-

30. Fran Ferder and John Heagle, *Tender Fires: The Spiritual Promise of Sexuality* (New York: The Crossroad Publishing Company, 2002) 111–12.

tation to fool around with someone other than your spouse. Instead of thinking about chastity in terms of what not to do, I think it is equally important, actually more important, to look at marital chastity in a more positive light. In my view, chastity is a means for ensuring that the sexual side of marriage will strengthen a couple's commitment to love and honor one another.

I doubt if there are many married people who have not struggled with sexuality issues in one form or another at various times in the course of their marriages. Once the initial euphoria of being in love wears off, I suspect it begins to dawn on all neophyte husbands and wives that most likely they are just not going to be having great sex night after night, no matter how adept they are at experimenting with different positions and techniques. Sooner or later it will be time to get down to the serious business of building a sex life that is as focused on honoring the dignity and uniqueness of the other person as it is in enjoying the benefits of having access to his or her body. The physical aspects of lovemaking, pleasurable though they may be, are only part of the picture. The intimacy of marriage is based on the ability to be deeply open to each other emotionally as well as physically. The joy of married sex has as much to do with the loving tenderness that exists between two people who are willing to be vulnerable with each other as it does with the thrill of reaching orgasm simultaneously. It seems to me that this is what chastity in marriage is all about—it is a way for us to be more mindful of what it means to be profoundly intimate with one another and to recognize that, like everything else about the gift of love, it comes from God.

Love is at the center of the vows we make regardless of whether we are making them as monks, nuns, husbands, or wives. We speak our vows in good faith, trusting that we will be able to remain faithful to promises we are making about a future we have yet to encounter. On our wedding day, Denny and I promised to be true to one another in good times and in bad, in sickness and in health. We promised to love and honor one another all the days of our life. It has not always been easy, because as Madeleine L'Engle says, marriage is the biggest risk in human relations that a person can take.

> If we commit ourselves to one person for life this is not, as
> many people think, a rejection of freedom; rather it demands
> the courage to move into all the risks of freedom, and the
> risk of love which is permanent; into that love which is not
> possession, but participation. It takes a lifetime to learn
> another person. When love is not possession, but participa-
> tion, then it is part of that co-creation which is our human
> calling.[31]

It takes a great deal of energy and work to create a marriage
that focuses on what is best for one another as individuals and
as a couple. Ironically, living with the sisters turned out to be one
of the best things I've done for my marriage in a long time. In
recognizing the wisdom contained in the vows of stability, obedience, and *conversatio morum*, I have come to a deeper understanding of what it means to be faithful to the vows I made on
the day I was married.

---

31. Madeleine L'Engle, *The Irrational Season* (San Francisco: Harper and Row
Publishers, 1977) 47.

CONCLUSION

I believe that the fact that lay people today feel attracted to the Cistercian charism and recognize themselves in it, can be understood as a sign that the Spirit also desires to share it with them, so that the charism receives an added secular form at this moment in history.[1]

> Dom Bernardo Olivera
> "Reflections on the Challenge of
> 'Charismatic Associations'"

Leaving the Monastery and Living the Life

April 10

This is the beginning of my last week. I'm looking forward to being home again but at the same time I dread having to leave. And I have a feeling it will probably be a lot harder making the transition back into my regular life than it was the other way around. I've loved living with the sisters and I know I am going to miss them. The big challenge about going home will be finding a way to make sure I don't forget everything I've learned while I was here.

As much as I hated to see the time I had spent with the sisters come to a close, there's no denying I was looking forward to going home. Not a day had gone by without thoughts of my husband and sons. I had missed them even more than I had thought I would and I couldn't wait to see them again and get back to living my normal life. The Cistercian path I had followed

---

1. Bernardo Olivera, ocso, "Reflections on the Challenge of 'Charismatic Associations,'" *Cistercian Studies Quarterly* 32.2 (1997) 230.

for three months inside the monastery was about to lead me right back out of it, back to where I had come from. It was where I needed to be and yet I knew it was not going to be easy adapting what I had learned from the sisters into my life. So during those last few weeks, I spent a fair amount of time thinking about what that would probably involve.

The Cistercian charism is a gift that lay men and women have also been invited to share, as Dom Bernardo Olivera, abbot general of the Cistercian Order, once remarked during a homily:

> You have no need to ask our permission to do this. The charism is a gift that we have received and embodied in history, but we are not the exclusive owners. I invite you to continue to take the risk of going beyond our borders. . . . We do not need you to be "copies" of the monastic version of Cistercians. Rather, we need you to embody the charism, to speak about it in different languages, to discover new ways of living it out, to re-inculturate it.[2]

Such a generous yet challenging invitation carries with it the responsibility to nurture that gift and use it appropriately. Not only did the three months I spent with the sisters help me gain a deeper understanding of the Cistercian charism itself but it also gave me some important insights into what I can do to "embody" it as a laywoman. I think the following key elements of their life have made the greatest impact on me and it is within this framework that I have been trying to follow their example.

Their Life Is Rooted in Prayer

When I went to live with the sisters, I knew that prayer was a central feature of monastic life and I was curious to learn more about what they do to stay so focused. What I discovered is that prayer takes various forms and many of them don't always involve *saying* words. Perhaps the greatest insight I've brought

2. Bernardo Olivera, ocso, Homily for the 2nd International Meeting of Lay Cistercians, Our Lady of the Holy Spirit Monastery (Conyers, Georgia: April 25, 2002).

back with me about prayer is the fact that my heart often knows more about it than my head does. I just need to trust it.

Sometimes, when I am able to quiet my restless and stubborn mind, prayer takes me to a place deep within where I can find the source of goodness in my life. And when I pay attention to what I find there, I am usually able to gain a clearer understanding of what I need to do to carry a little of that goodness out into the world.

But I have also discovered that prayer isn't always a pleasant experience. Sometimes I start out with the intention of praying only to end up being carried off in an entirely different direction by thoughts and distractions that are anything but prayerful. Even more disturbing are times when prayer takes me into places I would prefer not to go and forces me to confront things about myself I would rather ignore. Perhaps the hardest thing of all about prayer is that it sometimes seems dry and lifeless, and when that happens I am easily tempted to give up or to skip it entirely.

Living with the sisters has given me enough perspective on all this to recognize that if there is one rule to keep in mind about prayer, it's simply to keep on doing it, regardless of whether anything "happens" or not. I have come to the conclusion that prayer is a lot like life because I cannot predict what it is going to involve. Sometimes it's pretty ordinary and unexciting. On the other hand, there are times it is definitely quite a thrill. But most of the time I need to make myself at home in the very ordinariness of it. And I suspect that is one reason the sisters are able to make prayer such a central part of their lives. They have learned to be *right at home in it* because it is at the heart of their way of life.

Their Life Is Centered in Christ

The phrase "prefer nothing whatever to Christ" (RB 72.11) may sound like little more than a pious expression to those who don't take it seriously. But the sisters do take it seriously. It is the force that drives their lives. Like all Cistercians, the sisters are especially mindful that they have been created in the image of God and by using Christ as a model they try to remember that everyone else is too!

When I first arrived I'll admit it felt a little strange to hear them talking about Jesus as casually as other people talk about their friends and acquaintances. His name came up all the time and to hear them talk you could almost have sworn he had an apartment in Dubuque or had just been in touch via e-mail. The Christocentric aspect of the sisters' life means that Jesus is not simply a religious concept to them. He is undeniably real and that is why they have chosen to form their lives around him. They take him and his message very seriously. They try to follow his example and trust in his word. It's something I want to do as well.

But the truth is I have a long way to go. Maybe it is because reading about Christ is so much easier than following up on what he had to say. Taking his message to heart means responding to the needs of the poor and marginalized in our world as well as the vulnerable and the needy who make demands on my time and my energy.

And then there is the issue of forgiveness. The sisters say the Lord's Prayer aloud together frequently throughout the day because it's a part of the Liturgy of the Hours as well as Mass. It is a constant reminder of how important it is to forgive those who have hurt, disappointed, or annoyed them. After a few weeks of saying, "forgive us our trespasses as we forgive those who trespass against us" over and over again, I found myself thinking about those words a little more seriously. They often alert me to things I have done that I need to apologize for. Similarly, if there is someone who has done something recently that has hurt or upset me, those words are a reminder of how important it is to forgive him or her without harboring grudges, resentments, or bitterness.

By centering their lives in Christ, the sisters have found a way to live together more compassionately and charitably. That is not to say they never get upset or irritated with each other but rather that they try to handle those feelings in a more Christlike manner. They really and truly try to be patient with each other, to listen more and argue less, and to check their tendencies to be critical, judgmental, and quarrelsome. I've tried to follow their example (not always so successfully), especially when I encounter people with whom it is difficult to get along. The world is full of people who are selfish, rude, obnoxious, and downright unlov-able. A Christ-centered response is to forgive them and love them anyway.

They Live Their Lives Simply and Attentively

It is easy to romanticize the sisters' life by picturing the mon-astery as a place of gentle serenity and blissful peace. True, those words can be used to describe aspects of their lifestyle but it would be a big mistake to assume it is that way all the time. The sisters are well acquainted with the pressures and stresses that are part of needing to live and support themselves in a twenty-first-century world that operates according to tight schedules and complex technologies. They know all about the blight of busyness that infects just about everyone's life these days. And even though they are not immune to it, they have figured out how to spot it when it starts creeping into their own lives so they can keep it from spreading. It is one of the benefits of being com-mitted to a life of simplicity and it was one of the things I wanted to learn more about when I went to live with them.

It seemed to me that the simplicity of their well-ordered life was a tremendous asset because it enabled them to balance the many things they needed to do each day with the more important priorities that shape their lives. Their structured lifestyle helps keep work in perspective and gives them a way to avoid being consumed by tasks and projects that could easily overwhelm them otherwise. In my view, the order and consistency of their life is actually quite liberating because it provides them with the freedom to balance work, prayer, the responsibilities of com-munal life, and the joys of living in harmony with the rhythm of the seasons and the beauty of the natural world.

Living with the sisters gave me a chance to discover what it is like to move through each day attentively and mindfully. It was a wake-up call about the fact that I need to do something about my tendency to spend far too much time and energy on things that are not really that important, wanting things I don't really need, and worrying about things that don't really matter. I admired the sisters' approach to using time and resources wisely and came home hoping to do a better job of it myself.

It has meant struggling with obstacles to silence, moderation, attentiveness, and a prayerful approach to life, as well as a tendency to overlook the fact that as someone once said, there's more to life than increasing its speed. Unfortunately, my biggest obstacle is my own lack of self-control. I may decry the negative influences of a narcissistic culture that focuses on instant gratification, materialism, acquisition, and self-indulgence, but I still give in far too readily when tempted by messages urging me to go ahead and try it or do it or buy it because if I want it there's no reason why I can't have it. I once heard an abbot say that a life without some bite to it isn't very Cistercian. He was talking about asceticism, or to put it another way, he was referring to the importance of self-discipline. My own life falls far short of the mark. I know that if I am to free myself from the obstacles that prevent me from living a more balanced life, I must introduce a little more asceticism into it. I need to work harder to control my appetite and be sensible about what I eat, something I am definitely not very good at doing. I must do a better job of following through on things I know are good for me even though I hate doing them, and this applies to everything from physical exercise to scheduling regular checkups with the dentist and doctor. I must curb my tendency to avoid chores and tasks that are boring and tedious simply because I've got more interesting things to do. (Is it possible that cleaning out the refrigerator might actually be an ascetical practice?) And finally, I'm discovering that getting older brings all sorts of opportunities to exercise a little asceticism, provided I learn how to stop complaining about the pain and discomfort that goes along with the aging process!

Their Life Is Grounded in Reality

Once while preaching a homily to the sisters, Fr. Brendan Freeman made a comment that has stayed with me ever since. He said most of us probably do not consciously set out each day looking for happiness. It just happens naturally while we are doing what we are called to do. His words speak to the importance of coming to the truth of who we are, an important goal of Cistercian life.

I had a chance to get to know several of the sisters quite well because Gail had asked them to assist me in various ways during the time I was at the abbey. As my "guardian angel" during the entire three months I was there, Louise became a good friend and trusted confidante, who was always there when I needed her. In addition I met regularly with Kathleen, my spiritual director, who helped me keep everything that was happening to me in prayerful perspective. The "class" I took from Martha was a special treat because she was as much fun to be with as she was insightful. And not only did my weekly voice lesson make it possible for me to participate in choir but it also provided an opportunity to get to know Chris, my patient and enormously encouraging "vocal coach." Then there was Emma, without whose encouragement I probably would never have had the nerve to participate in the Cistercian forums and Saturday night Gospel sessions. And of course there was Sister Gail, who despite being busy with all her many responsibilities as abbess still managed to find time for me when I requested it. In addition to this little support network of encouraging and affirming sisters, there were so many others whose warmth and kindheartedness helped make my monastic experience such a rich one. When it came time to leave, it meant saying good-bye to a circle of women who had become very dear to me in the short time I'd known them.

People who visit the monastery sometimes use the word "radiance" to describe the sisters, even though I suspect such effusive language causes the sisters themselves to cringe. I have a feeling what visitors are seeing has to do with the fact that there is no artifice or pretentiousness about the sisters. They seem to be perfectly content and comfortable simply being who they are. Outside the monastery it's different. We get used to playing a variety of roles in an effort to impress (or perhaps intimidate) others, or we go to great lengths trying to be who we want others to think we are, or we create complicated defense mechanisms to prevent people from discovering things we don't want them to know about us, even though what we're doing is often pretty obvious to everyone except ourselves.

It was different living with the sisters. Granted, I wasn't there long enough to know for sure whether or not they were truly as authentic as they seemed. But I am usually able to spot a fake or a bluffer in a crowd, and I can quickly pick up the odor of artifice and pretense when I run into it. I didn't notice anything that came close to it at Mississippi Abbey. The sisters seem to have figured out a way to live together without constantly having to compete with each other or finagle devious little strategies for making sure their talents and accomplishments are noticed. Even more remarkable was their tendency to admit that they weren't the paragons of virtue they might have hoped they could be. Instead they were quick to admit their mistakes and weaknesses without trying to justify them or make excuses for themselves.

What impresses me about Cistercian people is the high priority they attach to the work of facing up to the truth of who they really are as opposed to who they want others to think they are. They trust their lived experiences to teach them about themselves and that means the sisters tend to take feelings and emotions very seriously. It's not a matter of being overly sensitive but rather of learning to recognize feelings for what they are—indications that something is going on inside that is worth paying attention to. I got the impression that the sisters do this in much the same way as they approach *lectio divina*. Instead of merely reacting to a particularly strong feeling there's value in reflecting on the message behind it and what it has to reveal.

Or maybe it's just as accurate to say that their years of mining the depths of Scripture has given the sisters the ability to pay attention to what their lived experiences can reveal to them. "For by the grace given to me I say to everyone among you," says St. Paul, "not to think of yourself more highly than you ought to think, but to think with sober judgment, each according to the measure of faith that God has assigned" (Rom 12:3). The ability to look at ourselves with "sober judgment" is surely a necessary step in the process of coming to the truth of who we are. It's why humility is such an important element in the spiritual life.

They Live Their Lives with Reverence

One of the things I miss the most about living with the sisters can be summed up in one word, and that word is "reverence." It was such a natural part of their life and it was expressed in just about everything they did. Maybe it was because they are so attuned to the many different ways God is present to us in the big and little moments of our lives. Whatever the reason for their reverent approach to life, it was a beautiful thing to experience and I miss it very much now that I have become immersed once again in a culture that has lost a sense of the sacred and forgotten how to be reverent.

Reverence showed up everywhere. Naturally, it was central to the liturgy. Everything about it is done reverently, beginning with the way the sisters use their bodies as expressions of prayer. They don't mosey into church, or stand there impatiently shifting from foot to foot, or plop themselves down in their choir stalls. They move with reverence, almost as if their every movement has been choreographed with reverence in mind. I loved watching the way they bowed, for example, dropping their heads gracefully while dipping their bodies forward from the waist, hands crossed at the wrist and placed lightly over the knees all in one fluid movement. It was a gesture of profound respect, a beautiful way of honoring what is sacred.

On Sundays, special feasts, and solemnities, there was always beautiful music, specially selected and carefully rehearsed, as well as a procession complete with incense wafting from the thurible at the bottom of the long chain Grace held in front of her as she approached the altar. How she managed to swing it back and forth in perfect sync with her own footsteps while somehow managing not to trip over it in the process was always a mystery to me. Sometimes the incense had been placed in a bowl that she carried in her hands, slowly lifting it above her head, then dipping it from side to side, sending smoky swirls drifting through the air, a symbol for prayers that rise from the earth to heaven.

These and other examples of liturgical reverence are sadly missing at the parish level where most people prefer a more relaxed and informal worship environment, arguing that it is more family friendly, warm, and welcoming. I'm not so easily convinced. There is something just a little too informal about all the talking that goes on up until Mass starts and as soon as the priest reaches the back of the church again afterwards. I once listened in appalled frustration to two women directly behind me as they discussed in graphic detail what takes place during a colonoscopy. Not nearly as offensive, but distracting nonetheless, is the choir that practices in the front of the church right up until the final few minutes before the entrance procession. Then there's the chorus of screaming children whose parents have opted against the crying room, making it impossible for the rest of us to get much out of the readings or the homily. Informality and family friendliness are one thing, but all too often going to Mass feels more like sitting in the bleachers at a soccer game than participating in a liturgical celebration. That's when I can't help thinking that a little bit of reverence would make a big difference.

But there's more to reverence than what happens during liturgies. It shows up in so much of what goes on at Mississippi Abbey because of the gentle mindfulness with which the sisters move through each day. I think possibly this is at the very core of what reverence is all about. It is a way of responding to the conviction that life is far too precious to waste by not living attentively. It is something I am determined not to forget. Gail's wise advice to make a point of spending some time outside each day has stayed with me as a vivid reminder that the natural world itself deserves to be approached reverently because of the many ways God is present in it.

The other lesson I'm determined not to forget has to do with the importance of slowing down in order to be attentive to those aspects of life that are worth reverencing. I feel life is far too short to waste by being in such a hurry. It is impossible to notice and appreciate what's significant if I'm constantly rushing right past it. Since coming back from the monastery, that much-touted time management technique known as "multitasking" makes absolutely no sense to me anymore. Why speed up the pace of my life by trying to accomplish several things at the same time if it means I'm not really going to be able to concentrate on any of them?

The sisters' reverent approach to the communal nature of their lives has also left an impression on me. It stems from their ability to look for what is sacred in one another even when confronted with the inevitable stresses and pressures of living in community. It's apparent in the way they acknowledge the impact of their words and actions, as well as the concern they have for each other's feelings and well-being. I've been trying to do a better job of taking the same reverent approach to the people in my life. It's not hard with the persons I enjoy being with or with those special people who are easy to love. It is all the others that make it a real challenge. Treating them with the reverence they are due—in spite of how downright unlikable they can be or how much their behaviors may irritate and upset me—is turning out to be one of the hardest of all the lessons I have tried to put into practice since leaving the monastery. But something tells me it is probably one of the most important.

Since coming home I have made a conscious effort to live a little more reverently, not only because so much of life is worthy of it, but also because it is such a good way to focus on what is sacred about the gift of life in the first place. In one of her books, Esther de Waal quotes a traditional Jewish proverb that goes like this: "On the day of Judgment God will only ask one question: Did you enjoy my world?"[3] I think that by approaching life with reverence I'll be able to answer that question in the affirmative.

A Sense of Vocation

April 22

This is my last night in the monastery and I have been thinking about a homily Fr. Neil gave earlier this week. He made the point that the relationship between who we are and what we do is central to our spiritual development because it's not enough to read and talk about the Christian life. We have to behave like Christians. I guess the same thing is true of what I have discovered during these past three months. It's not enough to have learned about the sisters' Christ-centered way of life, and thought about how relevant much of it is for me as well. Now I need to go home and live like a Cistercian to the extent that's possible for someone like me!!

3. Esther de Waal, *Lost in Wonder* (Collegeville, Minnesota: Liturgical Press, 2003) 72.

A few days before leaving the monastery, these words jumped out at me while doing *lectio*: "let each of you lead the life that the Lord has assigned, to which God called you" (1 Cor 7:17). A friend of mine says this kind of synchronicity has less to do with coincidence and more to do with what she calls "the sneaky spirit." In this particular case I had to agree. It was pretty obvious that message was filled with significance for me.

It was the word "assigned" that grabbed my attention. I was immediately reminded of the weekly chart that lists the various jobs the sisters are given in order to share the workload. Similarly, those of us who have been given a chance to share the wisdom of the Cistercian charism have been "assigned" different vocations in which to apply it. What I came to recognize and affirm for myself during the time I lived with the sisters is that although my specific "job assignment" as a wife and mother is quite different from theirs, it's no less important.

The path I am meant to follow twists its sometimes-rocky way right through the ups and downs of living a very ordinary life. I am fully immersed in what it means to cherish my husband and two sons as well as to preserve the bonds of love, friendship, and service that connect me to a large network of other people as well. I know that it is within this context that I can experience what is truly sacred about life, provided I am not swept along by the currents and tides of a spiritually illiterate culture. And this is why the Cistercian charism is such a gift. Living with the sisters has shown me the beauty of that gift and taught me that there is a place in my own life for the wisdom that goes along with it.

Looking back at the time I spent at Mississippi Abbey, I'm reminded that memories are beautiful things. The abbot of New Melleray is fond of an image Cassian uses in likening the memory to a jar that's been carefully put away in the cupboard of our hearts.[4] We can go there whenever we want to take down that jar, open it carefully, and inhale its beautiful fragrance.

---

4. Boniface Ramsey, OP, trans., *John Cassian: The Conferences* (New York: Paulist Press, 1997) 518.

That's what I have been doing with the memories I brought back with me from Mississippi Abbey. I've stored them away to be taken out and cherished again and again. And with each memory I'm reminded of the wisdom in Paul's words:

> [W]hatever is honorable, whatever is just, whatever is pure, whatever is pleasing, whatever is commendable, if there is any excellence and if there is anything worthy of praise, think about these things. Keep on doing the things that you have learned and received and heard and seen in me, and the God of peace will be with you. (Phil 4:8-9)

BIBLIOGRAPHY

American Academy of Pediatrics. Committee on Public Education. "Sexuality, Contraception, and the Media." *Pediatrics* 107, no. 1 (January 2001), http://aappolicy.aappublications.org/cgi/content/full/pediatrics;107/1/191.

Anselm, Saint. "The Proslogion." In *The Liturgy of the Hours*. New York: Catholic Book Publishing Corporation, 1975.

Baker, J. Robert et al., eds. *A Lent Sourcebook: The Forty Days*. Chicago: Liturgy Training Publications, 1990.

Barnes, Simon. *How to Be a Bad Birdwatcher*. New York: Pantheon Books, 2004.

Bernard of Clairvaux. Letter 142. In "Conversion of Life," Monk? Blog, posted July 21, 2005. http://monasticism.org/monk/2005/07/21/conversion-of-life.

———. *St. Bernard's Sermons for Seasons and Principal Festivals of the Year, Vols. II and III*. Westminster, Maryland: The Carroll Press, 1950.

Borland, Hal. *Seasons*. Philadelphia: J.B. Lippincott Company, 1973.

Brock, Sebastian, trans. *The Syriac Fathers on Prayer and the Spiritual Life*. Cistercian Studies Series 101. Kalamazoo, Michigan: Cistercian Publications, 1987.

Carson, Rachel. *Lost Woods: The Discovered Writing of Rachel Carson*. Edited by Linda Lear. Boston: Beacon Press, 1998.

Casey, Michael, ocso. *A Guide to Living in the Truth: St. Benedict's Teaching on Humility*. Liguori, Missouri: Liguori, 2001.

———. *An Unexciting Life: Reflections on Benedictine Spirituality*. Petersham, Massachusetts: St. Bede's Publications, 2005.

———. *Strangers to the City*. Brewster, Massachusetts: Paraclete Press, 2005.

———. *Toward God: The Ancient Wisdom of Western Prayer*. Liguori, Missouri: Liguori, 1996.

Cassian, John. *John Cassian: The Conferences*. Translated by Boniface Ramsey, op. New York: Paulist Press, 1997.

Catechism of the Catholic Church. Washington, DC: United States Catholic Conference, 1994.

239

Chittister, Joan, OSB. *The Psalms: Meditations for Every Day of the Year*. New York: Crossroad Publishing Company, 1996.

Constitutions and Statutes of the Monks and Nuns of the Cistercian Order of the Strict Observance. Rome, 1990.

Cummings, Charles, OCSO. *Monastic Practices*. Kalamazoo, Michigan: Cistercian Publications, 1986.

de Waal, Esther. *Lost in Wonder: Rediscovering the Spiritual Art of Attentiveness*. Collegeville, Minnesota: Liturgical Press, 2003.

Dillard, Annie. *Teaching a Stone to Talk*. New York: Harper Colophon Books, 1983.

Evdokimov, Paul. *The Sacrament of Love*. Crestwood, New York: St. Vladimir's Seminary Press, 2001.

Ferder, Fran and John Heagle. *Tender Fires: The Spiritual Promise of Sexuality*. New York: The Crossroad Publishing Company, 2002.

Fitzpatrick, Gail, OCSO. "Enclosure: The Heart of the Matter." In *A Monastic Vision for the 21st Century*. Kalamazoo, Michigan: Cistercian Publications, 2006.

———. *Seasons of Grace*. Chicago: Acta Publications, 2000.

Fox, Thomas C. "The Architecture of Simplicity." *National Catholic Reporter* 43 (January 26, 2007) 13–14.

Funk, Mary Margaret, OSB. *Thoughts Matter*. New York: Continuum, 1998.

Gilbert of Hoyland. *Sermons on the Song of Songs*. Cistercian Fathers Series 14. Kalamazoo, Michigan: Cistercian Publications, 1978.

Grün, Anselm, OSB. *Dreams on the Spiritual Journey*. Schuyler, Nebraska: Benedictine Mission House, 1993.

Holman, Jean. "Monastic Joyfulness in Gilbert of Hoyland." *Cistercian Studies Quarterly* 19.4 (1984) 320.

Hugh of St. Victor. *De tribus diebus*. Quoted by Constant J. Mews in "The World as Text: The Bible and the Book of Nature in Twelfth-Century Theology," *Scripture and Pluralism*, Thomas J. Heffernan, ed. Boston: Brill, 2005.

Jäger, Willigis. *Search for the Meaning of Life: Essays and Reflections on the Mystical Experience*. Liguori, Missouri: Triumph Books, 1995.

Kinder, Terryl N. *Cistercian Europe: Architecture of Contemplation*. Grand Rapids, Michigan: Wm. B. Eerdmans Publishing Company, 2001.

Lawlor, Anthony. *A Home for the Soul: A Guide for Dwelling with Spirit and Imagination*. New York: Clarkson Potter, 1997.

L'Engle, Madeleine. *The Irrational Season*. San Francisco: Harper and Row Publishers, 1977.

Lindbergh, Anne Morrow. *Gift From The Sea*. New York: Pantheon Books, 1955.

Louf, André, ocso. *The Cistercian Way*. Kalamazoo, Michigan: Cistercian Publications, 1989.

The Mass on the Day of Marriage. St. Paul: Leaflet Missal Co., 1967.

Meister Eckhart. In *Nearer to the Heart of God: Daily Readings with the Christian Mystics*. Edited by Bernard Bangley. Brewster, Massachusetts: Paraclete Press, 2005.

Merton, Thomas. *Contemplation in a World of Action*. Garden City, New York: Doubleday & Company, 1973.

———. *Thoughts in Solitude*. Boston: Shambhala, 1993.

Moyers, Bill. *The Language of Life: A Festival of Poets*. New York: Doubleday, 1995.

Nouwen, Henri. *Reaching Out: The Three Movements of the Spiritual Life*. Garden City, New York: Doubleday, 1975.

Olivera, Bernardo, ocso. 2003 Circular Letter: On Consecrated Celibacy and Virginity. Rome, January 26, 2003. http://www.ocso.org/HTM/aglet2003-eng.htm.

———. "Reflections on the Challenge of 'Charismatic Associations.'" *Cistercian Studies Quarterly* 32.2 (1997) 230.

O'Malley, William. *God: The Oldest Question*. Chicago: Loyola Press, 2000.

Origen. *The Song of Songs, Commentary and Homilies*. Translated by R.P. Lawson. London: Paulist Press, 1957.

Palmer, G. E. H., ed., *The Philokalia, Volume II*. London: Faber and Faber, 1981.

Panikkar, Raimon. *A Dwelling Place for Wisdom*. Louisville, Kentucky: Westminster John Knox Press, 1993.

Pastoral Constitution on the Church in the Modern World. St. Paul: Office for Social Justice. http://www.osjspm.org/majordoc_gaudium_et_spes_part_2.aspx.

Prou, Dom Jean, osb, and the Benedictine nuns of the Solesmes Congregation. *Walled About With God*. Translated by Br. David Hayes, osb. Herefordshire: Gracewing, 2005.

Sayers, Dorothy. *The Mind of the Maker*. London: Methuen, 1942.

Scholl, Edith, ocso, ed. *In the School of Love: An Anthology of Early Cistercian Texts*. Kalamazoo, Michigan: Cistercian Publications, 2000.

Shaw, Luci. "Art and Christian Spirituality: Companions in the Way." *Direction* 27, no. 2 (1998), http://www.directionjournal.org/article/?980. (Reprinted from The Swiftly Tilting Worlds of Madeleine L'Engle, ed. Luci Shaw [Wheaton, IL: Harold Shaw, 1998].)

Stokes, Bill. *The River Is Us.* Minocqua, Wisconsin: Northword Press, 1993.

Teilhard de Chardin, Pierre. *The Divine Milieu.* New York: Harper and Row, 1960.

Thomas, Dylan. *The Collected Poems of Dylan Thomas.* New York: New Directions Books, 1939.

Wong, Grace. "Ka-ching! Wedding price tag nears $30K." *CNNMoney .com,* May 20, 2005. http://money.cnn.com/2005/05/20/pf/weddings/.